D1462340

I WANNA BE A PRODUCER

I WANNA BE A PRODUCER

How to Make a Killing on Broadway . . . Or Get Killed

JOHN BREGLIO

Published in 2016 by Applause Theatre & Cinema Books
An Imprint of Hal Leonard Corporation
7777 West Bluemound Road
Milwaukee, WI 53213

Trade Book Division Editorial Offices
33 Plymouth St., Montclair, NJ 07042

Printed in the United States of America

Book design by F. L. Bergesen

Library of Congress Cataloging-in-Publication Data

Names: Breglio, John.
Title: I wanna be a producer : how to make a killing on Broadway or get killed / John Breglio.
Description: Milwaukee, WI : Applause Theatre & Cinema Books, 2016. | Includes index.
Identifiers: LCCN 2015051499 | ISBN 9781495045165 (hardcover)
Subjects: LCSH: Theater—Production and direction—Handbooks, manuals, etc. | Breglio, John. | Theatrical producers and directors—United States—Biography.
Classification: LCC PN2053.B63 2016 | DDC 792.02/32023—dc23
LC record available at http://lccn.loc.gov/2015051499

www.applausebooks.com

To Nan

But you know when the truth is told
that you can get what you want
or you can just get old.
You're gonna kick off before you even get halfway through.
When will you realize, Vienna waits for you?

"Vienna" from *The Stranger* by Billy Joel

Contents

Foreword

You are in good hands with John Breglio.

For over forty years, since the early 1970s, John has lived and worked at the heart of the American theater. Lawyer, producer, consigliere, and friend, he has helped countless producers and artists find their way through the confusing and often treacherous thickets of the Broadway world. In this book, he is offering you the same wisdom, clarity, and precision that he has given to some of the greatest and most groundbreaking leaders of the field, from Joe Papp and Marvin Hamlisch to John's great friend and colleague, Michael Bennett.

If you have ever wanted to produce, if you have ever been interested in the nitty-gritty of what creating a Broadway show demands, this book will be an indispensable aid. Nowhere else are the details, especially the contractual details, of commercial producing laid out with such clarity and completeness.

John spent the bulk of his career as a lawyer at Paul, Weiss, training under the legendary Bob Montgomery. By the mid-1970s he was the leading theatrical lawyer in the country, a position he retained for the next thirty years. During that time he put deals together for hundreds of Broadway shows, and represented artists, producers, investors and non-profit theaters. From *A Chorus Line* to *Fences*, John was at the center of many of the most significant theatrical productions of our era. He knows what went into making those shows successful, and in this book he is passing that wisdom on.

After producing the Broadway revival of *A Chorus Line*, which he lovingly put together in 2006, John left Paul, Weiss two years later to pursue his dream of producing full time. He has since added a decade of producing experience to his long service as a theatrical lawyer; that experience, too, has given him insights that few others possess.

This is not a gossipy book; John has too much class, and too much respect for his clients and friends, to write a tell-all memoir. But it is, inevitably, a personal book, and is filled with recollections and memories of theatrical figures great and small. Reading it, one comes to know the John Breglio I have known over the past decade: funny, smart, loyal, humane, and generous. When I returned to New York as Artistic Director of the Public Theater in 2004, John was a constant source of support, advice, prodding and clarity. To my great surprise, and great good fortune, I found that the Public's lawyer was the most reliable moral compass I had in charting our course. Although John left the law a year later, I have called on him often in the decade since, and he has always been generous with his time and brilliant with his insights.

I have benefited enormously from what John has had to tell me; I know you will, too.

Oskar Eustis
Director of the Public Theatre

Preface

I grew up in a family where no one ever cursed. We were observant, but not strict, Roman Catholics. Unlike many of my Irish American friends, my brother, sister, and I didn't attend parochial school, and none of our relatives became priests or nuns. But we went to church every Sunday and ate fish on Fridays. I also went to confession every month to be absolved of my venal sins (as opposed to a mortal sin, like murder). These were second-degree transgressions such as fighting with your sister, lying to your parents, or thinking impure thoughts. (I didn't know what an impure thought was until the age of eleven, when an older friend, Peter, clued me in.)

Anyway, cursing was just a lowly sin, but I never had to confess to it because neither my parents nor we kids ever thought about saying anything more than "nuts" to express frustration.

My parents loved popular music, especially musical comedies. They could see that it was in my DNA as well. I think the pomp and theatricality of the church served as a catalyst for my attraction to drama and music at an early age. My mother often told of searching the apartment for her six-year-old son only to find me behind the heavy damask curtains in the living room ringing a bell, genuflecting with a blanket around my shoulders, and muttering chants straight from a Sunday Mass. At first she worried that I was headed for the priesthood, but she soon realized this was my private fantasy playing out against the backdrop of the only dramatic event I knew—a church service, with its staging, music, costumes, and lighting.

I tell you this so you can appreciate the dilemma my parents faced when, several years later, they considered taking my sister and me to see our first Broadway musical, *Damn Yankees*. By this time we had moved to Garden City, Long Island. Things were looking up for the Breglios, as they were for many families who in the 1950s made their exodus from the outer boroughs of New York City to the new suburbs farther out on the Island.

Leaving aside the title of the show, they must have also been concerned about exposing their nine-year-old son and thirteen-year-old daughter to the show's content. Keep in mind, in those days, Broadway musicals were mostly meant as adult entertainment, in the best sense of the phrase. Ultimately, given my sister's and my infatuation with music and the theater, their determination to introduce us to musicals as soon as possible overcame their ambivalence. What's more, I think my father had his heart set on seeing the leggy star of the show, Gwen Verdon.

Still, when they told me we were going to see the show, I wondered whether I'd be allowed to say the title out loud. I soon figured out it was fine. After all, I'd only be referring to the play they were taking me to. So off we went in our new pale green Chevrolet Impala on a hot summer's evening in August of 1956.

Almost sixty years later, I remember every moment of that night. As we walked into the 46th Street Theatre (now the Richard Rodgers) I sensed that I was entering a sanctuary not unlike a church, but definitely more fun. Everyone was dressed up—all the ladies wore hats and the men wore suits, white shirts, and ties. The theater was dimly lit and seemed mystical. The walls were painted red with gold gilt and, in my memory, cherubs and angels were carved in the ceiling. I assumed there wouldn't be "smells and bells" (a phrase first heard from a WASP friend years later) as we had in a High Holy Mass, but the red plush seats were a lot more comfortable than pews.

The usher eyed us a bit suspiciously as she checked our ticket stubs since we seemed to be the only children coming into the theater, but the absence of other children only made me feel particularly grown-up. We were shown to our seats upstairs in an area my father referred to as center mezzanine. He told us with some authority that it was the best place to see a musical because it gave the clearest view of the direction and dancing. My five-foot-two mother also preferred being upstairs. She said the orchestra seats were meant only for tall people whose view wouldn't be blocked by the person in front of them. They were both right.

After I riffled through the *Playbill* and finally found the title page about a third of the way through, the lights dimmed and the overture began. The acoustic sound of the orchestra (no amps then) was like nothing I'd ever heard before. It was exhilarating and overwhelming. By the time the curtain rose, I was on such a sensory overload that my heart was pounding and my palms were sweating.

I won't belabor what I witnessed for the next couple of hours except for two things. When Ray Walston, who played the devil (my Catholicism was coming in handy), crossed his legs in his opening scene and revealed bright red socks, the audience roared with laughter at what is still today one of the most brilliant sight gags ever. Even I got the joke at the age of nine. But what struck me most, and has stayed with me all these years, was hearing for the first time some 1,200 people burst into spontaneous, loud laughter. Like the overture, it was a sound unlike any I'd ever heard.

My other distinct memory is of a scene later in the show, when Verdon, playing Lola, the devil's assistant, stripped down to a shimmering black, tight leotard as she seduced the young protagonist, Joe Hardy, and sang the signature song from the show, "Whatever Lola Wants." I'm sure, at that moment, my parents had second thoughts about having taken an impressionable prepubescent boy to see this risqué show. But when they looked at my face, they surely realized I was transfixed—I was being transported into another realm. After that scene, saying "damn" seemed quite innocent by comparison. I also realized I wasn't even remotely in a church.

From then on, the theater, particularly musical theater, took me over with a vengeance. As soon as my mother thought she could deal with my going into Manhattan alone, I used my allowance to travel by bus and subway to see show after show. These were usually solo escapades since most of my teenage friends had little or no interest in Broadway plays and couldn't afford to spend as much as $4.60 on a theater ticket—the price for the best seats in the house, by the way.

Fast-forward to years later in New Haven, Connecticut. I was a freshman at Yale when the nearby Shubert Theatre was still playing tryouts of new plays and musicals. A new show, *The Roar of the Greasepaint—the Smell of the Crowd*, starring Cyril Ritchard and Anthony Newley, was coming to town ahead of its Broadway opening. I rushed to get my single ticket—still having trouble finding theater companions—for the opening night weeks in advance. I specifically requested a center orchestra seat right off the aisle, near the front. By some miracle, that's what I got. I arrived early. Although I had seen dozens of shows since I was a boy, I had never been to an opening night. I wanted to have that experience even if it was out of town.

Sadly, entering the disheveled Shubert Theatre in 1965 wasn't anything like going to see *Damn Yankees* ten years earlier. There was paint peeling off the ceiling, the seats were worn thin from too many years of neglect, and there was an occasional missing light bulb. What was most disillusioning, however, was that the theater had empty seats scattered all around both downstairs and up. On opening night! There wasn't exactly a buzz in the audience, but I tried to erase all those disappointments from my mind and focus instead on watching the opening of a new musical never seen anywhere before.

When I sat down, there was one seat vacant in front of me. Probably for a critic, I thought. I had read somewhere that they always came late, perhaps in Moss Hart's book, *Act One*. The audience was restless and the curtain was late. After all, this was New Haven, not Broadway, where everyone would have been happy just to be invited to an opening night.

Then it happened. Bounding down the aisle, in black tie and patent leather evening slippers, came none other than David Merrick, Broadway's most notorious and successful producer. Somehow, I had forgotten that this was his show. He took his seat directly in front of me. Seconds later, the houselights dimmed and the overture began. Nothing goes on in his theater until he's ready, I thought. During the show, he barely moved. And, not unlike the transfixed nine-year-old boy I had once been, he seemed oblivious to everything except each line spoken and each song sung on the stage. So this was what it was like to be a producer.

I appreciate that these vignettes may not be particularly unique. Anyone who has ever become infected with the theater bug can recount every detail of his first sighting of a Broadway show. When you are exposed to one for the first time, you're either possessed or not. Either you know it's something that must be part of your life, or you can take it or leave it.

I knew, from the age of nine, that somehow the theater would have to be part of my life. I didn't know in what guise, but details didn't matter then. The intoxication was so strong, I can recall saying to my college roommate, "I'd be happy just to pull the curtain."

None of us can foresee how we will get from here to there in our lives. Little did I know that becoming a producer myself would require that I first act as an entertainment lawyer and consigliere to artists and producers for more than thirty years.

Introduction

I've never considered myself a writer. As a lawyer, I've filled reams of paper, writing memos and letters on behalf of my clients, but writing a book such as this one called for a different skill. Moreover, by writing a how-to book, I was taking on the role of a teacher, an equally daunting proposition. I've guest-lectured and even taught a graduate school course on producing, but I wanted to avoid writing an academic text book.

While struggling to come up with a palatable solution, I was reminded of a quotation from a George Bernard Shaw play: "I'm not a teacher: only a fellow traveler of whom you asked the way. I pointed ahead—ahead of myself as well as of you."[1] Perhaps his advice might show me the way. Having spent four decades witnessing the business from so many perspectives, I hoped to offer a road map of the hows and wherefores, dos and don'ts of producing a Broadway play, interspersed with relevant memories from my own career.

One thing I knew for certain: theater people bring to their work a passion and dedication unparalleled in most other professions. I thought I could share my knowledge and experience of the industry with those who might want to produce and with others who are curious about the backstage reality of the theater. I will consider this book well worth writing if I have conveyed practical information set against the real-life stories of those who have devoted their lives to the theater.

Some Fundamentals

Dramatic Plays vs. Musicals

Plays are divided into two types: dramatico-musical (commonly referred to as musicals) and dramatic (commonly referred to as straight plays).[2]

---

[1] The quotation comes from Shaw's play *Getting Married.*

[2] These terms are used to identify musicals and plays in the Dramatists Guild's Approved Production Contracts, which will be examined and discussed in greater detail later in the book. The term *straight play*, coined many decades ago, has today taken on a curious connotation. The uninitiated may ask, "As opposed to a gay play?"

Although the basic principles and issues that apply to producing on Broadway pertain equally to both types, generally speaking musicals are more complex, particularly from a legal and business point of view. For one thing, musicals are anywhere from four to five times more expensive to produce than straight plays and can cost more than twice as much each week just to pay the bills. There is usually one author—the playwright—for a straight play. For musicals you normally have three authors: bookwriter, composer, and lyricist, although one person may perform two or all three roles (music and lyrics by Stephen Sondheim; book, music, and lyrics by Jonathan Larson). Additionally, the director in a musical often collaborates with the authors early on in the creative process and can become, in effect, another author.

Whereas straight plays are usually based on a playwright's original idea, musicals are more commonly derived from another work—a novel, movie, sound recording, or the life story of a celebrity or other well-known personality. Consequently, writing a musical requires, at the very outset, the acquisition of copyrights and other rights held by the owners of those other works.

As for the economics overall, a play employs a coterie of creative personnel and staff to get it up onstage; a musical requires a legion of people.

Collaboration

As I'll discuss in more depth in chapters seven and eight, musicals also depend on the success of the artistic give-and-take among the authors. The playwright holds supreme in the production of a straight play. Even the director ultimately bows to the playwright's concept and vision of what he means to convey to the audience. On the other hand, with musicals, it is of paramount importance that all the authors work closely and communicate regularly with one another from the very outset. Added to this mix is the participation of the director or, preferably, the director and choreographer (roles often performed by one person), who ideally should contribute to the work as early as possible in the creative process. Without a good working collaboration among those responsible for the primal elements of a musical—book, music, lyrics, direction, and choreography—the show will fail, regardless of the brilliance of any one of those elements.

And the collaboration doesn't end there. All the great musicals integrate the literary and musical material seamlessly with the designs of the show. Imagine the original productions of *Dreamgirls*, *The Phantom of the Opera*, or *Sunday in the Park with George* without Robin Wagner's spare design of revolving towers, Maria Björnson's sumptuous color palette, or Tony Straiges's ingenious scenic adaptation of Seurat's painting *A Sunday Afternoon on the Island of La Grande Jatte*, respectively.

For musicals, by virtue of the greater number of artists involved in creating the work, the producing chores become more complex, not only in dealing with more personalities (and temperaments) but also in managing the legal and business elements associated with the production of the show.

The Business of Producing

What's often forgotten is that every show is a new enterprise essentially built from the ground up by bringing together hundreds of theater professionals for the purpose of presenting a new work of art. A show's business foundation consists of the contracts between the authors and the owners of the underlying literary and musical material, and a team consisting of a producer, lawyer, general manager, stage management and crew, and advertising, marketing, and press agencies, all of whom provide the supporting framework. This book will examine in detail all of these contracts and the relationships that are established between the business and artistic sides of the equation. Not unlike any other business, the theater has its own words of art whose application we will consider whenever appropriate.

Developmental Work

Every show needs to be given sufficient time for the authors and other creative personnel to shape and experiment with a new work before it's presented on Broadway as a finished piece to the critics and the public. Readings, workshops, and out-of-town regional productions are prerequisites to reaching that final goal. Thanks to the unique alliances that have developed over the past six decades between the not-for-profit and commercial theaters, these smaller venues more often than not serve as the breeding grounds for most Broadway straight plays and musicals.

Financing

Producers must bring their own money and best salesmanship skills to raise the financing necessary to realize the artists' intentions for the play. If you are not experienced in raising money, this book will introduce you to the customary financing vehicles employed to solicit funds from the public and to related federal and state securities laws and regulations. Gaining the trust and confidence of your investors can be achieved only by providing for experienced management and preparing financial documents that contain realistic projections and expectations.

My objective throughout this book is to be comprehensive but not exhaustive or exhausting by getting into minute details. Although a few chapters might seem heavily technical or analytic, contained within each are concepts that will serve you well as a producer, in spite of the gory details. Every show is unique—you can never have enough knowledge or experience in the quest to do your job well.

Ultimately, my goal is to give the business of producing the respect it deserves. It is a profession that requires numerous skills, both business and creative. It demands relentless fortitude and optimism, and it should never be assumed casually without recognition of the enormity of the task.

1

The Idea

Free as the Air

You're in the shower or driving your car and you have an idea. You're pretty sure it's something no one has ever thought of before. What's more, you think it's a great inspiration for a Broadway musical.

That's one way a musical may get its start. The idea doesn't necessarily have to originate with you, the producer. It can come from anyone—a composer or lyricist, a director, an actor, or even your mother-in-law. But it's your job as the producer to make it come alive.

Musicals are either original or based on another work, such as a novel, a movie, a straight play, or someone's life story—*Les Misérables*, the Victor Hugo novel; *The Producers*, Mel Brooks's movie; *La Cage aux Folles*, the French straight play by Jean Poiret; *Hamilton*, the life story of Alexander Hamilton.

Probably the most famous original musical is *A Chorus Line*, first conceived by the legendary director and choreographer Michael Bennett. In 1974, Bennett and a dozen other Broadway dancers met in a rehearsal room on the Lower East Side of Manhattan and spent the next twelve hours recording anecdotes and memories from their childhoods and professional careers. In the beginning, Bennett didn't know what would come out of these sessions; it might be a documentary film, a book, or perhaps a play. He knew only one thing: he would call it *A Chorus Line*.

Even though it is not based on a book, movie, or other copyrighted material, even *A Chorus Line* is based on source material—the interviews recorded in that rehearsal room. To permit the bookwriters, Nicholas Dante and James Kirkwood Jr., and the lyricist, Ed Kleban, the freedom and legal right to use this material for the show, Bennett obtained written consent from each dancer to do whatever he chose with the material in exchange for one dollar. (Bennett would later voluntarily give all the dancers who participated in the interview sessions and the subsequent workshops a share of his income from *A Chorus Line* in recognition of their contributions to the show. We'll talk more about this in chapter eleven, "Workshops.")

Protecting Your Idea

Unfortunately, no matter how brilliant or original you may think your idea is, it cannot be protected legally from anyone coming up with the same idea.

In a landmark US Supreme Court case in 1918, Justice Louis Brandeis wrote, "Ideas are . . . free as the air."[1] As a further embodiment of that maxim, the copyright law of the United States provides that the law does not protect facts, ideas, systems, or methods of operation. What the copyright law *does* protect is the manner in which these things are expressed. For example, if a producer obtains permission from the owner of the rights in a novel to adapt it as a musical, then the actual expressions—the book and lyrics—created by the bookwriter and lyricist will be capable of being protected by copyright.

Over the years, major motion picture studios have had to defend countless lawsuits in which a plaintiff has alleged that his idea was "stolen" by a studio. To prevail in such a case, the plaintiff would have to prove that the studio had contractually agreed to compensate him for the use of his idea even though it wasn't capable of copyright protection. This is something to which no studio would ever agree. In fact, as a rule, studios, and many writers and producers, will not accept unsolicited manuscripts or ideas from unknown third parties for fear that at some point down the road that person will claim his idea was stolen. Most such allegations are considered nuisance claims, but often they have to be defended with all the attendant legal costs and expenses.

Along a similar line of reasoning, titles are not generally protectable, except in certain circumstances. Let's assume someone wants to produce a musical entitled *Rent*. Prior to the opening of the now world-famous musical of the same title, anyone could have used the word *rent* as the

[1] International News Service v. Associated Press, 248 U.S. 215, 250 (1918).

title for a musical. It was, as Justice Brandeis said, "free as the air." However, the situation today is quite different. If anyone now tried to use the title *Rent* for a new play or musical, the owners of the estate of Jonathan Larson (the composer, lyricist, and bookwriter) would most assuredly commence a lawsuit seeking to prohibit its use. And they would prevail.

That's because the musical *Rent* has now achieved a level of protection which would undoubtedly be recognized by courts of law. Allowing someone else to use that title for another musical would confuse the public and permit that musical to compete unfairly in the marketplace with the Tony Award–winning play. In effect, the new musical with the same title would be trading on the success and popularity of the 1996 show.

To achieve this level of protection the title itself must have established "secondary meaning," which means that whenever one reads or hears the title, one associates it with the title of the famous work. Hearing the words *gone with the wind* immediately conjures up Margaret Mitchell's Civil War saga. The same holds true for *Gypsy*, *Wicked*, *The Lion King*, and *The Sound of Music*—all titles of famous musicals comprising simple English words. These titles have all established a secondary meaning beyond the actual meaning of the words themselves.

To prove "secondary meaning," the owner of the play, movie, or other literary work is required to prove that a reasonable person, when hearing the words of a particular title, will identify those words with a specific copyrighted work. That kind of recognition is based on the degree to which the specific work has achieved a high level of success, not only nationally but globally as well. The factors taken into account are the length of its run on Broadway and elsewhere throughout the world, box office success, Tony and other awards, critical acclaim, and widespread advertising, marketing, and merchandising.

Another factor to keep in mind is that secondary meaning, once attached to a title, applies only to a specific industry or business. Although the owners of *Rent* could prohibit another play or movie from being produced with the same title, they could not prohibit a moving van company, for example, from using the word *rent* as part of its business name. No reasonable person could confuse one use with the other and, consequently, there could be no confusion or unfair competition between the musical and the moving company.

Here's a real-life example of title confusion.

The Elephant Man vs. *The Elephant Man*

In 1977, the playwright Bernard Pomerance wrote a straight play entitled *The Elephant Man*. It was originally produced at the Hampstead Theatre in London, later in New York by the York Theatre Company at Saint Peter's Church, and then on Broadway, at the Booth Theatre, in the spring of 1979. It was produced by Richmond Crinkley and the team of Elizabeth I. McCann and Nelle Nugent.

The play told the true story of Joseph Merrick (called John Merrick in the play), who lived in Victorian England in the late nineteenth century. Merrick was born with a serious body deformity that caused him to have misshapen limbs and an enlarged skull—so large in fact that his hat measured three feet in circumference. At the time, doctors diagnosed Merrick with elephantiasis; hence the name the Elephant Man. Medical science continued to study Merrick's condition long after his death, eventually coming to the conclusion that he most likely suffered from a rare disease known as Proteus syndrome.

The play was a huge success in the 1978–79 season. It won the Tony Award, the Drama Desk Award, and the New York Drama Critics' Circle Award for Best Play. It ran for 916 performances on Broadway, toured the United States and Canada, and was produced throughout the world. It has also had two revivals on Broadway featuring star performers (Billy Crudup and Bradley Cooper) in the title role.

Although Pomerance's play was based on a real person and included other characters who lived and interacted with Merrick while he was alive, the play was also partly a work of fiction, being the product of Pomerance's fertile imagination.

In 1980, Mel Brooks's motion picture company, Brooksfilms, announced it was planning to produce a full-length feature motion picture entitled *The Elephant Man*. The press release said that it would not be based on the Pomerance play. At that time, the play had not yet been sold to any movie company, but it was still running on Broadway and would continue to run for over two years. As the lawyer representing the play, I was contacted by Pomerance and the producers, who sought my advice about the upcoming film. Their concern was that Brooks's film would be confused with the Broadway play and effectively eliminate any possibility of a future film sale for the play. They also felt that it was unfair of Brooks to play freely off of the huge success of their play and exploit its notoriety for the benefit of his film.

Beyond the obvious issue of the similar titles, this case had a further wrinkle. Not only was *The Elephant Man* based on a man who lived in the nineteenth century, but he himself was also referred to at that time as the Elephant Man. Therefore, although Brooks didn't gainsay the play's success or its worldwide recognition, he argued, nonetheless, that no playwright could take an actual person's name or sobriquet and use it exclusively as his own. It would be as if a playwright tried to restrict the use of Abraham Lincoln as the title of a play.

There was, however, an important factor in favor of Pomerance. Although Merrick might have been known some one hundred years earlier as the Elephant Man, one would be hard put to identify even a few people who had known him or ever heard of the Elephant Man before 1979.

Would the courts permit Pomerance to, in effect, remove Merrick's name as a title from use by any other author or producer by virtue of the success of the play? As discussed earlier, to do so, Pomerance would have to establish a strong secondary meaning for his title and demonstrate that permitting Brooks the right to use the same title would cause confusion in the public's mind and deprive the play of future income.

During the pretrial discovery phase, we took lengthy depositions of Brooks in my office. At one of these sessions, Brooks had already been grilled for several hours when my litigation partner went at him full force, declaring that he had stolen outright the title of the Broadway play. After several moments of contemplation, Brooks leaned forward in his chair and wagged a finger in my partner's face. "You," he said, "are sooo *mean*." The lawyers called it a day.

Pretrial discovery dragged on for months—there seemed no end in sight. While the lawyers thrashed it out, Brooks had moved ahead with filming and was nearing post-production. The film was a negative pickup

The original poster for the Mel Brooks film, *The Elephant Man*. Note the legend in the box distinguishing the movie from the Tony Award winning play. *From the authors collection.*

deal, which meant Brooks would have to deliver a completed unencumbered film to the studio in order to recover its production costs. Under the cloud of litigation, Brooks would be unable to deliver a clean title to the film or get it released. Ultimately, practical and financial pressure brought Brooks to the settlement table. The terms of settlement were confidential. What history shows, however, is that the film was eventually released with appropriate language distinguishing it from the play: "Based upon the life of John Merrick, the Elephant Man, and not upon the Broadway play or any other fictional account."

If the case had gone to trial, it would have been one that tested in a novel way the legal theories of unfair competition and secondary meaning. In my view, if it were not for the fact that Joseph Merrick had actually been known as the Elephant Man, Pomerance would have undoubtedly prevailed on his claim that the title of his play had established secondary meaning. However, I believe the court would have required a very high degree of proof, not only that the play was inextricably identified with the man but also that, in his time, Merrick was known as the Elephant Man by only a relatively small segment of the British population and never achieved any widespread international notoriety.

An interesting question: What if the Internet and social media as we know it today existed during Merrick's lifetime? Would he have become a cause célèbre of international fame and thereby been known to generations after his death as the Elephant Man? If that had been the case, his name would not be unlike that of Julius Caesar—free for anyone, including Shakespeare, to use as the title of any number of books, plays, or movies.

Here's another story.

Once in a Full Moon

At my law firm, we had what was referred to as the Full Moon Committee, the members of which were usually the younger partners. Their job was to conduct a preliminary interview with unsolicited clients who appeared on our doorstep without a referral. I believe it was in the early eighties when a call from a woman was referred to me as the newly appointed member of the committee. The woman told my secretary, Ann Scaffidi, she needed to discuss a matter of some urgency. Ann tried to get some specifics from her, but the woman refused to offer any details other than that it required immediate attention. Being a junior partner and ambitious to widen my practice, I told Ann to book an appointment the next day.

When this rather mysterious woman arrived, she was shown by Ann to my office. Although her name has not stayed with me, I remember her very clearly. She was nervous and shifty-eyed—not unlike Mary Astor in *The Maltese Falcon* when she first meets Humphrey Bogart in his office.

We exchanged a few awkward pleasantries, after which she said she needed my advice about an exceedingly confidential matter. She'd come up with an idea that would be the basis for the greatest musical in Broadway history and would undoubtedly make her and me (as her lawyer) very rich people. I now grew suspicious since the only way my fortunes could be tied to hers was if I agreed to take a contingency fee[2] for my services, rather than an hourly rate. I was about to tell her that because she was not yet a client, any communication between us would not technically fall within the confidentiality privilege. But I refrained from saying anything, as I assumed that the idea she was about to share would warrant as much secrecy as the air we breathe.

My visitor then looked around the office, moved her chair closer to my desk, and lowered her voice: "I want to produce a musical based on a very well-known movie."

I waited a few beats and said, "Yes, I understand. Can you tell me the name of the movie?"

"*King Kong*."

I don't recall precisely how I reacted but I'm sure I did something like touch the fingers on one hand with those on the other hand and lower my head in deep contemplation. As it happened, at that time there was a rumor floating in Hollywood that the first film remake of *King Kong* was going to be produced. I told my lady friend about the remake and warned her that it was highly unlikely the film studio that held the

[2] In most cases, lawyers are paid fees based on hourly charges. On occasion, a lawyer may charge a percentage contingency fee (usually 5 percent or 10 percent) of the money earned by a client from a transaction negotiated by the lawyer.

rights would be willing to grant a license to anyone to produce a stage musical, much less to someone who had no experience producing anything. I also pointed out that any such license would require a substantial up-front payment of at least five figures, not to mention my legal fees, which, I was quick to say, would be based on the many hours it would take me to track down the rights. None of these warnings seemed to dissuade her, although I'm sure I noticed a wince when I mentioned my fees.

Then I thought I would ask her a very practical question which would surely disabuse her of her fantasy and get her out of my office. "Well," I said in what I thought was an appropriate conspiratorial tone, "how do you intend to portray the beast onstage?"

She searched the room with her eyes again and said, slowly and emphatically, "I have a very big friend."

To this day, I'm not sure if she thought her most valuable idea was *King Kong* or her big friend.

I now realized nothing I said would get her out of my office and so I resorted to a surefire tactic. I told her that I would think about our meeting and, if I thought I could help her, I'd send her our retainer letter along with an invoice for our up-front down payment.

As I write this, there is indeed a musical based on *King Kong* threatening to come to Broadway. Perhaps that very same lady who visited me over thirty years ago is involved, having found a more solicitous lawyer, but no doubt continuing her friendship with the very big friend.

2

Get Thee to a Lawyer

The first thing we do, let's kill all the lawyers.
—*Henry VI*, part 2, act 4

Shakespeare notwithstanding, the first thing any producer, fledgling or veteran, must do if he wants to move beyond fantasizing about a show is hire a lawyer—and not just any lawyer, but an entertainment lawyer.

When I first entered law school, I had never heard of entertainment law. Most specialties are defined by a body of law such as taxes, corporations, trusts and estates, or litigation. I would learn that entertainment isn't so much a body of law but rather an industry requiring lawyers with an expertise in copyright and trademark laws, contracts, and financing. Today, you also need to familiarize yourself with all aspects of the internet, online services, and streaming programming.

I Found My Job in the *New York Times*

In the fall of my second year at Harvard Law School, I read in the *New York Times* a profile of a lawyer in New York, John F. Wharton, who was a founding partner of the firm Paul, Weiss, Rifkind, Wharton & Garrison. He was trained as a corporate lawyer, but his avid avocational interest in the arts caused him to carve out a specialty representing playwrights, directors, composers, and actors. At the time the article appeared, Wharton was undisputedly the dean of entertainment lawyers. On his seventy-fifth birthday, the Shubert Theatre on West Forty-Fourth Street shut down so the entire community could celebrate his illustrious career. None other than the playwright Arthur Miller, one of Wharton's clients, gave one of the testimonials.

A year after joining Paul, Weiss as a summer associate in 1970, I was invited to join the firm as a permanent associate and began working with Wharton and another partner, Robert H. Montgomery Jr., a preeminent motion picture lawyer.

To give you an example of the through-line of these two lawyers' careers, it was Wharton who had come up with the idea that a limited partnership[1] could be used by producers to raise capital and produce plays and musicals. It was, like all innovative ideas, quite simple, but one that revolutionized the theater-production business. For years, individual investors (or so-called angels) had handed over their money to producers with little or no paperwork, and with no apparent protection from lawsuits or other shady practices that might occur in connection with the show. By using a limited partnership, the investors' liability would be "limited" to the amounts they actually put into the play, regardless of the number of lawsuits brought against it and the damages that might be awarded. Limited partnerships, a commonly used legal entity in other businesses, such as real estate, gave theater productions a legitimacy and credibility for the first time. Today, nearly seventy years later, many theater professionals still refer to this form of theatrical limited partnership as the "Wharton form."

Montgomery, who worked in the 1950s with Wharton and another Paul, Weiss lawyer, John C. Taylor, took Wharton's idea one step further and applied it to independent-film financing. The same principles and benefits accruing to theater investors would apply equally to film investors. One of the first films to use the limited partnership as its financing vehicle was the 1970 film *Diary of a Mad Housewife*, directed and produced by Montgomery's client Frank Perry. Today, the limited partnership, or limited liability company (a close relative), remains the principal financing vehicle used by filmmakers for the production of independent films.

So I sat at the feet of both these men, regarded as the best theater lawyer (Wharton) and film lawyer (Montgomery) in the country. Since the firm had dozens of clients involved in all aspects of the entertainment and media worlds, I was exposed to the music-publishing, sound-recording, and book-publishing businesses as well. I became immersed in the complexities of contract drafting and was soon negotiating one-on-one with

---

[1] As we'll see later in chapter fifteen, "Finding the Money," the limited partnership is still used today to raise money for most Broadway plays.

other lawyers and agents for rights and services in just about every facet of the entertainment business. I owe my career to these great teachers and all the other lawyers at Paul, Weiss who made it possible for me to represent a wide variety of artists.

A Trusted Ally and Friend

But what does an entertainment lawyer really do besides negotiating and drafting contracts? By and large, clients seek out entertainment lawyers not only for their legal skills but also for their business judgment and acumen, their professional contacts, and their knowledge of what is current and relevant in the business at any particular time.

If a fledgling producer came to me with a great idea for a show (but had little or no experience), I'd initially help guide him and arrange for the acquisition of rights in a particular book or movie, and then I'd introduce him to writers, composers, or directors who could potentially be a good match, regardless of whether or not they were my clients. I'd instruct him on the rules and principles governing the raising of money for a show and the necessary legal requirements. I might even introduce him to potential investors or other financing sources.

Perhaps most important, I'd become, in some ways, his most loyal and steadfast friend and confidant throughout the whole process. As I've said to many of my clients, everyone associated with your show will have a contract with you and could, at some point down the road, become your adversary. Your lawyer can be trusted to hold as confidential all of your affairs and should work only in your best interests whenever there are disputes—and there will be many. Your lawyer needs to be a shoulder to lean on. There aren't that many shoulders around, particularly when things aren't going so well.

In addition, your lawyer must be able to guide and advise you both legally and practically from the inception of your idea to getting your show up on the stage. She should be experienced in securing stage and other related rights in the copyrighted material, such as books (both fiction and nonfiction), movies, other plays, sound recordings, and life story rights of real people either living or dead that often form the basis for musicals. Building on those rights, she must be conversant with the forms of agreement that secure the writing services of the bookwriter, composer, and lyricist of the show. When it comes to financing the production, she needs to be aware of the laws, both federal and state, that govern the raising of money from the public. That necessarily involves the organization of the proper investment vehicle to represent the producer's and the investors' financial stakes in the production. She also needs to have a background in copyright and related intellectual property law, such as unfair competition, and all forms of the new media and the Internet.

Besides having the requisite legal and business skills, a producer's lawyer should ideally have acquired a reputation among theater owners, talent agents, managers, and other producers as a trustworthy member of the community familiar with the customs and norms of the industry.

A lawyer should also identify areas of weakness in her client's profile. For example, if a client inexperienced in producing came to me with what seemed like a good idea, I might suggest he team up with a seasoned producer, particularly if the client didn't have his own financial resources to fund the up-front developmental costs of the project. Otherwise, I couldn't responsibly represent to agents or theater owners that my client was capable of bringing the necessary expertise or financing to the table. Moreover, if it was going to be necessary to acquire rights in a valuable underlying book or movie, the owners of those rights might be understandably reluctant to hand over a valuable property to a first-timer.

Usually the producer has enough resources to hire a lawyer, acquire the necessary underlying rights, and hire the authors. That's not inexpensive, often requiring anywhere from $25,000 to $100,000. As a rule of thumb, it's always advisable for the client to develop the property on his own for as long as he can in order to leverage a more advantageous deal with partners later on.[2]

Like any professional, a good lawyer with the right experience does not come cheaply. On the whole, entertainment lawyers charge their producer clients an hourly fee that, for senior members of the bar, can range from $500 to $1,000. The fees can be broken down in stages:

---

[2] In chapter fifteen, "Finding the Money," we'll also discuss the raising of so-called front money, which can be used to finance early developmental costs.

First, your lawyer will probably ask for a retainer as an advance against her hourly fee—somewhere around $10,000. She will then begin by acquiring the necessary underlying rights and securing the services of the writer, composer, and lyricist. You will also be advised to hire a general manager fairly early on to begin the process of budgeting the show, although this can't really be done practically until at least a first draft of the work is completed. To reach that point you will have spent a significant amount of money; the underlying owners will require an advance, perhaps $25,000, the writers will get at least $18,000 ($6,000 each), the general manager $10,000, and the legal fees to get that far could be as high as $25,000. You're now up to $78,000 and you've barely begun.

Once the show is written and ready to be produced in a workshop, an out-of-town tryout, or on Broadway, the general manager will prepare budgets that include an estimate of legal fees for the production. Those fees can vary considerably depending on any developmental pre-Broadway productions and the scope and complexity of the show. The legal fee line item in most production budgets for a major Broadway musical is rarely less than $100,000 and can be higher. These fees and any other monies spent during pre-production will be included in the original capitalization for the show and can be either invested by the producer or reimbursed to him once he has raised all the money from his investors. During the run of the play, the lawyers receive a weekly fee to cover day-to-day miscellaneous legal issues that may arise. These fees range from $750 to $1,000 per week or higher, again, depending on the magnitude of the production.

I'll have a lot more to say in later chapters about general managers, budgeting, and financing.

Artists and producers are needy souls. Helping to bring the written word to the stage or screen and the actor's or director's talent to the public, and guiding a producer around the shoals of the business, are what good entertainment lawyers do every day.

The practice of entertainment law can be intense and stressful, particularly representing talented artists who can be ego-driven and self-possessed about their careers and not much else. But more often than not it can also be exceedingly rewarding, particularly when you find yourself representing someone who's creating exemplary work.

There was nothing more satisfying for me than acting for the likes of Stephen Sondheim, August Wilson, and Michael Bennett, to name a few—what giants they were and continue to be, in the case of Steve. To be there for whatever they might need to get their work seen and heard always seemed a privilege to me. True artists are rare beings who transform sometimes ordinary ideas into works of art that enrich and illuminate our lives. Listen to Sondheim's song "Move On" from *Sunday in the Park* with George, or read Wilson's act 1 monologue for Bynum in *Joe Turner's Come and Gone*, or watch Bennett's staging of "At the Ballet" in *A Chorus Line*. To experience these moments is to appreciate what it is to be an artist.

If I sound like a fan, it's because I am in the truest sense of the word. After all, what could be more fun than to be a fan of your own client?

3

The Eye of the Tiger

In any successful lawyer-client relationship, it is essential that your lawyer gain your trust and confidence. Conversely, if your lawyer is to protect and serve you well, you must be forthright and honest with her. These relationships can be particularly fulfilling and can endure for many decades. My most satisfying representations were those in which my clients and I developed a high degree of mutual respect for one another so I could not only act as a close confidant on their entertainment matters but also be there for them, along with my partners, for divorces, estate planning, and litigations.

All the more reason a client should sever the relationship with a lawyer he suspects of disloyalty or in whom he has lost confidence. And a lawyer should end a representation—in effect fire the client—if she finds herself working at cross purposes or, worse, compromised by the actions of her client.

Many years ago, I was approached by a producer, Ms. X, whom I knew by reputation but had never encountered in any business matters. She was a relative newcomer to Broadway. Her early forays had brought her a mixed bag of middling success and some disappointments. At the time, she was also in the middle of a nasty lawsuit.

I was wary of taking on Ms. X as a client, since I had heard gossip about her aggressive nature and litigious predisposition. To some extent the reputation of a lawyer can be a reflection of the clients he or she represents but the reverse can also be true. A lawyer who has the right credentials and high credibility can be an enormous asset to a client, particularly for someone who is an unknown commodity. I made a few calls—to agents and theater owners—to find out if this was something I should pursue. I was told to be cautious, but no one said anything that set off alarm bells.

I eventually agreed to meet with Ms. X and told her my due diligence revealed she had a somewhat checkered reputation around town.

She said she was aware of the rumors but she assured me they were unfounded. She was determined to change any negative perceptions and enter the top tiers of producing on Broadway. Since there was no contract between us except our mutual goodwill and intentions, I said that if either of us found the relationship wanting for any reason, we could terminate it at will.

I assigned Ms. X to one of my more experienced associates. The first few matters proceeded smoothly, but, several months into the representation, she came to me with concerns about Ms. X's behavior. "I don't know how much longer I can continue to work on her matters," she said. "She's asking me to take positions I'm not comfortable with and I'm not sure she's being straight with me." I asked her to give the client some slack for the time being, but to get back to me if things got any worse. Now alarm bells *were* beginning to go off.

Then I had an encounter on a subsequent matter that was, to say the least, unsettling. I was negotiating for Ms. X against one of the most powerful talent agents in the business. The deal was fraught with problems and it wasn't clear my client would win the day. In order to clinch the deal, Ms. X asked me to make a representation to the agent that turned out to be false. When the agent discovered this, he exploded. "For over twenty years, John, I've known you to be a tough adversary, but never a dishonest one."

It was the straw that broke the camel's back. When I told my associate what had happened, she expressed no surprise but, rather, seemed relieved that it had all finally come to a head.

I called Ms. X and told her that we'd have to go our separate ways. She was astonished. She didn't understand what the issue was, so I invited her to meet with me and my associate in my office. I reviewed the entire episode and concluded by saying that her lying to me had compromised my integrity and placed me in an unfavorable light with an important member of the community. Again, she expressed surprise and said she didn't understand the problem.

I asked, "What don't you understand?"

She then proceeded to tell me her philosophy of the ideal lawyer-client relationship. It went something like this: "When I retain a lawyer, I expect him to be a tiger." She wanted her lawyer to be tough and aggressive. Fair enough, but then she said, "If I had told you the truth, you wouldn't have been able to be a tiger and get me the best possible deal." Her philosophy was pure and simple: the ends justify the means, even if it means lying to your own lawyer.

I looked at my associate, who had by now grown ashen-faced, and then turned to Ms. X and said, "And that's why we can no longer represent you."

4

The General Manager

An Unsung Hero

Equally important to retaining a lawyer from the beginning is hiring a seasoned general manager (known as a GM) for your musical. When I decided to produce my first show, I knew I needed the best possible GM by my side, particularly since I was going it alone. Alan Wasser was someone I had worked with and observed for many years. I respected his steady hand and knowledge of the industry. I knew I would be entrusting him with all of the day-to-day details of the production and, as my closest business associate, he would be the face of the production to the outside world. Alan, along with his associate Aaron Lustbader, proved to be everything I had hoped for and more.

GMs are the backbone of the producing business. They are the equivalent of a line producer in a film. Here's a list of their most important duties:

- Prepare production and operating budgets
- Along with your lawyer, negotiate the deals with the authors, the director, the choreographer, the star, the arrangers and orchestrators, and the theater owner; on their own, negotiate dozens of contracts with the cast, crew, and staff, including the ad agency, press agent, and marketing group
- Know the intricacies of and abide by the union rules governing the actors, musicians, stagehands, ushers, box office treasurers, stage and company managers, and press agents
- Maintain your financial books and records and, with the production's outside accountant, prepare monthly and annual reports for your investors
- Prepare payroll and administer payment of royalties to the creative team

- Monitor the daily activity at the box office and the income for the show from all other sources
- Organize opening night and the party along with an outside planner
- Provide advice for best practices in marketing and advertising
- Manage ticket inventory and pricing policies
- Field inquiries for additional productions
- Overall, act as the producer's surrogate for any and all matters that require attention when he is unavailable

The GM shouldn't be confused with the company manager, production stage manager, or stage manager.

- The company manager, usually hired on the recommendation of the GM, attends to the needs of the cast and crew. He or she attends each performance, works closely with the house manager (the theater owner's employee), and reports the number of seats sold and the daily income for the show. The company manager usually also manages house seat requests.[1]
- The production stage manager (often referred to as the PSM) is the director's right-hand associate. The PSM attends and manages every rehearsal while beginning to prepare the stage manager's script containing the director's blocking and other performance notes. When the show goes into technical rehearsal at the theater (before previews), the PSM, alongside the director, will take charge of the dozens of designers and stagehands as the set is put into operation for the first time and the lights are focused. All of the intricate setups are recorded by the PSM as "cues" in the stage manager's script.
- The stage manager runs each performance of the show from a small upright desk in the wings, armed with the stage manager's script. The PSM may run the show during previews and even thereafter until the crew are comfortable with their assignments. After the opening, the PSM is usually retired and the stage manager takes over. Each cue is called by the stage manager and communicated through headsets to the lighting, sound, and

---

[1] See chapter 5 for an explanation of house seats..

stage crews. The stage manager and the company manager are in charge backstage after the PSM leaves. After each performance, the stage manager will prepare a written report that's sent to the producer, director, and several key personnel, summarizing the quality of that performance overall, any absences, audience response, and other pertinent information.

The GM's Contract

Most GM contracts are similar in form and substance. The GM's duties as outlined above are performed within the approved budgets and with the consent of the producer (except for day-to-day ministerial duties).

The GM's compensation includes a fee of anywhere from $40,000 to $60,000 and, in special cases, more, payable in installments beginning on signing of the contract and ending at the completion of rehearsals. If the project is abandoned at any stage, only the payments up to that date are retained and the balance, if any, is forfeited. There may be time limits on the GM's services, so that if the development process goes beyond three or four years, the GM can ask for additional payments to take into account the protracted time period.

Additionally, a weekly salary of $5,000 to $6,000 is paid for the run of the play. Again, built-in increases may be included after the first two or three years of a run. Rarely, if ever, does the GM receive a royalty, but it is not unknown for a highly experienced GM to receive as much as 5 percent of the net profits,[2] though it is more commonly in the range of 2 percent, rising to 3 percent after recoupment of the show's production costs.

GMs may also request that they be hired to manage additional companies of the show. A producer who has no experience working with a particular GM may be reluctant to commit in advance to this obligation. Of course, if for any reason the GM is in breach of the contract, the producer can terminate the relationship. On the other hand, the GM may have performed the duties of the job satisfactorily but had poor rapport with the producer or a personality conflict with the director. A compromise is to commit to hiring the GM at least for the first US national

[2] The term *net profits*, as it applies to Broadway shows, will be discussed in greater detail in chapters dealing with financing and the various production contracts.

tour. Other smaller tours and foreign companies (London, Europe, and Asia) should be excluded since in such cases the producer may partner with other producers who may want to use their choice of GM.

⬥ ⬥ ⬥

I can't emphasize enough the value of a good GM. This is the "go-to" person in all respects. By and large, GMs in New York are all competent, although some may be more experienced in managing straight plays rather than big-budget musicals. And some have greater expertise Off-Broadway as opposed to Broadway. You should interview as many as you can and go with the one with whom you feel most comfortable and who has the time to devote to your project.

Musicals regularly congratulate themselves for a particularly long run—ten, fifteen, or more years—by holding special-invitation performances for family and friends. At one such performance I attended, the producer came onstage to address the audience. He generously thanked everyone, from the cast to the attendants in the ladies' room, but he never mentioned the GM and his staff. It might have been an oversight. I was stunned nonetheless and I told the GM as much later on at the party. Everyone can be forgiven when they slip up on their thank-yous, but this wasn't any ordinary omission.

Too often GMs don't have their praises sung. These men and women, who usually have worked their way up through the ranks, are as critical to the success of a show as anyone else, maybe more so. They tend to be self-effacing and are happy to stay out of the limelight. Many GMs ease their way into producing as they mature in the business. They find it increasingly frustrating sitting on the sidelines while they observe novice producers enter the arena with little or no knowledge or experience. In that case, their office serves a dual function—that of a shadow producer and GM.

Objectivity is not the strong suit of a producer in the midst of battle. In fact, it may be a hindrance when what's needed is a headstrong and relentless leader. At such times, there is no substitute for having an independent GM at your side who can be clearheaded and vigilant about any missteps. No one knows better the shoals and sharks lurking everywhere. Your GM is your rudder and ballast.

5

Securing the Rights

Without foundations there can be no fashion.

—Christian Dior

Now that you've formulated your idea for a musical, retained a lawyer, and hired a GM, you're in a position to secure the rights in the underlying property on which your musical will be based.

As discussed earlier, the majority of musicals are based on some other copyrighted or otherwise protected literary, musical, or factual material,[1] rather than an unprotected idea—straight plays, less so. Musicals are drawn from many different kinds of underlying works—novels, nonfiction books (including biographies and life stories of celebrities and well-known historical characters), motion pictures, dramatic plays, operas, sound recordings, and even poems. Notable examples are: *The Lion King* (film), *Rent* (opera), *Evita* (sound recording), *Cats* (poem), *La Cage aux Folles* (play), *Hamilton* (life story), and *The Bridges of Madison County* (book and movie).

The task of securing the necessary rights to underlying material is fundamentally the job of your lawyer, although your lawyer may also call on your GM for advice, and confer with you if you have experience from other shows or have some special connection to the owner of the underlying material. Otherwise, you'll rely on your lawyer who will call upon not only her legal expertise but also on her familiarity with precedents from other deals and her relationships with the agents, lawyers, and business affairs executives with whom she will negotiate the deal.

[1] If the underlying work is in the public domain, its copyright has expired. It is then available for anyone's use without payment. Your lawyer will conduct a copyright search to determine to what extent the work is legally copyrighted or in the public domain both domestically and internationally.

The underlying rights deal is perhaps the single most important legal document you will sign as a producer. It is the foundation on which every other important creative contract will rest; it defines the extent of the exclusive rights granted to the producer, both temporally and geographically, and governs the creative relationship among the owner of the underlying rights,[2] the authors of the musical, and the producer. When negotiating these deals, it becomes necessary to contemplate all the twists and turns down the road as you develop the show so that the terms of the deal, and any restrictions or constraints contained therein, do not become hindrances or, in some cases, outright obstacles to the show's creation.

An underlying rights agreement can be broken down into ten parts:

1. Grant of primary rights
2. Options and advance payments
3. Royalties
4. Additional and subsidiary rights
5. Merger
6. Credit or billing
7. Expenses
8. Representations, warranties, and indemnities
9. Opening night seats and house seats
10. Agency clause

Grant of Primary Rights

The grant of rights in the underlying work (let's assume it's a novel) is commonly expressed in the following terms:

> The exclusive option to develop, finance, produce, and exploit, initially in the United States and Canada and, thereafter, throughout the world, a musical for one or more first-class, live stage performances based on the underlying work.

---

[2] Throughout this book, whenever I refer to the "owner" it will mean the owner of the rights in an underlying work as compared to "author(s)," which will refer to the bookwriter, composer, and/or lyricist of the musical.

There is a lot of substantive content in that one sentence. If you understand the meaning of this sentence, you can master the essential terms of any grant of rights in underlying material.

Let's start with a question frequently asked and rarely, if ever, adequately answered: What constitutes "first-class performances" or "first-class productions"? Oddly enough, no such definition exists either in common or statutory law, nor is there any industry-wide consensus on a definition. Nonetheless, the reference to "first-class performances" or "first-class productions" appears in virtually every contract for a Broadway straight play or musical. As an exercise in futility, try asking any theater professional for a definition of a "first-class production." See what you get.

There is, however, one way of piecing together an understanding of this fundamental term of art. The Dramatists Guild (a collective of playwrights, composers, lyricists, and bookwriters) promulgates standard contracts for the production of Broadway straight plays and musicals known as the Approved Production Contract (both referred to as the APC). These contracts pertain to the engagement of the authors of a straight play or musical, not to the licensing of underlying rights. However, many of the terms embedded in the APC are quite similar to those found in an underlying rights agreement. In chapter twelve I will explore the APC in depth, but it's worth noting here that there is a definition of first-class performances on the first page of the APC:

> *First-Class Performances* shall mean live stage productions . . . in a first-class theatre in a first-class manner, with a first-class cast and a first-class director.

How's that for clarity? It would be easier for a blind man wearing a blindfold to find a needle in a dark room than for anyone to figure out that definitional vicious circle.

Here's my considered take on how to make some sense of this phrase. Although the APC doesn't give you much help with the other "first-class" references, industry practitioners understand that a "first-class production" generally means (a) hiring a cast under the actors' union's (Actors' Equity Association) Broadway contract (the "Production Contract"); (b) hiring a "first-class director" under the directors' union's

(Stage Directors and Choreographers Society) Broadway contract; and (c) booking a first-class theater with a seating capacity of five hundred or more located within the area west of Sixth Avenue, east of Ninth Avenue, south of Fifty-Fourth Street, and north of Forty-First Street.[3] Generally speaking, only straight plays and musicals that open in those theaters are eligible for the much coveted Tony Award nominations.[4]

Remarkably, in virtually all underlying rights agreements, the grant of rights simply makes reference to "a first-class production as generally understood in the legitimate theater business." It is in effect saying: we all know it when we see it. But try that in a court of law if a dispute should arise on the exact meaning of the phrase. You wouldn't get very far.

So now you've agreed to produce a "first-class production." In the first instance, the primary rights are commonly limited geographically to the United States and Canada. Producers can open their play initially in an out-of-town tryout or even on the West End of London. But, ultimately, most first-class productions have their eyes fixed on Broadway.

As we'll discuss later, provided the producer has opened the musical on Broadway and it has run for a few performances, the underlying work (the novel) will become conjoined or merged, if you will, with the new musical adaptation written by the authors. As a consequence, the musical can then be produced throughout the world, not only in first-class productions but also in smaller venues with both professional and amateur actors, and be further exploited in film and all other media. I'll have a lot more to say about merger and these additional and subsidiary rights in chapter twelve.

Options and Advance Payments

As compared to an outright sale, underlying rights agreements are licenses for a limited period of time and are subject to the holder making certain "option" payments at specific intervals.

---

[3] Lincoln Center's Vivian Beaumont Theater, although outside these boundaries, also qualifies as a first-class theater.

[4] As a producer, you are also bound to embrace the less coveted privilege of paying higher union rates to most of your employees if you play in a Broadway, Tony-eligible theater.

An example might work as follows: the first option period is normally for one year or eighteen months upon payment of anywhere from $10,000 (or less for an obscure work) to $100,000 (or more for a well-known work). This payment is considered an "advance," which means it will be recouped or paid back against future royalty payments from performances of the play. If, for example, the owner of the underlying material were entitled to $4,000 as a royalty based on box office receipts for the first week of performances, that royalty of $4,000 would not be paid to the owner but instead would be subtracted from the $10,000 advance, leaving a balance of $6,000 to be recovered from future weekly royalty payments.

As a lawyer, I normally advised my producer clients to obtain up to five years' worth of options in the underlying material. Any veteran producer will attest to the fact that it can easily take three to five years or more to develop, finance, and open a Broadway musical. Even after a musical has been fully developed and the producer has obtained all of his financing, he could sit on the sidelines for a year or more waiting for a suitable theater to become available. Andrew Bergman, the successful screenwriter and playwright (*Blazing Saddles*, *The In-Laws*), recently reminded me that I warned him in 2004 that it would take at least five years for him to see his film *Honeymoon in Vegas* realized as a Broadway musical. The musical finally opened more than ten years later, in 2015, and sadly closed a few months later. So I say to anyone who has ever thought of producing a musical: *Do not quit your day job!*

With each extension of the option period, an additional advance must be made. If the initial payment is $10,000, the additional yearly option payments will likely be a similar amount, thereby totaling $50,000 if the entire five years are optioned.

Owners of underlying rights will usually resist tying up the stage rights, particularly for highly sought-after books or movies, for as long as five years. Your lawyer will have to convince those owners of the necessity of giving the producer a long period to develop the musical. One way of compromising on this issue is to offer the owner what's commonly referred to as "progress to production" payments, a phrase borrowed from the film industry. In other words, the producer is not permitted to extend the option period merely by making a payment. He must also have advanced his development of the property—that is, made some progress, in some meaningful way—if he wishes to get more time.

As an example, a contract may state that to extend his option for a second year, the producer must have secured a commitment during the first year from a composer, bookwriter, and lyricist to write the show. To get a third year, the producer must have had delivered to him a completed book and at least ten songs during the second year. For a fourth year, he must have presented a full reading or at least a two-week workshop during the third year. By the end of the fifth year, the play must have opened on Broadway. These conditions can vary from contract to contract. The important point is to give assurances to the owner that the producer is not going to sit on the rights for five years by making modest advance payments but no real progress toward realizing the production of a show. If the producer fails to satisfy the condition specified at the end of any particular time period, the contract terminates and all rights granted to the producer revert to the owner.

This is critically important to owners since no matter how high the advance payment, the *real* money lies in the show opening and running for many years, not only on Broadway but in other cities throughout North America and the rest of the world. As compared to the film industry (where a screenwriter can receive seven figures for a screenplay regardless of whether or not the film is ever released), in the theater grasping the golden ring is having the show open in a venue in midtown Manhattan and run for many years. Without exception, as compared to the royalties earned over many years, the amount of up-front advance monies in the theater business is almost always inconsequential and, for the owner (as well as the authors), often barely enough to pay a few months' rent.

The underlying rights option is exercised once the play is produced and all the option payments have been made. As mentioned above, the rights are then merged with the musical play written by the authors for exploitation on Broadway and elsewhere throughout the world.

Before we move on to a discussion of royalties, I'd like to address the unusual situation of attempting to acquire rights in a series of books, such as Harry Potter or James Bond, as compared to licensing rights in a single book.

The owner of a highly successful series of books will be reluctant to grant the producer anything more than the bare minimum of rights necessary to produce one play, reserving as much as possible for himself. But the producer who is seeking to adapt the series needs access to all of the characters and the many different stories in the series so his authors can create a unique amalgam of these elements in crafting the book of the musical. This can lead to a complicated tug-of-war in which the owner attempts to limit the producer's access to all of the material in the series while the producer attempts to tie up as much as he can for his authors' use.

There aren't a lot of precedents dealing with this peculiar issue. In order to give minimal protection to the producer and the authors, the owner would have to concede at the very least that, while the musical was being developed during the option period, he would not grant to any third party the right to produce another musical based on the series. Without that guarantee, the producer would never be able to finance his show. A competing work opening before or at the same time as his play would be devastating.

In addition, if the producer can identify characters for inclusion in the show other than the lead characters in the first book, the owner should grant him the nonexclusive right to incorporate those characters in the play. As for storylines, hopefully the authors would create something original, rather than ape the exact storyline of the books, although there would be similarities such as locations.

This then leads to another critical issue. As a general rule, a producer must guard against agreeing to any third party having the power, by contract or any other means, to legally stop the development or production of the play. Let me illustrate this idea by applying it to the underlying rights agreement. If the series of books has been a massive success, the owner will most likely be particularly protective of his work and wary about the manner in which this producer and his authors plan to adapt it into a Broadway musical. The film *Saving Mr. Banks* portrays the tensions that often exist between a highly protective owner (in this case P. L. Travers, author of the book *Mary Poppins*) and a relentless film producer (Walt Disney) who is determined to acquire the rights to adapt the book into a Hollywood movie. Travers (played with suitable British aplomb by Emma Thompson) is initially skeptical and suspicious of Disney (played with suitable American aplomb by Tom Hanks), but she's ultimately won over by his promise to respect the integrity of her work and her belief that he'll enhance it with an infectious musical score.

The owner might well demand that he have the absolute right to approve not only the composer, lyricist, and bookwriter, but also each of the elements themselves—that is, the music, lyrics, and book. As producer, by agreeing to these approvals you would in effect be ceding control of your project and its fate to the owner. There are few, if any, authors who would agree to write a musical knowing that the owner retained control over the new material. When, for example, is that approval final? After the first draft, after you're in rehearsals, or maybe the night before the official opening? And what if subsequent changes are not approved? What happens? Do you have to close down the show and give back $16 million to your investors?

Your lawyer should fight tooth and nail to resist giving these approvals away. They are what lawyers often refer to as "nonstarters." As we'll see later on, there are a number of approvals that remain within the exclusive purview of the authors of the show, but to cede control of the creative process to the owner is a prescription for disaster. It is nonnegotiable.

So, how to compromise? One fairly common solution is to offer the owner approval of the choice of bookwriter, composer, and lyricist but not the material. The producer might add that any author who has received a Tony Award cannot be disapproved by the owner. In the end, a producer wants the owner to be happy with the choice of authors. In fact, it may be advisable for the producer to disclose to the owner the authors he's considering during the negotiations of the deal. In this way, the owner will feel part of the process from the beginning and the producer won't be blindsided later by the owner's refusal to approve established and respected authors.

Another compromise is to give the owner the right to approve a first draft or précis of the storyline for the musical. The owner understandably wants to ensure that the spirit and integrity of his work are preserved. Ian Fleming's estate doesn't want James Bond to become a pimp on Charing Cross Road. There is some danger in giving this right of approval, but if the producer and the bookwriter both intend to be faithful to the integrity of the original work, then they shouldn't have too much trouble agreeing to this. However, the contract must be clear: once the owner has approved the outline, he will forgo any further right to impede the creative evolution of the show, provided the authors do not deviate in any substantial way from the approved précis. The owner must ultimately trust that his material is in good hands and, whether or not the show proves to be a critical or financial success, he won't be embarrassed for having licensed the rights.

I want to stress that the terms I've just outlined are rare and are granted only to very successful authors of world-renowned material. In most underlying rights deals, the owners do not have the negotiating leverage to obtain such rights. They simply give the producer an option with the freedom to adapt the work free of any approval or encumbrances and, upon payment of the required advances, they are happy to attend opening night.

Royalties

The theater and movie businesses are, in so many ways, the opposite sides of a coin. One way of demonstrating this is to compare royalties paid to the owner and the creative team in the theater (weekly compensation based on the level of business at the box office) to the so-called back end or net profits in films. In the theater, any agent will warn his client, particularly one new to the business, that she'll never make a living wage on up-front fees or advances. If the show's a hit, payday comes from royalties earned from the run of the show in New York and elsewhere around the globe. On the other hand, that same agent will advise a new screenwriter to take as much as possible up front, since it's assumed the writer will never see a nickel from a percentage participation in the net profits, even if the studio offered 100 percent.[5]

Once a show opens on Broadway and becomes a certified hit, the bounty of the participants can be extraordinary and the basis for those fortunes rests with the payment of royalties. These are payments based

[5] A handful of very powerful stars and directors in the film business receive percentages of gross (so-called distributor's gross), but the vast majority of the creative talent receive their back-end compensation based on a percentage of net profits—an illusory concept in most cases.

largely on the level of weekly box office receipts, made to the owner, authors, director, choreographer, designers, orchestrators and arrangers, and possibly a regional not-for-profit theater that produced an early tryout version of the musical. There may be other royalty participants, but this list contains the most common ones.[6]

Dating back to the first days of the modern American theater, royalties were based solely on a percentage of gross weekly box office receipts. You might think that the term means exactly that: the gross amounts (without any deductions whatsoever) received from 100 percent of the dollars paid by a customer for a seat in the theater. Not so. Deducted from those dollars are any local governmental taxes (there used to be an amusement tax on theater tickets in New York, but no more), payments to the labor unions' pension and welfare funds, credit card charges, theater party discounts, and a restoration fee paid to the theater for each ticket purchased (it's two dollars per ticket right now). The latter is a deduction devised by the theater owners about fifteen years ago to help maintain their old landmarked houses.

GMs will tell you that as a rule of thumb these deductions usually amount to about 10 percent of the true gross. So the industry calculates the true gross (referred to as gross gross) and then, after making the deductions, calculates the net figure (referred to as net gross). It is on the basis of net gross that the percentage royalty payments are made. This is just one example of why learning about the theater's words of art is essential.

For many years, *Weekly Variety*, the entertainment industry's trade magazine, regularly reported the net gross for every show on Broadway. Several years ago, in response to pressure from the industry, *Variety* began reporting gross gross instead. Broadway producers wanted to be able to boast to their investors (and to each other and the public) how much money was actually coming in from public sales, without deductions. But while gross gross is the total amount actually collected from ticket sales, the only number that's meaningful, in terms of figuring out how much money is available for the creative talent or the investors, is net

---

[6] As discussed later in chapter eighteen, the producer also receives a weekly royalty as part of his compensation package.

gross. It is the number on which a percentage participant relies in order to calculate his weekly financial piece of the pie.

The percentages of net gross paid to all of the royalty participants in a typical musical today can be anywhere from 15 to 20 percent, depending on whether the show has had a workshop or not-for-profit tryout and other factors. So, for example, if the gross gross for any week of the run is $1.5 million, the net gross (after deductions of 10 percent) would be $1.35 million. If the owner is entitled to receive 2 percent, his royalty for that week would be 2 percent of $1.35 million, or $27,000, and if the authors as a group are entitled to receive 6 percent, their royalty would be 6 percent of $1.35 million, or $81,000. Not a bad take for one week.

With a few exceptions, however, shows on Broadway, both straight plays and musicals, have not calculated royalties on the basis of net gross or any other kind of gross amount for over thirty years. Instead, by and large, Broadway shows today pay royalties on the basis of what are referred to as weekly operating profits. As a consequence, all of the royalty participants, along with the producer, share in a pool of monies that reflects the weekly operating profits of the show (not gross monies) remaining after all of the weekly operating costs have been deducted from the net gross. Hence, the word of art: *royalty pools*. In the case of the owner, his share of the pool would be calculated based on a ratio his 2 percent bears to the total percentages paid to all of the creative talent. So, for example, if the total royalties paid to everyone were 16 percent, then the owner would receive one-eighth (two divided by sixteen) of the pool of monies allocated for royalties to all of the creative participants.

I'll have a lot more to say about royalty pools, their origin and various formulations, in a later chapter devoted entirely to that subject. For now, to give a concrete example, I think it may be helpful to relate my experience acquiring the rights in the underlying material that formed the basis for the musical *La Cage aux Folles*.

La Cage aux Folles: Broadway vs. Hollywood

To set the theatrical scene in a historical perspective, 1978 was a time when the theater was still enjoying the huge successes of *A Chorus Line*, a consistent sellout at the Shubert Theatre, and *Annie*, also drawing capacity audiences at the Alvin Theatre (now named the Neil Simon). The prolific Stephen Sondheim, with newcomer John Weidman as bookwriter, offered up *Pacific Overtures* in 1976 and would write his masterpiece *Sweeney Todd* with bookwriter Hugh Wheeler in 1979.

It was in early 1978 that I received a call from Allan Carr, a relatively new client of mine who had recently co-produced the movie *Grease* with another client, Robert Stigwood. The movie was based on the stage musical and starred John Travolta and Olivia Newton-John.

In Hollywood, where colorful and outsized figures are as common as palm trees, Allan was second to none. He was one of the town's most flamboyant talent managers (Ann-Margret, Paul Anka, and Marvin Hamlisch were among his clients) and could be seen at every important event, many organized by him, wearing one of his multicolored caftans which covered, but hardly hid, his substantial physical proportions. Allan was plagued by obesity throughout his life and was one of the first to undergo a medical procedure to remove a portion of his stomach (gastric bypass surgery) so as to reduce his caloric intake. The operation was only partially successful and may have contributed to his untimely death in 1999 at the age of sixty-two.

Although Allan lived in LA for most of his career, he was a Broadway baby at heart. He lived and breathed the film business and was steeped in all the glamour and notoriety of Hollywood and Vegas, but his dream was to one day produce a big Broadway musical comedy.

So it was on a cold and snowy day in early January that Allan telephoned me to say that he wanted to obtain the rights to adapt the foreign-language film *La Cage aux Folles* into a musical. Although I had not yet seen it, the French-Italian film had recently opened in New York and Los Angeles to unanimous raves. For an independent foreign film, it broke all sorts of box office records and won the Golden Globe for Best Foreign Language Film.

Allan told me to stop everything I was doing and get over to the 68th Street Playhouse, an art house cinema, to see the film. I did as I was told and attended a matinee, something I hadn't done since I was eight years old. The theater was vacant except for me and a handful of other patrons probably seeking shelter from the cold.

The movie was hilarious. Its European sensibility, combining the best of Franco-Italian humor, suited the subject matter perfectly. For those readers who are mysteriously unaware of this film, the plot centers on the dilemma of a gay couple, Albin, a headliner drag queen, and Renato, a cabaret proprietor whose son from a previous marriage announces he is engaged to the daughter of an ultraconservative and naturally homophobic politician. When the son, Laurent, says that he plans to bring his future in-laws to the house to meet Renato and Albin, everyone (except Albin) recognizes that Laurent's fiancée's parents will never accept Albin for who he is and what he represents. In the tradition of commedia dell'arte, they decide to disguise Albin as Laurent's mother and avoid the truth of Laurent's life. The consequences of this ill-fated deception and the chaos that ensues are worthy of the best farces ever written for stage or screen.

After seeing the film, I rushed back to my office and called Allan to tell him that I thought his idea was brilliant. This clearly was an extremely funny movie and, with its cabaret setting and Albin's larger-than-life character, it was perfectly suited to be adapted as a stage musical.

There was one problem—a very serious one. Allan's idea was ingenious, but I had to secure the underlying rights in the film quickly if I was going to protect him from the possibility of another producer having the same idea and beating him to the punch. After investigating the ownership of rights to the film, I discovered that the film was an adaptation itself; it was based on a French play with the same title written by Jean Poiret.

The safest and most expensive option for Allan was to acquire rights both in the original French play from Poiret and in the film adaptation from its producer, Marcello Danon. I immediately contacted Poiret's New York agent, the late Elisabeth Marton, an elegant and well-connected New York literary and theater agent who represented many European writers, only to find out that, while Poiret was happy to consider having his play adapted as a musical, Danon, the film's producer, had no such interest.

If that wasn't enough, Marton also told me if Allan wanted to make a deal with Poiret, I had better move quickly, since she was already in negotiations with none other than David Merrick, who also wanted the rights. I pleaded with Marton not to close a deal with Merrick until I got back to her, which I promised to do within twenty-four hours.

When I reported all this to Allan, he barely flinched and instructed me to do whatever was necessary to get the rights. I explained to him that he would not be able to use anything in the movie that was not in the original play, since that new material was owned solely by the film producer. Allan was confident, even though he hadn't read the play, that there would be sufficient material in it (with the same plot and central characters) to create a new stage adaptation. In effect, the musical would leapfrog over the film and go back to the original French play for all the rights it needed. I remained skeptical, as I hadn't read the play either, and to ignore the film was something I had never faced from a legal point of view. To my knowledge, it had never been done before, and it hasn't been done since.

The fact that Merrick wanted the rights made Allan all the more determined to go after them. It's an old saw that no one ever bids to buy something until someone else wants it. Fools rush in (when others do). But in this case, Allan was no fool. Merrick's interest not only confirmed his instincts that this was a great idea, but it also played directly into Allan's lifelong dream to be a Broadway producer.

What followed was for me one of the most stressful and tense negotiations I've ever encountered.

Most important was money—how much would Allan have to pay for the initial year's option? Merrick had already offered $25,000, a not insubstantial sum in 1978, especially when one considers most option payments even today are in the range of $10,000.

Allan upped the ante to $50,000. Merrick quickly met that. We feared we'd lose the bidding war since Merrick had substantial personal resources as compared to Allan, who had not yet realized the financial benefits of his hit movie, *Grease*. But we were aware of two important things: (1) Merrick didn't know what Allan was capable of paying—all he knew was Allan's Hollywood reputation, and (2) it was well known that Merrick wasn't accustomed to throwing his money around. When Merrick came to call, his reputation was usually enough to get him whatever he wanted. He didn't engage in bidding wars.

Allan threw the dice and offered $100,000, an amount unheard of as an advance for underlying material. The gamble worked. Marton called me back within hours of our proposal to say Merrick had dropped out of the bidding and *La Cage aux Folles* was now Allan's.

In addition to paying a huge advance, we also agreed to give Poiret a royalty of 3 percent of the gross weekly box office receipts. There were no royalty pools at the time, just straight gross deals. This was also much higher than the customary 1.5 or 2 percent of the net gross reserved for the owners. So this was a very rich deal indeed. But Allan had snatched it from the jaws of Merrick. For Allan, that was in and of itself a victory.

La Cage opened on Broadway at the Palace Theatre on August 21, 1983. It was an unqualified success, winning six Tony Awards, including Best Musical, Best Original Score, and Best Book. It ran for over five years in New York before closing somewhat abruptly as the AIDS crisis came to a crescendo. There was uninformed, rampant fear about the virus and the cause of its spread. Suddenly, audiences weren't particularly interested in seeing two gay men flaunt their sexuality onstage in a musical farce.

The worldwide anxiety and ignorance about the disease became evident to me when I was in Sydney, Australia, for the opening of *La Cage* in late 1985. In spite of positive reviews, the box office was not doing well and no one knew why. Then we began to hear rumors. Among others, we heard that the box office treasurers were being asked by patrons if gays were coming to the theater and if they should be concerned about sitting in the same seats. Australians had heard of AIDS and they weren't eager to see a show from Broadway, which they viewed as a hotbed for the disease. I don't think this degree of irrationality existed in New York, but it was not uncommon during the early stages of the epidemic for fear and ignorance to overcome compassion and understanding everywhere.

Now let's return to a discussion of the other important provisions in underlying rights agreements.

Additional and Subsidiary Rights

In addition to acquiring the primary rights of producing the musical as a first-class stage production, if the show is a success, a producer will want to mount additional companies within North America (touring companies) and other parts of the world and benefit from the future exploitation of the musical in non-first-class productions (local civic and amateur groups) and motion picture and television adaptations. A producer will also want to obtain the right to arrange for the recording of an original cast album and sell merchandising (T-shirts, key chains, tote bags, and all the other stuff you see peddled at the back of the theater). The owner and the authors of the musical are considered as one group for purposes of determining the division of monies among them. Going back to my initial discussion of royalties earlier in this chapter, I provided for a royalty of 2 percent for the owner and 6 percent for the three authors, for a total of 8 percent. The ratio of the owner's royalty of 2 percent to the total of 8 percent is 25 percent. Therefore, any monies received from the exploitation of subsidiary rights (non-first-class productions, film rights, etc.), cast album, and merchandising sales would follow the same percentages: 25 percent for the owner and 75 percent for all the authors.

Merger

Any discussion of additional and subsidiary rights leads to a discussion of the critical issue of merger. Once the musical has been produced on Broadway, the producer and the authors will want to exploit the show on the stage throughout the world, in all venues, with professionals and amateurs, and will want to see their musical adapted for film, television, and other media.

To achieve this, the musical must be merged or conjoined with the underlying work thereby forming a new copyrighted work consisting of copyrighted material from the underlying work and the new musical's book, lyrics, and music. That combined new work can now be sold, licensed, and exploited throughout the world by the authors for the full term of copyright in the new work with all the monies received therefrom being divided among the owner and the authors, as well as the producer and his investors. Without merger, the separate rights in the underlying work could be licensed to other producers and third parties by the owner for competing works, thereby denying the producer and the authors the right to reap the full benefits of future income from the musical.

For most underlying works, the minimum number of performances the musical must run in order to qualify for a merger is twenty-one in New York, with a maximum of eight previews being credited to the total.

The owner of a particularly valuable underlying work may not want to agree to merger unless he's assured the musical is a success of sufficient magnitude to justify merging these valuable rights with the new musical. Therefore, the owner will often require, as a condition of merger, that the musical not only open on Broadway but also run for an extended period of time thereafter, perhaps as long as six months, to demonstrate its "hit" status.[7] In this way, the owner can be more confident that the play is truly *the* best musical version of his work. Otherwise, if the musical is short-lived, the owner would have given away the right (potentially forever) to realize another musical based on his work.

Even after the show has run its course on Broadway for an extended period of time, the owner may require additionally that the musical generate each year a minimum amount of money received from the sale and licensing of subsidiary rights in which the owner participates if the merger is to continue. That yearly minimum may be as low as $100,000 or as high as $250,000. It is also often expressed in terms of an average yearly amount over a five-year period so as to adjust for any unusual wide fluctuations of income from year to year. If the musical fails to meet these minimum financial thresholds, a demerger, or uncoupling of the underlying work and the musical, may come into play.

Simply put, when demerger occurs, the joint nature of the new musical is undone and the underlying work reverts to being a separate and distinct work from the musical. Although demerger clauses appear in quite a few agreements, I am not aware of any musical where a demerger has actually taken place. The fact is, if the show's a hit on Broadway, it will likely continue to be licensed and performed throughout the world for years to come, earning income well above the minimum thresholds. It then is in the best interest of everyone, including the owners, to have only one musical available for licensing.

A corollary to this issue is the right to produce a sequel or prequel to a musical. This refers to a new adaptation of an underlying work based on the original musical, with similar characters but a new storyline; a story predating the original musical is a prequel and a story postdating the original is a sequel. Although producers and authors consider these to be valuable rights, there have been very few prequels or sequels ever produced in the theater.

---

[7] It is not enough that the play just run for this period. It must also be running on a profitable basis—that is, the show must be earning weekly operating profits. The owner wants to be sure the musical is long-running *and* making money in order for it to be merged with his work.

About twenty years ago, a sequel to *Annie* was produced and disappeared rather quickly. There was also a sequel to *The Phantom of the Opera* in the West End of London (*Love Never Dies*) but it too was not successful and never reached Broadway, although a revised version was produced in Australia two years later and fared somewhat better. Other than those two shows, one would be hard-pressed to think of any other sequels to Broadway plays or musicals.

This is somewhat surprising when you consider the penchant in Hollywood for sequels and their success: *Jurassic Park*, *Star Wars*, *Rocky*, *Superman* and countless others were followed by successful sequels. But not in the theater. It's hard to figure out the reason for this stark difference between theater and film. I know that if a musical is very successful, the sequel tends to remind the audience of the original well-known score; the sequel's music, for whatever reason, usually pales in comparison. Ironically, when the audience leaves the theater after seeing a sequel, they're often heard humming the songs of the *original* musical.

Credit or Billing

Credits identify the individual creator or creators of a particular element (book, music, or lyrics) as well as the owner, the director, the producer, and the other creative participants and management associated with a project.

The words *billing* and *credits* are used interchangeably. Billing originally referred to the tradition of listing major headliners in the bills or handouts that were distributed to the public and plastered around town and outside of theaters. Today posters found in subways and other outdoor locations are referred to as *two-sheets* or *three-sheets* depending on their size. *Credits* is a more expansive term since it can be applied to posters, print and television advertising, and, most important, the title page in the official *Playbill* program distributed in the theater.

The three issues associated with credits are: size, where, and when.

By and large, the size of a credit is a function of the size of the title. No one in my experience has ever received billing greater in size than the title of the musical itself. The underlying owner's credit usually appears after the authors' credit and is customarily half the size accorded to the authors, which in turn is usually 50 percent of the size of the title. On rare occasions, the owner's billing may be 60 percent of the size of the authors' credit.

The owner's credit usually appears whenever or wherever the authors' credits appear. If the owner's credit is particularly lengthy, the producer may want to limit where and when it appears in order to preserve space and reduce costs. This is always a matter of negotiation. On the other hand, the producer may wish to have the owner's credit appear at all times for marketing purposes.

For the musical based on *La Cage aux Folles*, the credits read as follows:

LA CAGE AUX FOLLES

[50 percent size of title]:

Book by Harvey Fierstein, Music and Lyrics by Jerry Herman

[25 percent size of title]:

Based on the play by Jean Poiret

All negotiations over billing are based on the producer's desire to accord credit only when he thinks it will be effective in selling tickets versus the talents' desire to give credit to themselves for their contributions, regardless of their fame or notoriety. As we'll discuss later, the Dramatists Guild insists on certain minimum billing requirements for authors of straight plays and musicals. These usually are not controversial and are accepted by most producers. If those credits are used as a benchmark, credits to the designers and others usually follow those parameters but can vary depending on the bargaining power of a particular artist.

Expenses

The owner, as well as all other creative and production personnel, are entitled to have their expenses reimbursed whenever they are traveling away from their primary residence at the request of the producer.

In addition, the owner's contract will provide that he is entitled to attend opening night on Broadway and to round-trip airfare (usually business class), first-class hotel accommodations, a per diem (or daily expense allowance) of approximately $100 to $150 for three days, and private car transportation to and from all airports. An owner might also request attendance at final rehearsals or preview performances, for which he would receive reimbursement on the same basis. Well-known owners might also request attendance at openings for the first national tour, as well as in London and other major European and Asian capitals.

When a musical has most of its creative talent residing in and around New York City, these expenses aren't a major concern for budgeting purposes. However, for musicals that are imported from the West End of London with a British creative team and perhaps a British star, these expenses can be exceedingly high. The producer and GM will want to keep a tight lid on this line item in the production budget. Foreign living and travel costs can be as much as 2.5 percent of an overall production budget of $10 million.

Representations, Warranties, and Indemnities

The purpose of including representations, warranties, and indemnities in the owner's contract is to protect the client and the creative team if it should turn out the owner does not actually own the rights he has granted to the producer, or has violated the copyright or other personal rights of a third party. If the true owner or aggrieved party should emerge and sue the producer, the authors, the theater owner, and just about everyone else, the owner is responsible for defending those lawsuits and covering the costs of litigation, including legal fees and any judgment obtained against the show.

These provisions are somewhat technical in nature and are negotiated between the lawyers for both sides. Although no non-lawyer producer is expected to fully comprehend the many complications associated with these clauses, it is important to understand their legal import. If, for any reason, the owner is unable or unwilling to stand behind his grant of rights in the contract, your lawyer will have to assess the level of

[8] The production's insurance broker will advise that errors and omissions insurance be taken out, which will protect the production, in most cases, from third-party claims of copyright infringement and violation of privacy and publicity rights.

risk you will be assuming if you nonetheless elect to proceed with the production.[8]

Opening Night Seats and House Seats

The major creative talent all receive specifically assigned seats, known as house seats, for each performance of the show. The owner may receive two pairs, except for certain benefit performances to which he'll receive only one pair. These seats are usually in very good locations in the orchestra section of the theater. They are not free except for the opening night performance, for which the owner will receive perhaps as many as five complimentary pairs. For all other performances, house seats are sold at the regular, published box office price and are held in reserve for the owner to purchase a minimum of forty-eight or seventy-two hours prior to the performance.

For a big hit, this is a valuable commodity, particularly with the current trend of charging premium prices (well above the highest regular price) for prime orchestra seats. For the hottest tickets, it is not unusual to charge $250 or as much as $450 for a premium seat, as compared to the price of a regular seat of $145. More important, having the luxury of being able to wait until two or three days before a performance to buy the best seats in the house is, at any price, invaluable. The regular ticket buyer may have to wait to see *Hamilton* on a Saturday night. The owner will be able to purchase his house seats for himself or his family and friends at the regular price of $145 as late as three days before the performance.

House seats that have not been sold are usually released two or three days prior to a performance. Often, producers will hold on to the unsold house seats until a day or so before the performance date, particularly for Friday and Saturday nights, so they can sell them at premium prices to last-minute, well-heeled shoppers. I know savvy theater veterans who try to time their arrival at the box office of a sold-out performance a few hours before curtain time in the hope that they might be lucky enough to snag a couple of unsold premium seats at regular prices.

Agency Clause

Without exception, any established talent in the entertainment business is represented by an agent, manager, or lawyer, and sometimes by all three. Even a first-time composer will probably retain an agent once he has nabbed a producer for his project. Most contracts contain an agency clause, which specifies that all monies paid to the owner or writers are paid directly to their agent, who first deducts his or her commission and then remits the balance to the client.

An agent typically works on a contingency basis for a percentage and not a fixed fee. On occasion an agent might ask for expenses, but that happens only in rare cases. In return for an agent speculating on a client's future success, she will normally receive 10 percent of the gross monies earned by her client. In the case of an owner, that 10 percent would apply to the advance payments payable under the option agreement, as well as all royalties and any other income derived from the exploitation of the musical's subsidiary rights. For a very successful musical, that 10 percent can amount to a veritable fortune. Consider the composer of a megahit that has grossed in the tens of millions of dollars. His agent will become a multimillionaire by virtue of her 10 percent agency share. But those megahits are exceedingly rare. Most agents spend many years early in their careers earning little more than modest four-figure commissions. Advance payments made to a first-time composer may be as low as $6,000 for the first year and only a few thousand dollars for the next several years. If he's lucky enough to have the show produced five years later, his total advance payment might amount to $30,000. For his agent, who has also been biding her time those same five years, the commission is a grand total of $3,000.

In Hollywood, where top-tier screenwriters can earn guaranteed seven-figure fees, agents' commissions amount to substantially more money and are realized up front, whether or not the film is produced. If the writer is powerful enough to get a strong back-end deal based on the success of the film, the agent will also realize a huge bonus from her 10 percent share. In the theater, the payback for the talent, as well as for the agent, is realized only if the production runs for years on Broadway, spawns additional companies, and realizes income from the exploitation of subsidiary rights.

One New York agent I met early in my career was Jerry Talbert. Jerry was a true company man, having made his career at the venerable William Morris Agency. He was an aggressive and persistent negotiator for his clients. With a sense of humor rarely apparent, Jerry's no-nonsense negotiating style let you know without a doubt what was most important to him in any deal. Once the first draft of an author's contract was completed and approved by my producer client, I would send it (in those days usually by hand) to Jerry for his review and comments. I'd estimate how long it would take the messenger to deliver the contract to Jerry's office, which was only a few blocks away. Within an hour after the contract arrived, like clockwork, Jerry would call with one observation: "That contract you just sent over? I haven't read the whole thing yet, but I have read the agency clause and here are my comments." No matter how many times I tried to kid Jerry about this, he never took the bait, nor would he concede there was anything to joke about. He was dead serious about the importance of the agency clause. It was William Morris's lifeblood and, without the agency clause being drafted as airtight as possible, there was little point in going any further with the deal. Don't get me wrong. After he reviewed the entire contract, Jerry would be equally aggressive about getting everything else he could for his clients.

Summary

We've covered a lot of ground in this chapter. Many of the words of art, concepts, and issues we've addressed will reappear when we look at the authors' contract (the APC) as well as the other creative talent's contracts. For some readers, it might not have been an easy read. But this book is a primer on how to produce a musical. Anyone who is even half serious about trying his or her hand at producing must understand the underpinnings of the business. Would you build a house without knowing how to construct a foundation?

Some will say that they leave the contract negotiations and details to their lawyer and GM and, of course, to some extent, that is appropriate and sensible. But being ignorant or uninformed about the asset you've invested in is foolhardy and can even be dangerous. If things go wrong, as producer, you're on the line and answerable to your investors, the creative team, and the cast.

What's more, the theater business is, inescapably, a public spectacle. Whether a new car dealership or fast food franchise succeeds is of minor public concern. The abject failure of a Broadway musical, however, attracts widespread interest from the media and the public at large. A commercial failure resulting from those things over which you and your colleagues have no control is understandable. But there is no excuse if a show fails due to a producer's ineptitude and ignorance.

6

In Pursuit of the Holy Trinity

Selecting your bookwriter, composer, and lyricist is perhaps the most important decision you will make as a producer. Here are some of the considerations you should weigh:

- Who is best suited to appreciate and translate the unique sensibilities of the underlying work in the musical play?
- Who will be most simpatico with the owner and listen and respond to his concerns?
- Has any of the authors collaborated with any of the other authors before?
- Do you go for the most experienced authors or strike out and hire artists who have shown promise but have not yet been tested on Broadway? Do you try to mix and match tyros with veterans? Will you enjoy working with them?
- Who's available to write the show within the time frame of the option periods? Is any of them overcommitted?
- Can you afford to pay them? Will their agents' demands put them out of your reach?

If you are new to the game and not familiar with the players, how do you go about finding all three authors?

First, familiarize yourself with the shows currently running both on and off Broadway and in the regional and not-for-profit theaters. In other words, do your research. Get to know the authors' styles and artistic temperaments. Listen to recordings of old shows no longer running. By immersing yourself in the art form you will eventually develop your own taste and, more important, begin to appreciate the kind of writing that will be most suitable for your project.

If you're adapting an underlying work, such as a novel, it is probably wisest to initially seek out a bookwriter whose take on the musical is consonant with your and the owner's intentions. An experienced book-writer may want to work with composers and lyricists with whom he has collaborated on other projects. Producers often seek out famous writing teams such as Rodgers and Hammerstein, Lerner and Loewe, and, today, Shaiman and Wittman (*Hairspray*) and Ahrens and Flaherty (*Ragtime*). Engaging an established "team" for your show may seem convenient or expeditious, but, as the producer, you need to be certain all the authors have the right sensibility for your project.

When considering a new author, producers may request that the bookwriter prepare a précis or a sample scene, or that the composer and lyricist write two or three songs. Established authors usually won't agree to "audition," so to speak. But, in order to get their first Broadway show, many new writers may be willing to accede to this request. This gets a bit tricky legally. The writer's agent will insist that any new material written by his client be owned by him, including any copyrights. If the writer isn't ultimately hired to do the show, the producer must be careful not to use any of this material so as to avoid any claim of infringement.

As you seek new or established talent, take advantage of the contacts and experience of your GM and lawyer. They'll probably know of the availability of certain authors and will be able to put you in contact with the authors' agents. They may also be aware of the reputation of the artists you wish to approach—is she a difficult personality, in spite of her genius; is she a team player, open to criticism from her co-authors and producer; does her agent conduct every negotiation as if it were World War III?

Here's a page out of my book of not-to-be forgotten experiences.

When Enough Is Enough

The original creative team chosen by Allan Carr to do the musical adaptation of *La Cage aux Folles* comprised Maury Yeston for music and lyrics, Jay Presson Allen for the book, Mike Nichols to direct, and Tommy Tune to choreograph. Flora Roberts, a member of the old guard of female agents, represented Yeston. All of the others were represented by the agency International Creative Management, with its senior agent, Sam Cohn, acting as their spokesperson.

From the outset, it seemed as if Sam needed to make history in terms of getting more money for his clients than ever before. It was the dawn of royalty pools,[1] about which I will have a lot to say later on, but Sam would hear none of it. As we have already seen, in an earlier chapter, Allan had already made a very rich deal with Jean Poiret for the underlying rights in the French play. He wanted each of these authors to be well compensated, but, in the end, the financial projections for the show had to make some economic sense.

Sam went from deal to deal for each of his clients on this project trying to extract higher and higher royalties. None of the artists he represented wanted to be treated less favorably than the other. In my experience with Sam, he usually tempered his aggressive negotiations with a realistic assessment of what a show could bear and then moderated his demands accordingly. But this time, his demands seemed to spiral out of control.

After nearly six months of negotiations, I advised Allan that he could not afford to move forward with the project unless everyone took a 25 percent cut in their royalties. I sensed we would never be able to come up with a royalty package that would support a sensible and viable investment. The negotiations were also taking forever, and Allan was running out of time on his option on the underlying French novel. I finally quoted Mike Nichols to Allan: "Life's too long."

Allan came to New York and requested I accompany him to a meeting with Sam. When we arrived, Sam was sitting back in his chair, with both feet propped up on his desk, wearing his somewhat tattered, cable-stitched, preppy sweater and brown penny loafers. We all exchanged brief pleasantries. Despite his deal-making style, Sam could be quite charming and funny, particularly in the presence of someone like Allan whose reputation for gossip and quick repartee knew no bounds. But Allan was uncharacteristically serious, almost somber, as he began to lay out his agenda. He was brief and to the point: "Sam, there are no artists for whom I have more respect than those you represent in this deal. They are a dream team. But the drama of our negotiations over the past six months

[1] Royalty pools replaced royalties being paid on net gross, with the creative team and the investors sharing in the weekly profits of the show. See chapter nine for a more detailed discussion.

is the only theater we're going to see—this deal is over. I'm withdrawing all of my offers and I plan to hire a completely new team for *La Cage*."

There was dead silence. Sam stood up, stopped chewing on some Kleenex (which he did regularly), and laughed nervously. Allan assured him he was being completely serious. Allan shook Sam's hand and asked him to please convey his gratitude to everyone for considering the project. With that, we left Sam's office and returned to mine. I had never seen Sam nonplussed before. I can only imagine the ensuing phone calls with his clients.

What Sam didn't know was that Allan had already contacted Jerry Herman (*Hello, Dolly!*, *Mame*, and many others), who had expressed a passionate desire to write the score for *La Cage* months earlier. Herman told Allan he was ready to start writing immediately. That gave Allan enough confidence to walk away from Yeston and Sam's clients and build a new group.

Eventually, Allan hired the legendary Arthur Laurents as director and Harvey Fierstein as bookwriter. Fierstein had just written his first Broadway play, *Torch Song Trilogy*, for which he had won the Tony Award for Best Play. For choreography, Allan took a chance on a Las Vegas choreographer, Scott Salmon, who had never worked on Broadway, but had a style and flair for the kind of showy and glitzy dances Allan envisioned for the club's musical numbers. It was a very smart combination of old-timers (Herman and Laurents) and newcomers (Fierstein and Salmon). The result was a musical crafted in the best traditions of the American musical theater with a freshness and a contemporary point of view. *La Cage aux Folles* went on to win three Tony Awards, including Best Musical, and ran for over five years on Broadway.

Who's to say if Allan had stayed with the original creative group whether it would have been a bigger hit or perhaps not so great? What's important to learn is that Allan, a newcomer himself to Broadway, followed his instincts based on the advice he got from others. He knew that he somehow needed to move on once the negotiations with Sam got out of control. For all of Allan's apparent flamboyance, deep inside he was conservative financially and very protective of his own resources. He was intent on raising financing for the show from others and ultimately kept his own investment to a minimum.

Final thought: you can never make a good deal unless you're willing to walk away from the negotiating table. That's a true axiom for any business. In the theater, however, it is particularly difficult to walk away once you have been wooed and seduced by the talent you seek to hire for your show. To analogize to real estate, you can let emotions enter your negotiations only when purchasing a home for yourself—if you're in love, another 5 percent added to the purchase price shouldn't let you pass up your dream house. On the other hand, a real estate investment should cede no room to sentimentality. Either it makes financial sense on paper or it doesn't. There must be a drop-dead price beyond which you simply won't go.

I suppose for most theater producers there is a middle ground. After all, producers get involved in a play not in spite of, but because of, their passion and love for the art. There are many other businesses that carry less risk and will generate greater returns than the theater business. Unless money is no object, and it's your *own* money, a sensible economic foundation needs to be considered when producing any commercial show.[2] What good is it to produce a great play, only to see it flounder and disappear because of its inability to survive as a viable and profitable enterprise?

A Calculated Risk

> "Teacher says, 'Every time a bell rings, an angel gets his wings.'"
>
> —*A Wonderful Life*

I recall my early conversations with producer Nick Vanoff in the early part of 1988 about choosing the lyricist for his new musical, *City of Angels*. For Vanoff, although an experienced TV producer, producing a Broadway musical was alien territory. The musical's book was to be written by one of Hollywood's and Broadway's most prolific and successful comedy writers, Larry Gelbart, and the music would be composed by the Emmy and Tony Award–winning Cy Coleman (*On the Twentieth Century*, *Sweet Charity*, *Barnum*).

---

[2] As for the economics of not-for-profit theaters, the financial incentives may be secondary to other objectives, as we'll see later, in chapter thirteen.

Coleman and Gelbart at first wanted to find a lyricist with a proven track record.[3] Coleman eventually reached out to a young and unknown lyricist, David Zippel. Zippel was a graduate of Harvard Law School with aspirations of becoming an entertainment lawyer. (Sound familiar?) After having written a few songs for the Tony Award–winning actress (*The Music Man*) Barbara Cook with her pianist, Wally Harper, Zippel decided to leave his law school training behind and pursue a career on Broadway. (I can imagine Zippel's mother being reminded of the Noël Coward song "[Don't Put Your Daughter on the Stage,] Mrs. Worthington.")

Vanoff had his concerns and, as his lawyer, I shared them. Was this never-before-heard Zippel sophisticated enough to complement two of the most seasoned veterans in the business? Could he write lyrics that would effectively carry the storyline alongside Gelbart's razor-sharp wit? Coleman had seen Zippel's Off-Broadway show, *Just So*, and although it was not well received, Coleman thought the lyrics showed talent and great promise. He was satisfied Zippel had the right sensibilities and instincts to deliver the kind of lyrics that would propel the show forward and match the shows style. To allay Vanoff's concerns, Coleman and Gelbart were prepared to audition a few songs for him before he finally committed to producing the show. Vanoff invited me to accompany him to the audition. These are the kind of perks that occasionally come your way as an entertainment lawyer.

Coleman banged out the songs on the piano, singing the lyrics with Zippel, and Gelbart summarized the plot. I can't remember which songs we heard, but it was quite obvious that the whole enterprise was going to be witty, urbane, and infectious. It would be an uphill battle to convince investors and others that Zippel was the right man for the show, but Vanoff knew, in the end, the strong pedigrees of Gelbart and Coleman would win over any doubters. What's more, after hearing Zippel's work and getting to know him, Vanoff became a believer and was quite comfortable, indeed excited, to move forward with Zippel.

---

[3] Coleman had worked on three previous shows with one of Broadway's most famous lyricists, Dorothy Fields, who, by the time of her death in 1974, had written over four hundred songs for stage and screen.

Fast-forward to the night of the Tony Awards, when *City of Angels* won six awards, including Best Musical and Best Original Score for Coleman and Zippel. Against all odds, a first-time producer had produced the biggest hit of the 1989–90 Broadway season. And what Zippel achieved, by winning a Tony for his first show, was something that has eluded so many others for their entire careers.

* * *

A sad footnote: when Vanoff first hired me to represent him, I jokingly warned him he needed a strong heart to get through the process of producing his first Broadway show. Vanoff told me it was no joke—he had recently had a triple bypass heart operation and his doctor had advised him to avoid stress. I expressed concern and was worried Vanoff might not be in a condition to deal with the arduous challenge that lay ahead for him.

Less than a year after accepting his Tony for Best Musical, Vanoff died of heart failure at the age of sixty-one. I don't think producing *Angels* was the cause of his death, although he did go through a number of crises along the way that would have taxed the healthiest of men.

Producing a Broadway musical had been a lifelong dream for Vanoff. I know if he had to do it all over again, he would.

Après the Pursuit

After you choose your authors, your lawyer will begin negotiating the agreement for them to write the show. In your initial meeting, your lawyer will probably have made reference to the Dramatists Guild and two contracts—one for musicals and one for straight plays, both referred to as the Approved Production Contract, or the APC. These are the model contracts used by the vast majority of producers to hire playwrights for straight plays and bookwriters, composers, and lyricists for musicals. They are model contracts in that they set out much of what lawyers refer to as "boilerplate," or standard, non-controversial clauses that will require few changes, such as the approvals accorded to the authors, the basic grant of rights, additional and subsidiary rights, definitions of basic financial terms, billing, and expenses.

The APC will have attached to it a rider that amends and expands on many of the standard terms and adds additional terms not covered by the APC. For example, the credit provisions are often expanded to permit certain exemptions for the producer to advertise the show without according authorship credits, and there are additional options added for the producer to present the play in foreign-language-speaking territories.

As we will see in detail in a later chapter devoted exclusively to the APC, many of its provisions deal with the same issues addressed in the underlying rights agreement. The APC must complement and be compatible with that seminal agreement so that there are no conflicts that could disrupt the orderly construction of the other creative contracts and financing documents for the show.

7

Collaboration

A Conspiracy among Artists

If "location, location, location" is real estate's mantra for the best house in the neighborhood, then "collaboration, collaboration, collaboration" is the theater's sine qua non for a successful musical.

Under the US Copyright Act, a musical play may be registered as a joint work comprising the individual copyrights in the book, music, lyrics, and the material taken from the underlying work. The creation of that joint work is the product of collaboration among the bookwriter, the composer, the lyricist, the underlying rights owner, and, very often, the director.

Collaboration may begin before the authors are hired. The producer may meet with the owner of the underlying work to see if their respective visions of a musical adaptation resonate with each other. During the negotiations on *La Cage aux Folles*, Allan Carr spoke directly to Jean Poiret, the author of the underlying play, not to discuss money but to assure him that he, Allan, wanted to benefit from Poiret's familiarity with the material and seek his creative input. Allan's charm, infectious sense of humor, and respect for artists undoubtedly impressed Poiret and helped cement the deal for Allan.

In the case of a fledgling producer, he needs to assure the owner of a valuable underlying work that he can pull off the production of a major musical. Having the financial resources to mount the show is only part of the equation. To close the deal, the owner needs to know that the integrity of his work will be protected and the producer will have the good judgment and taste to hire experienced creative and production teams capable of following through on the producer's promises.

A theme I've repeated over the years to my clients is the need to build personal bonds of trust and confidence at the outset with those you plan to work with. Those bonds are built by being willing to listen and respond constructively to what others have to offer, avoiding the temptation to become blindfolded by your own agenda and point of view.

In the theater, especially in the writing of a musical, collaboration takes on a unique dimension and goes to the very core of how an artist practices and hones his or her craft.

The Chicken or the Egg?

Although there are some musical authors who perform more than one role (Jonathan Larson, book, music, and lyrics for *Rent*), in this section I'll assume there are three authors, each being responsible for only one of the three elements of a musical.

What comes first? Some composers need to see lyrics, or at least the idea of a song, before they can compose the music. It's the opposite for others. The composer charts a melody based on the emotional needs of a specific moment in the story and then the lyrics follow. In the case of a musical based on a book, it seems natural that the storyline come first and the songs be laid in afterward. But even that is not a given.

What comes first can also be governed by other practical factors. Who's available to begin work on the show? One or more of the three authors may be tied up with another show. If the owner of the underlying work has the contractual right to approve a summary, outline, or even a scene or two, then the bookwriter must start working first. Even so, the bookwriter ought not to begin before all the authors and the producer have arrived at a consensus concerning the style and tone of the piece and exchanged ideas about when and how the music will be interlaced with the dialogue.

As for tone, will the musical be in the tradition of the musicals of the fifties and sixties, à la *The Pajama Game, Damn Yankees*, or *How to Succeed in Business without Really Trying*? Will it lean more heavily on the popular British musicals of the late eighties and nineties, with a greater emphasis on high drama, such as *Les Miz* (as it's affectionately called), *Miss Saigon*, and *Sunset Boulevard*? Or will it take its cue from more recent shows such as *Spring Awakening* or *Hamilton*, melding several musical styles including rap and other contemporary genres? As for integration with the score, since the book forms the dramatic framework for the show, the authors should have some idea about where the dialogue ends and the music and lyrics pick up. This is particularly important for a first-time bookwriter, or even a successful novelist or screenplay writer. The writer needs to develop characters who take their shape alongside the score and a narrative that relies as much on the lyrics to drive the storyline forward as the dialogue. It's an art in and of itself peculiar to musicals and one dramatically different from the writing of a novel, screenplay, or even a straight play.

The Who and Why of a Musical

The collaborators need to consider the question: Who's the audience? Ideally, every show wants to attract theatergoers from every walk of life. One of the reasons for the enormous success of *The Lion King* and *The Phantom of the Opera* is that they attract a widely divergent audience, old and young, and domestic and international. And viewers return time and time again. In contrast, *Spring Awakening* primarily appealed to teenage and young adult audiences, a possible reason for its modest success on Broadway in spite of winning a Tony Award for Best Musical; likewise, *Grey Gardens*, a critically acclaimed but short-lived musical, appealed mostly to adult, urban audiences.

Why Make This into a Musical?

I've had clients who wished to adapt a film to the stage assume that the music and lyrics are all-important and that the book should be a relatively easy assignment. After all, the characters and story already exist. What worked on the screen simply needs to be translated to the stage. That's a serious mistake. In fact, the opposite may be true.

I've routinely asked producers and authors who wanted to adapt a famous movie: *Why?* The film was a blockbuster, its star won an Oscar, and critics said it was perfect—writing, direction, acting, cinematography, editing, and design. What's the point? You'd be surprised to learn that very few, if any, producers and not many authors have a good answer to this question. To play off the notoriety of the original work by having a carbon-copy book with the same characters singing and dancing is a shortcut to failure. Having the inspiration to produce a musical because of the worldwide familiarity of a title is just the beginning of realizing a musical with its own raison d'être. And that imperative may need to come primarily from a book with a different perspective than that of the movie.

Even if the producer hasn't thought it through, it surely is the authors' job to come up with the artistic justification for the adaptation. Before a word or note is written, the three writers need to investigate the why and wherefore. *Cats* rests on its own dramatic construct, separate and apart from T. S. Eliot's poetry. *My Fair Lady* exists independently of the dramatic social commentary of George Bernard Shaw's *Pygmalion.* And Tony and Maria of *West Side Story* seem torn from the headlines of a 1950s tabloid newspaper rather than being based on characters from a sixteenth-century Elizabethan drama.

These legendary shows, and many others, grew out of a collaborative creative process that began with extracting from the underlying work its emotional and dramatic essences so that they could be incorporated into the fabric of the musical's book and score. I'm not suggesting that this is all accomplished at the outset. All of the elements may not be in sync at first. But it is through the development process that ultimately the musical will emerge, benefiting from and relying on its source material, and standing on its own so that it will exist as a newly conceived collective work of art.

Enter the Director as "Author" and Catalyst

The collaborative process isn't limited to the authors.

All of the great musicals of the past have relied on the vision and concept of the director. The five decades from the forties through the eighties gave us Jerome Robbins, Michael Kidd, George Abbott, Gower Champion, Moss Hart, Hal Prince, Bob Fosse, and Michael Bennett. They're all gone (except for Prince, who's still working in his late eighties), but they all left behind a rich legacy of breakthrough work that will probably never be equaled in invention or surprise, at least in what may soon become known as the grand *old* tradition of musical comedy. They left scores of musicals, a legacy passed down to our current stable of American directors, such as James Lapine, Michael Mayer, Jerry Mitchell,

Casey Nicholaw, Susan Stroman, and an extraordinary newcomer, Lin-Manuel Miranda, to name just a few, so that they could each discover and invent their own brand of musical theater.

With the director steering the boat, he may bring on board, early in the process, the designers (sets, costumes, lighting, and special effects) so that his concept will begin to take shape visually. The director becomes the creative catalyst for the whole endeavor. Indeed, as we'll discuss in a later chapter, the director in effect becomes a fourth "author," along with the composer, lyricist, and bookwriter. Although he may not actually put pen to paper, his collaboration with the authors becomes endemic to the point that it will earn him the right to become a partner with the creative team, both practically and legally. The great directors/choreographers often receive the credit, "Conceived, directed, and choreographed by," with the "conceived" credit reflecting the director's participation in the conceptualization and writing of the show.

In the best cases, what ultimately emerges from this complex amalgam is a musical that is greater than the sum of its parts.

I'm always reminded of Marvin Hamlisch when I discuss the end result of a successful collaboration. After *A Chorus Line* opened, it won every award known to man. The show got universally rave reviews, although a few critics said Hamlisch's music had a film underscore quality and lacked a big, standout, popular hit. In truth, what *A Chorus Line* represents is an organic collaboration of every artistic element of the show, with no one element overpowering or dominating the stage at any one moment. The fact that Hamlisch's score served the whole rather than being a so-called hit score is a testament to its worthiness.

Consider the song "At the Ballet." Three women, Sheila, Bebe, and Maggie, tell of their early, dark childhood memories set against the common backdrop of going to ballet class, where their prosaic, everyday existence was transformed and everything and everyone was beautiful. Near the end of the number, Hamlisch and Kleban have Maggie repeat three times, on ascending notes, the title "At the Ballet"; Robin Wagner's black box set reveals a wall of mirrors; Tharon Musser's lighting paints a Mondrian-like palette; and the full company bends, turns, and leaps balletically, dressed in Theoni Aldredge's simple yet evocative audition clothes—all in a mere ten seconds. The audience cheers and there are few dry eyes in the house. It all comes together effortlessly and seamlessly. For director Michael Bennett, it was the defining moment of the show.

But what is truly special about this moment is that no one element dominates the stage—not the score, not the sets, costumes, lighting, or Bennett's staging or choreography. The impact is visceral and organic.

Going back to the criticism a few leveled at the music, Hamlisch elevated on Broadway the art of movie underscoring, which, when employed in *A Chorus Line*, is by definition secondary to the narrative of the book. And when he wrote a song such as "Sing!" for Kristine and Al, the intent was not to deliver a top-ten tune but, instead, to give support to Kleban's narrative-like lyrics and to define a character's motivation.

It's ironic that the one song in *A Chorus Line* that achieved a popular "hit" status was "What I Did for Love." Stylistically, the song is quite different from the rest of the score. Joseph Papp, who produced the original production, never liked the song. He thought it was overly sentimental and cut across the vérité of the rest of the piece. But Bennett and others were being told the show needed its eleven o'clock number. Collaboration is compromise.

Collaboration Can Breed Unhappiness, to Say the Least

A successful collaboration is not devoid of conflict or controversy. Whenever theater insiders hear that the early work on a show is going well, that everyone is happy and there are no arguments, they assume the show must be in a lot of trouble. Actually, more often than not, the best work will come out of the battle among big egos and strong-minded artists who will argue passionately for their own opinions and contributions, but ultimately know that they may have to subordinate their own agenda to what is most effective for the piece overall.

Crises will occur. The lyricist may get another show and be suddenly hard to reach. The bookwriter may hit a wall and struggle to find his way around it. Or worse, all three authors may not want to be in the same room with one another.

If serious obstacles arise, for whatever reason, the producer needs to address them and find a solution quickly. He may even have to replace one or more authors or the director. Although draconian, this measure may become unavoidable when a recalcitrant member of the creative team is unable to work constructively with the others. As a last resort, this solution is far better for a producer than wasting years of development watching his idea evaporate and his options expire due to the artistic team's failure to collaborate for a common good.

In the end, personal, creative, and practical considerations will dictate whether or not the collaboration successfully results in the authors completing a strong, workable first draft. Unless a producer keeps watch for signs of discord, he may wake up one day to find the collaboration has collapsed into serious disputes and irreconcilable differences. He needs to walk the fine line between being insufficiently engaged in the process and meddling or interfering unnecessarily.

A Broadway producer once told me that, in order to get his way, he felt it was often useful to instigate conflicts among the authors, pitting one artist against another. "Out of conflict comes great work," he said.

If the conflict among the authors arises naturally from the give-and-take of collaboration and compromise, then that can be a positive and useful development. But a producer manufacturing or manipulating artists for his own ulterior motives strikes at the very heart of maintaining the trust and confidence of those involved in the show. It will and should end in failure.

A Dimly Lit Ballroom

After *A Chorus Line*, Michael Bennett decided to develop a musical entitled *Ballroom* based on the successful TV movie *Queen of the Stardust Ballroom* written by Jerome Kass and starring Maureen Stapleton and Charles Durning.

Kass thought he had hit the lotto jackpot getting Michael, the most sought-after director in town, to adapt his teleplay into a Broadway musical. Kass also wanted to write the book of the musical, to which Michael agreed. So Kass would play double duty, thereby avoiding any possible conflict between the bookwriter and the underlying owner.

As for the composer and lyricist, Michael and Kass turned to the Oscar-winning couple of Marilyn and Alan Bergman for the lyrics and Billy Goldenberg for the music. None of them had ever written a Broadway show, but the Bergmans were legends in Hollywood and Goldenberg had a long list of impressive film credits. They seemed like a natural choice since they also had written the score for the TV movie. After all, Hamlisch and Kleban hadn't written a show before *A Chorus Line* either.

The love affair among all of these artists was immediate and intense. No one was more seductive than Michael, especially with artists and actors. And the Bergmans, particularly Marilyn, took on the role of Mother Goose, bringing bagels, lox, and other comfort food whenever they worked on the show at Michael's duplex penthouse overlooking Central Park. Michael loved to identify everyone with whom he worked as a family member—Kass and Goldenberg became siblings, Marilyn Bergman a mom, and the inscrutable Alan? Not sure. Maybe a distant cousin.

The first meetings seemed to go well, although one of the problems Michael saw early on was that no one, including himself, had figured out the "Why?" Why adapt this rather serious, sentimental TV movie into a musical?

The story was quite simple. Bea, a late-middle-aged woman (based on Kass's mother), at the urging of her friends, tries to get out from under her recent widowhood by going to the local dance hall, where she meets an older married guy (Al), has an affair, and discovers there may be more left to live for. Just when it seems that it's all going to end happily, her paramour dies. Roll the credits.

Although Michael worried no one had found a reason for the adaptation, he continued with its development if for no other reason than he felt the ballroom dance sequences would be a great excuse to give employment to many older unemployed dancers with whom he had worked for many years. One of his reasons for developing *A Chorus Line* back in 1975 had been to give employment to out-of-work theater gypsies at a time when Broadway was at its nadir in terms of invention and productivity. But giving jobs to out-of-work dancers isn't a good enough reason to mount a million-dollar musical.

As for an overall visual conception, Michael had a rather prosaic idea of dividing the play into two halves: Bea's antique shop, where she spent most of her dreary existence, and the Stardust Ballroom, where her life became magical and fantastical. Michael's longtime design collaborator, Robin Wagner, would execute that concept.

Meanwhile, the Bergmans, Goldenberg, and Kass were writing a musical adaptation that essentially took what was on the TV screen to the stage. Michael insisted that traditional "book songs" be written that would move the narrative along. But the Bergmans wanted to keep a number of the songs from the movie in the play, which served little purpose other than providing background music for a tango, rumba, or waltz for the ballroom scenes. Kass, whose story was both fiction and memoir, also didn't want to veer too far from his original teleplay. Michael thought the play tended to be too morose and eventually insisted, against Kass's objection, on bringing in Larry Gelbart to liven up the proceedings.

The collaboration began to degenerate as Michael made increasing demands. Egos prevented the collaborators from being open to seeing others' points of view. It was no secret that Michael could be patronizing and dismissive of writers—they existed to serve the work and he became increasingly irritated and impatient with the authors' unwillingness to see it his way. The Bergmans were established Hollywood royalty. They weren't accustomed to being dictated to by anyone, not even Michael, whom they began to view as an irritant rather than a valuable collaborator.

Kass, while in awe of Michael, was torn between trying to please him and remaining loyal to his collaborators. Kass wasn't interested in fundamentally changing *Ballroom*. In the TV version, Al dies at the end, leaving Bea alone again. Michael insisted the ending be changed to be more upbeat. The final decision was to have Bea accept her relationship with Al as an ongoing, secretive affair (in the song "Fifty Percent"), while Al remained married. A pretty improbable and unsatisfying ending for upper-middle-aged women and men—the dominant demographic for Broadway audiences.

Goldenberg more or less did what he was asked to do. He remained loyal to his co-authors but had great respect for Michael's insights and experience. He recognized that for all of his and his partners' success in the film world, Broadway musicals were a new venue for them. He appreciated that listening to Michael, who was fast becoming a legend in his own time, was something they all should be embracing. But Goldenberg could not bridge the gap between the indomitable Marilyn Bergman and the tyrannical Michael.

Michael became more and more disheartened as the show completed the workshop phase and was slated to open at the Majestic Theatre in December of 1978. Michael had vowed after *A Chorus Line* never to green-light a show to Broadway until he was convinced it had been workshopped and honed to perfection. In his gut, he knew *Ballroom* wasn't ready, but he was under enormous pressure from the Shuberts, who were holding the Majestic Theatre for him.[1] If he wanted the prince of Broadway theaters, he had to commit by the early fall.

After I attended an early preview in Stratford, Connecticut, Michael confessed to me backstage that he knew all along *Ballroom* would fail—not only because he thought the show wasn't terribly good, but because, according to him, no one was allowed to be as successful as he was after *A Chorus Line*. He said, "They will have to cut me down. I'm just too successful." Michael often referred to "they." He meant the "community"—all those "friends" and other colleagues afflicted with schadenfreude and, of course, the critics.

Opening night was as much a wake as a celebration, since Michael and most everyone else knew at an early hour that the reviews were generally bad. A show's fate was largely a function of the critics' reviews in 1978. The power and influence of the *New York Times*, in particular, was such that a review in that paper could seal the fate of most Broadway plays. To get a lukewarm review or, worse, a pan from the *New York Times* was a death knell. That power would only increase exponentially when Frank Rich became the chief drama critic in 1980. The combination of the paper's worldwide readership and prestige, along with Rich's insightful criticism and trenchant writing, effectively made the paper the primary arbiter of most plays' success or failure.

Ballroom closed after a brief run of 116 performances. Michael personally lost a million dollars, equivalent to $10 million or more today. He had financed *Ballroom* single-handedly because he didn't want anyone to lose a dime on a show he instinctively knew would fail.

Scars remained. The authors and Michael went their separate ways. The Bergmans were bitter and blamed Michael for the failure. Kass

[1] "The Shuberts" were Bernard Jacobs and Gerald Schoenfeld, president and chairman, respectively, of the largest and most powerful theater chain on Broadway.

became disillusioned and no longer saw Michael. Billy Goldenberg took it in stride and went back to working in Hollywood.

Was Michael right? Would "they" have killed the show regardless of its merit? Looking back and trying to figure out why a show failed, at least financially, is an exercise no more satisfying than listening to a Monday morning quarterback tell you why your team lost the day before.

The truth is, an unsuccessful show results from a combination of factors. From Michael's point of view, the musical simply wasn't good enough and, what was worse, there had never been a good reason to make the film into a musical in the first place. The authors would have said that Michael never trusted the original material and wanted the play to be more about his dancers and the ballroom than about the story of Bea and Al. One thing is certain: the collaboration failed.

Another contributing factor might have been the lack of an independent and seasoned commercial producer. Michael not only put up all the money but was also the lead producer with final control over all producing decisions. Maybe he had taken on one too many roles?

Finally, everyone could find solace in blaming the critics. After all, what do they know?

There have been a few attempts to mount a revival of *Ballroom*. The writers have revised and added new material. Finding a director who has a vision that syncs with the authors' ideas will be key to having a successful collaboration. As the legal representative of the Bennett Estate, I'd be happy to see the show have a new life, although I can't help but be somewhat skeptical. If the collaborators can find the answers to the questions asked, but never answered, in 1978, and the collaboration takes hold, they may have a shot. *Merde*.[2]

Coda

Great collaborations are not exclusive to musical plays.

There is a scene at the end of act 1 of *The Elephant Man* in which Mrs. Kendal, the famous actress, visits John Merrick, the title character, for the first time. When they say good-bye, Mrs. Kendal extends her hand to

[2] "The French word for no. 2.

Merrick as a sign of her friendship and her compassion for his condition. The audience understands from Merrick's reaction to that simple gesture that no one else before has shown such kindness to this misshapen man. In that brief moment, all the emotional underpinnings of the play come to the fore. Every time I've seen this play, at the moment when their hands touch, a collective chill rises up the backs of the audience.

In the original Broadway production, that effect was achieved by the instructions of the playwright (Bernard Pomerance), the staging of the director (Jack Hofsiss), and the execution by the actors (Philip Anglim and Carole Shelley). Would that scene have had the same power without any one of these collaborative contributions to the overall effect? I think not.

8
The Authors' Collaboration Agreement

What usually comes first is the contract.

—Ira Gershwin

Authors tend to resist entering into a formal agreement with one another before going to work on a musical in the same way couples shy away from entering into a prenuptial agreement. For couples, signing a legal document that contemplates divorce seems to belie the love and commitment each of them will invoke in their marriage vows. Similarly, expecting the authors to address the consequences of dissolution at the very outset of their collaboration may seem to be at odds with building trust and confidence among them.

Prenups are rare, as they should be, and are usually reserved for the well-to-do or for other peculiar circumstances. Collaboration agreements, on the other hand, are essential in almost all cases. Authors need to remind themselves that they are in business with one another. Much is at stake; money, yes, but also reputations and ownership of one's literary and musical property. Addressing what happens when the joint venture unravels is only one part of the understanding. Equally important is clarifying the authors' legal relationships to one another and their respective rights and privileges so as to avoid future ambiguities and disputes.

It is also in the producer's best interest to have these matters worked out in advance among the authors so that any disagreements arising thereafter will not impede the development process or the exploitation of the play.

The lawyer for one of the authors will usually prepare the first draft of an agreement. Each author needs to have legal representation to protect his or her rights in the agreement. If one or more of the authors do not have the money to hire a lawyer, the producer or one of the other authors may advance money to that author which can be repaid later on from royalties.

The document is rather straightforward. Its most substantive terms are:

1. Ownership and approvals
2. Term
3. Compensation
4. Voting
5. Credits
6. Expenses
7. Arbitration

Ownership and Approvals

The bookwriter owns all rights in the book, including copyright and the sole and exclusive right to make any changes or modifications. The same holds true for the lyricist and his lyrics and the composer and her music.

During the development period, each author will, in the give-and-take of the collaboration, contribute ideas and sometimes written material to the others. By agreeing to respect the integrity of each author's ownership rights, the bookwriter will not lay claim to any of the lyrics nor will the composer lay claim to any of the book regardless of the ideas each may have contributed to the other.

Of course, it may turn out that the bookwriter is contributing more than an occasional suggestion or idea to the lyricist. In that case, the agreement can always be modified or amended to provide a sharing in the ownership and proceeds from the lyrics. Otherwise, under the original agreement, the lyricist is protected against any claims to his lyrics, and the bookwriter has to accept that his contributions to the lyrics, no matter how extensive, will become the lyricist's property.

Term

The agreement usually remains in effect until a merger of the book, music, and lyrics occurs, in which case a joint work is created for the life of its copyright.[1] If merger does not occur within a specified period, say five or six years, then the agreement terminates and each of the authors is thereafter free to exploit his or her respective contribution without any further obligations to the others.

Upon merger, the authors will agree that none of them will sell, license, or exploit the book, lyrics, or music separate and apart from the other elements of the musical without the approval of all three authors. The one major exception is that the composer and lyricist will reserve the right to exploit the separate musical compositions with their music publisher for the sale of sheet music, sound recordings, movie synchronization, and other so-called small performance rights, often referred to as the non-dramatic rights, administered by one of the three major licensing organizations, ASCAP, BMI, and SEASAC. There may be holdbacks and other restrictions on the licensing of these rights, but they are generally not considered to be competitive with the exploitation of the so-called dramatic or grand rights in the musical for the stage, film, or any other media.

When does merger occur? We saw in chapter five, "Securing the Rights," that the merger of the underlying work with the musical play occurs either after a few performances on Broadway or, in the case of a famous work, after the musical has run profitably for a substantial period of time on Broadway. Merger among the three elements of the musical usually occurs no later than the first performance of the musical as a first-class production. In effect, there are two mergers: the first among the book, music, and lyrics (the merged musical) and the second between the underlying work and the merged musical. Keep in mind it is absolutely critical that the first merger occur at some point early on so that none of the authors can pick up his or her marbles and abandon the project prematurely, leaving the other authors high and dry. Similarly, the producer needs to make certain that each of the authors is committed to the work and that no competing works will emerge before all of his options have been exercised.

It becomes a balancing act between having the elements of the musical merge whenever it becomes clear the musical is moving forward with a commercial production, and waiting long enough so that, if the collaboration should fail, the authors are free to move on with other creative partners.

---

[1] See chapter five, "Securing the Rights," for an explanation of merger.

Compensation

Provided merger occurs, the proceeds derived from the musical are most commonly shared in equal thirds among the three authors. There can be exceptions, particularly if the bookwriter, for example, is a Tony Award–winning writer with precedents giving him above-average advances and royalties and the other authors are getting their first chance to do a show. In that case, the split might be 40 percent to the bookwriter with the remaining 60 percent divided equally between the composer and lyricist. Obviously, there can be many permutations of the split. The important thing is for each author to feel content with his share and, if there are any underlying tensions or misgivings, have them aired and resolved early on.

The proceeds from the small publishing and performance rights in the songs are divided between the composer and lyricist on a 50/50 basis. This can also be adjusted but it rarely is.

If the book of the musical is sold separately in print or digitally, the bookwriter usually receives 100 percent of the proceeds or he may offer the others a share of 10 percent or so. If the book and lyrics without music are published, then the bookwriter and lyricist split the proceeds with a small share perhaps going to the composer. If merger never occurs, and the authors go their separate ways, each will own 100 percent of future proceeds derived from his or her own authorship.

Voting

Each author customarily has one vote in the disposition of rights to the work as a whole and such dispositions usually require unanimity. Occasionally, the authors may agree that decisions are to be made by two out of three, but it's rare that any author is willing to be outvoted on important issues dealing with the whole work, such as the sale of motion picture rights or the disposition of other subsidiary rights.

These votes also extend to the exercise of author approvals of creative matters, such as the choice of cast, director, choreographer, and designers. Decisions as to anything affecting only one element of the musical, such as the choice of musical director, rest only with the author of that element, in this case, the composer.

A variation on the above may occur when there is a highly experienced and powerful director or director/choreographer involved in the show, particularly if he has been involved in the collaboration from early on in the development process. He may require an equal vote along with the other three authors on the disposition of rights in the play as a whole. With a fourth vote, unanimity becomes an even greater hurdle to affect the sale of rights. The producer will be affected by this, since he doesn't have a vote but he does share in the proceeds derived from any disposition and wants to avoid any deadlocks on those deals. As such, he may try to insist that the four parties agree to a majority vote but that may not win the day. It will come down to the relative bargaining strengths among the group.

Credits

As we've seen in chapter five, "Securing the Rights," the authors' credits appear in a size equal to 50 percent of the size of and below the title and any credits to the stars:

TITLE OF MUSICAL

[50 percent size of title]:

Book by ______, Music by ______, Lyrics by______

As a general matter, most of the details concerning the authors' credits will be set out in the Dramatists Guild APC, which we will discuss later. The collaboration agreement sets out the basic phraseology of the billing and the placement of the authors. The order of the billing among the authors can be arranged in any way they choose, but in most cases the bookwriter comes first, followed by the composer and lyricist.

Expenses

Each author will be entitled to reimbursement for his travel and living expenses, but the actual amounts are deferred until the author enters into the APC with the producer. On occasion, one or more of the authors may have expended money for the recording of a demo or arranging for a reading, for example, before the producer enters the picture. In that case, the parties can agree that the author will be reimbursed for such expenses by the producer upon entering into the APC.

Arbitration

Most collaboration agreements contain an arbitration clause, which provides that, in the event of a dispute between or among the authors, it will be adjudicated by arbitration under the rules of the American Arbitration Association, rather than in a court of law. For one thing, arbitration is usually less costly and more expeditious, but that's not always the case. Speed may be crucial especially in cases where a conflict could impede the progress to production or the exploitation of the show.

Summary

The best collaboration agreements (or contracts in general, for that matter) are those that are signed and never looked at again by the parties. In the ideal situation, during the course of their collaboration, the authors will compromise and find middle ground on the most important creative issues, and, if their agents and lawyers are experienced, the sale of rights to the play as a whole will arise out of the representatives' consensus on the best price and most attractive non-financial provisions.

But disputes do arise from time to time. Having a collaboration agreement that sets out everyone's expectations and interests gives clarity and protection to each author, but also gives the producer confidence that any disputes will be resolved expeditiously so that his investment is not held hostage to the authors' legal wrangling, legitimate or not.

Compromise Is the Hallmark of Collaboration

Collaboration agreements are often signed after the authors have begun their work, sometimes even following completion of the play. Here are a few examples of compromises reached among authors, drawn from my experiences negotiating collaboration agreements:

- The bookwriter gave considerable help to the first-time lyricist. The bookwriter isn't asking for any share of the lyricist's royalty, but he wants credit. The lyricist objects since most of the lyrics were written by him alone.

✓ Compromise: The bookwriter takes a credit below the lyricist's credit in smaller print as follows:

Lyrics by Joe Blow
Additional Lyrics by John Smith

- The composer had the idea for the musical and wants a "conceived by" credit in addition to her composer credit. The bookwriter objects. He thinks "conceived by" diminishes his contribution to the project as bookwriter. He argues that the composer's idea, while a helpful starting point, did not rise to a level of authorship justifying a separate credit.

✓ Compromise: The composer drops her request for the "conceived by" credit and accepts instead a credit that will appear below the title as follows:

Based on an idea by Jane Doe

- The musical is mostly sung through (à la *Les Misérables*) and the bookwriter doesn't feel "book by" accurately reflects his extensive contributions to the storyline. He maintains it is difficult to discern the difference between the lyricist's work and his narrative that is both spoken and recitative (halfway between speaking and singing) and underscored by the music.

✓ Compromise: The bookwriter receives a credit more commonly used in opera but occasionally used in musicals:

Libretto by John Doe

- All three authors write music and all three feel they have contributed to some degree to the book and lyrics.

✓ Compromise: Credit book, music, and lyrics to all three authors, probably listed alphabetically.

- The director/choreographer has won multiple Tony Awards, having directed and choreographed several hit musicals. He has worked on the show from the outset and the authors have already agreed he is entitled to receive a share of the authors' subsidiary rights proceeds. Therefore, the director wants an equal vote with the authors when disposing of rights to the musical. He also does not want any one of the authors to be able to stop the sale of any of the rights if he and the others wish to move forward.

✓ Compromise: In order to exploit any rights in the musical, both the director and a majority (two out of three) of the authors must approve the deal. This places the director in a very strong position, since nothing can be disposed of without his vote, regardless of how the three authors vote. Also, provided he and two out of three of the authors agree, the one dissident author cannot hold up the sale.

- The book and lyrics are written by a husband and wife and the music is composed by their son.

✓ Compromise: Don't do the show.

All for the Common Good

Negotiations among authors can be fraught with tension. No author likes to be accused of being ego-driven, but that is often the basis for disputes such as the ones cited above. However, these disagreements often reflect fundamental truths, if you will, about the authorship of the show. In the majority of cases, the three authors should be satisfied with their respective credit for book, lyrics, or music. The goal is to ensure that each feels comfortable offering suggestions to the others without being concerned that he or she is encroaching on another's territory. Conversely, each author shouldn't fear that accepting an idea from another author may jeopardize the ownership of his or her contributions. There is one common goal: the creation of a seamless, integrated musical.

9

Royalty Pools

Gross is our birthright. You don't touch that.

—Peter Stone, former president
of the Dramatists Guild

As I explained earlier in chapter five, "Securing the Rights," royalties payable to the play's creative team (the owner, authors, director, designers) were traditionally paid on the basis of gross weekly box office receipts. We saw how the total gross received for any one week of performances (the gross gross) was reduced by deducting local governmental, federal, and other admission taxes (there are no others right now), payments to the labor unions' pension and welfare funds, credit card charges, fees for group sales and theater parties, and a restoration fee paid to the theater owner. The amount remaining is referred to as the net gross. As I also explained earlier, the net gross (about 10 percent less than gross gross) is the only number that's meaningful in figuring out how much money is available for payment of royalties to the creative talent, for the return of investment, or for the realization of net profits following recoupment. It's the number that everyone relies on to calculate their weekly financial piece of the pie.

In 1980 the total net gross payable to the authors, the other creative talent, and the producer for a big musical based on a famous underlying work could be as much as 20 percent, and that didn't include theater rent (6 percent) or a star's percentage (10 percent).[1]

If the gross gross for that week was $500,000, the net gross, after deducting 10 percent, would be $450,000. If the authors were entitled to receive 6 percent of the net gross, they would be paid 6 percent of

[1] As we will see in chapter eighteen, "The Producer's Deal," the producer also receives a weekly royalty in consideration of his services during the run of the play.

$450,000, or $27,000. Pretty good for one week, particularly in 1980. That would be the equivalent of $75,000 in 2016.[2]

Today, with few exceptions, Broadway shows, both straight plays and musicals, no longer pay royalties on the basis of a percentage of the net gross. Instead, royalties payable to the creative team, as well as to all other royalty participants, are paid on the basis of a percentage of the "weekly operating profits." All of the royalty participants, along with the producer, share in a pool of monies that reflect the weekly operating profits of the show that remain after all of the "weekly operating costs" have been deducted from the net gross. Hence the word of art *royalty pools*. I'll illustrate how these royalties are calculated below, but first some history.

Cause Célèbre of the Year

The impetus for the industry to devise and accept a more palatable alternative for paying royalties was a November 1981 front page article in the *New York Times* focusing on a long-running musical, *Woman of the Year*, starring Lauren Bacall, based on the motion picture of the same title. The show was budgeted at $2 million (a lot of money in those days) but it encountered cost overruns along the way and ultimately cost nearly $3 million by the time it opened on Broadway. Originally, all of the royalty participants were paid on the basis of net gross. At the time the *New York Times* article was written, the show had returned barely any money to its investors, in spite of the fact it had been running for nearly nine months. Based on the numbers reported by the *New York Times*, it wasn't difficult to calculate the millions of dollars earned by the creative talent, the producer, and the theater owner while the investors sat on the sidelines receiving financial statements month after month which showed no meaningful return of their investment. As a result, pressure was brought to bear on the royalty participants and the royalty structure was renegotiated, putting a royalty pool in place.

The article quickly became a cause célèbre within the industry. The media suddenly became interested in Broadway economics (a first), and producers realized that if they were to survive and find future investors,

---

[2] Based on Consumer Price Index.

they had to address what appeared to be the inequity between the royalty participants and the investors. Many read the article as an indictment of a system that unfairly burdened the production by paying gross royalties to talent, the theater, and the producer as a first priority before paying any of the other bills, leaving little or nothing for the investors. Not exactly Max Bialystock, the double-dealing producer in Mel Brooks's *The Producers*, and certainly not illegal, but perhaps a distant cousin.

The article spurred an industry-wide hue and cry to address this apparent injustice to the investors, particularly when investments were becoming harder and harder to come by. The *New York Times* piece plunged a stake through the heart of every offering circular being distributed to potential investors for new shows at the time.[3] The solution, to the dismay of the creative talent, was to cease paying royalties based on net gross starting from the first performance and to construct another formula based on a pool of net operating profits for paying the creative talent, the investors, and, in some cases, the theater on a more equitable basis.

This all led to a sharp debate between the authors and the producers. When interviewed for the *Times* article, the late Gerald Schoenfeld, chairman of the Shubert Organization at the time, put the conflict this way: "When you're dealing with gross, you [the authors] don't give a damn what net profits are. If the show is still running, you're still getting royalties. Is this the most efficient way, for people to get paid large amounts even though the play is not making money?"

The other side of the debate was expressed by the late Peter Stone, bookwriter for *Woman of the Year*, president of the Dramatists Guild, and staunch advocate for authors' rights. With the introduction of royalty pools in the 1980s, Stone became a bulwark railing against what he considered to be the unbridled avarice of the producers and theater owners. To his mind, eliminating authors' royalties based on gross was tantamount to undermining every author's God-given right to a decent living. He saw no reason to rest the burden of realizing net profits on the shoulders of the dramatists or any of the creative team. Getting gross was just the

[3] An offering circular is part of the package of financing documents distributed to potential investors in a show. We'll discuss this in more detail in chapter fifteen, "Finding the Money."

way it had always been, he argued: "If it was fair then, it's fair now. We asked for ten percent [of the gross] when Eugene O'Neill was a member of this guild. . . . Gross is our birthright. You don't touch that."

By the early eighties, royalty pools became ubiquitous, although their construction and application have remained controversial subjects, repeatedly scrutinized, adjusted, and debated within the industry over the decades. In spite of many people's dislike of these formulae, they have survived and been accepted reluctantly by the creative community, as a result of economic necessity. Simply put, without adjusting the traditional formulation of paying royalties based on gross, the industry would have collapsed financially under the sheer weight of providing for preferential treatment of the artists over any other costs or the return of capital.

How Are Royalty Pools Constructed?

If you are, or want to be, a producer on Broadway, you must become conversant with the rationale for, and the mechanics and nuances of, royalty pools. They form the very core structure of the economics of most shows. Although few investors, and even some producers for that matter, truly understand the intricacies of a royalty pool, the first question many investors nonetheless ask is, "Do you have a royalty pool?" You'd better say yes. If you don't, then you'll have to explain why not. The common perception is that without a royalty pool, the show will not have a shot at recovering its production costs.

When I represented Blake Edwards, the Oscar-winning Hollywood director and bookwriter of the musical *Victor/Victoria*, and John Scher, his co-producing partner, we would periodically convene in my office to discuss royalty pools, not so much because Blake and John wanted to learn about them but rather for some comic relief from the day-to-day pressures of producing a musical. There was no end to their amusement as I explained in excruciating detail the definitions of gross gross, net gross, weekly operating expenses and weekly operating profits. As John would say to me more often than not, "Don't give me a headache. I'll just leave it up to you." And Blake would simply shake his head, confounded at what he considered the inanity of Broadway economics as compared to Hollywood's more straightforward approach to compensation—big payouts up front and almost never any income from a share of net profits or other back-end arrangements.

Regardless of the difficulties involved, I'll try to set out the most important elements of royalty pools. Let's consider a typical breakdown for an average musical *prior* to 1980.

ROYALTY PARTICIPANT	PERCENTAGE OF NET GROSS
Underlying rights	1.5%
Bookwriter	1.5%
Composer	1.5%
Lyricist	1.5%
Director	2.0%
Choreographer	0.75%
Set, costume, lighting designers	2.0%
Orchestrator	0.25%
Actors' Equity Association (workshop)	1.0%
Not-for-profit theater (pre-Broadway tryout)	1.0%
Producer	2.0%
Total	15.00%

After recoupment (the point at which production costs have been recovered and the investors have been paid back their investment), the above percentages would usually increase by as much as one-third, bringing the above total of 15% to 20%. Moreover, as I pointed out at the beginning of this chapter, due in no small part to rampant inflation during the seventies, the artists' demands for a greater percentage of net gross, even prior to recoupment, began to mushroom.[4]

However, even using the above more modest royalties, it becomes quickly apparent that the economics of a big musical paying royalties on the net gross was exceedingly unattractive for an investor. For example, if the weekly net gross was $275,000 (a hefty amount in 1978), royalties of 15 percent would equal $41,250, the star at 10 percent would get $27,500, and the theater at 6 percent would receive $16,500, for a grand

[4] By the time *Woman of the Year* opened, it was not unusual to have as much as 20 percent of the gross being paid out to the royalty participants prior to recoupment, and, as noted earlier, that excluded an additional 10 percent for the star and 6 percent for the theater.

total of $85,250. Deducting that amount from the $275,000 net gross would leave $189,750 to pay all of the show's fixed expenses ($175,000), leaving a balance of $14,750 to repay the investors their capital investment for that week. At that rate, a $2 million show would have to run nearly three years or 136 weeks just to recoup.

Now consider a royalty package of 20 percent plus a star at 10 percent and the theater at 6 percent. Using the same costs as above, the bottom line is that the show barely meets its weekly breakeven with nothing left to pay the investors after paying weekly costs, while the royalty participants, the star, and the theater are enjoying bountiful returns.

The Birth of the Royalty Pool

As I said previously, the solution for correcting the inequity among the investors, the creative royalty holders, and the theater was to devise a sharing arrangement among all the parties whereby the net gross, after deducting the weekly operating costs, would be divided into three parts: (1) royalty participants, (2) theater, and (3) investors.

It was assumed that a major star would not be willing to participate in the pool, but rather would continue to insist on getting a percentage of the net gross, an expense that would be included in the show's weekly operating costs.

Initially, the pool of money to be split among the participants for straight plays was 40 percent to the royalty holders, 20 percent to the theater, and 40 percent to the investors. When the pool was applied to musicals, in order to provide sufficient money to return the much higher costs of production, the royalty holders were reduced to 35 percent, the theater stayed at 20 percent, and the investors' share rose to 45 percent.

To go back to our example above, assuming a net gross of $275,000, weekly expenses of $175,000, and a star at 10 percent ($27,500), for a musical that would leave $72,500 to be split in a pool of money among the three groups below:

Royalty participants (35%)	$25,375
Theater (20%)	$14,500
Investors (45%)	$32,625
Total pool payments	$72,500

As for the royalty participants, their share of the pool ($25,375) would be divided among them proportionately based on their respective percentage of net gross royalties (referred to as "points" in the pool). For example, if the director was entitled to 2 percent of the net gross out of a total royalty of 15 percent without a pool, he would get two-fifteenths or 13.33 percent of the pool money allocated to all of the royalty participants (13.33 percent of $25,375, or $3,382). Without a pool, that same director would have gotten 2 percent of the net gross, or $5,500.[5]

Most important, however, is that the investors are now getting nearly $33,000 each week, thereby making it possible to recover the capital costs of the production ($2 million) in about a year's time, as opposed to three years without a pool.

The theater owners at first agreed to be part of the pool. But as the business improved, due in no small part to the emergence of megahits from Britain starting with *Cats*, the theater owners reverted to insisting on getting their rent based on net gross. That left only the creative team and the producers to share in and divide up the royalty pool pie.

Without the theater sharing in the pool, the division of the pool for musicals was normally 35 percent to the creative team and 65 percent to the production. As for straight plays, the customary split was 40 percent to the creative team and 60 percent to the production. As an aside, the British were late coming to the idea of royalty pools. Most of the big musicals from England were so successful that they had no need for a pool. Their weekly grosses were more than sufficient to pay all of the talent and the theater's rent while still leaving a goodly amount to pay to the investors for recoupment and eventual net profits. As those shows got weaker, however, the British also converted to royalty pools to take advantage of the sharing arrangements between artists and investors.

Here are a few other refinements to the royalty pool structure:

- The royalty participants receive guaranteed minimum weekly fixed payments regardless of whether the show has any operating profits for that week. Originally, the minimum was equal to $500

---

[5] As a further complication, under the directors' union collective bargaining agreement, minimum payments are required to be paid to directors and choreographers even under royalty pool arrangements. See chapter sixteen, "The Director."

(later increased to $750) for each percentage of net gross (or points) the artist was entitled to receive under a net gross deal. For the authors, who would have gotten a minimum of 4.5 percent of the net gross prior to recoupment, their minimum under a pool would be three times $750, or $2,250 per week.

- When the theater owners decided to no longer participate in the pool, the Dramatists Guild unilaterally promulgated certain minimums and other safeguards for its members, the most significant being that the authors would have to receive a minimum of 15.56 percent of 100 percent of the weekly operating projects for the pool prior to recoupment and 17.78 percent thereafter.[6]
- Prior to recoupment the 35 percent payable to the creative team is often capped at an amount equal to what they would have received if they were being paid on the net gross. If a show is a sold-out hit, 35 percent of the pool, after paying the fixed expenses, could be greater than 20 percent of the net gross. Normally there is no cap on the pool shares payable following recoupment.
- The percentage split between the two groups changes after recoupment: 35 percent rising to 40 percent for the creative team and 65 percent going down to 60 percent for the investors, for musicals. For straight plays, the pool increases to 45 percent for the creative team and the investors' share is reduced to 55 percent. In some cases, this post-recoupment adjustment favoring the creative group is delayed until the investors receive anywhere from 110 percent to 125 percent of their investment back.
- Royalty pool payments are normally payable based on the weekly operating profits over a four-week period rather than on a week-to-week basis in order to offset big swings in the weekly grosses. For example, if the operating profits/loss for a four-week period were +$75,000, –$25,000, +$10,000, and +$15,000, the aggregate net operating profits used to calculate the royalty pool for that four-week period would be $75,000.

[6] It was Peter Stone who came up with these seemingly arbitrary percentages. During negotiations, he would painstakingly explain the logic and math behind these numbers to producers, but he rarely got a sympathetic reaction from them.

The 1982 Tony Awards: David vs. Goliath

On December 20, 1981, Michael Bennett's production of *Dreamgirls* opened at the Imperial Theatre. There were good reasons for the street's high anticipation for the show. Anything Michael did was big news; the show was said to be inspired by (not based on) Diana Ross and the Supremes; Jennifer Holliday, the young gospel singer playing the leading role of Effie, was rumored to have a voice the likes of which had never been heard before on Broadway; and then there was the powerhouse producing team of music mogul David Geffen and the Shubert Organization alongside Michael and his longtime collaborator, Bob Avian.

The *New York Times*'s chief drama critic, Frank Rich, filed a rave review the day after the opening, showering the show with the kind of praise most artists only dream about: "When Broadway history is being made, you can feel it. What you feel is a seismic emotional jolt that sends the audience, as one, right out of its wits. While such moments are uncommonly rare these days, I'm here to report that one popped up at the Imperial last night. Broadway history was made at the end of the first act of Michael Bennett's beautiful and heartbreaking new musical, 'Dreamgirls.'"[7]

When I saw Michael at the opening night party, he pulled me aside and said, "They're still out to get me"—again, his reference to those amorphous outside forces he could somehow never elude. He had seen Rich's review, but he'd also seen several others that were not as kind. I told him that, with the over-the-top Rich review and the other positive ones, the show was bound to be a huge hit. Michael was not convinced. He remained pretty despondent the rest of the evening.

The next morning, after all the reviews had come in, Michael spoke with Bernard Jacobs, president of the Shubert Organization and lead producer, and me by telephone, yelling over and over, "Do I have a hit?! Do I have a hit?!" He wanted and needed to hear, particularly from Bernie Jacobs, as his producer, that the show would have a long run and be profitable. At first Bernie was noncommittal, which only increased Michael's anger. Bernie finally relented and assured Michael he had a

---

[7] Rich was referring to Holliday's explosive rendition of the closing song, "And I'm Telling You I'm Not Going."

hit. Bernie went on to say that *Dreamgirls* would win the Tony for Best Musical. Not a risky bet given the rest of the musicals slated to come in before the Tony deadline in May.

What Michael was really doing was challenging Bernie (and the other producers) to support the show with fresh capital in order to mount an advertising and marketing campaign big enough to overcome any negative reviews or publicity. Michael was brilliant in concealing a motive behind what appeared to be aberrational behavior.

Meanwhile, a month later, a new musical, with book by Arthur Kopit and music and lyrics by newcomer Maury Yeston, was being workshopped by director/choreographer Tommy Tune. The musical was *Nine*, based on Federico Fellini's semiautobiographical film, *8 1/2*.

Tune presented portions of the show to producers and potential investors at the old New Amsterdam Theatre on Forty-Second Street. This predated Forty-Second Street's transformation from a dirty, crime-ridden haven for prostitutes and drug dealers to its present incarnation as a more tourist-friendly destination. With generous tax incentives being offered by the city, Disney kicked off the whole regeneration of this infamous street by restoring the New Amsterdam to its past glories and splendor. Broadway hadn't seen the likes of a theater this beautifully ornate and spacious for decades. Everyone thought it was a bright omen for Times Square's future.

Today, one can judge for oneself whether Forty-Second Street's transformation has reestablished it as one of New York City's unique cultural venues or whether it has become another nondescript neon-laden boulevard of franchise food stores and the carnival-like attractions (Ripley's Believe It or Not and Madame Tussauds) commonly found in many other cities. What cannot be disputed is that it *is* safer, attracts millions of tourists each year, and is no longer a street of hookers and pushers.

In some ways, back in 1981, presenting *Nine* in this ramshackle environment made it shine even more. The overwhelmingly positive reaction of those who attended the presentation reverberated throughout the theater community. The opening number, "Overture Delle Donne," set to Yeston's haunting music, had Tune's chorus of long-legged beautiful women spinning, kicking, and stretching on small black pedestals. It was sexy and stunning in its simplicity.

Most people at the time still thought that nothing could compete with *Dreamgirls* for that season's top honors. James Nederlander, owner of the second-largest theater chain on Broadway, offered Tune the much sought-after 46th Street Theatre (later named the Richard Rodgers), provided the show opened before the Tony deadline in early May.

Time was very short. Tune needed six weeks of rehearsal and one month of previews, which meant all the deals and the full capitalization needed to be completed within two weeks. The commercial rights to the show were held by Michel Stuart, the actor who originated the role of Bobby in *A Chorus Line*, and Harvey Klaris, a young lawyer-businessman who had previously co-produced Tune's Off-Broadway play *Cloud Nine*. Neither had the personal financial resources to mount *Nine* as a Broadway show.

But, soon after the workshop, *Nine* began to gather a momentum all its own. Led by veteran theater owner Nederlander, a handful of new kids on the block were eager to take on the king of the hill, *Dreamgirls*. They included Roger Berlind, a savvy investment banker who turned his attention to producing on Broadway in the late seventies; Francine LeFrak, daughter of the legendary real estate tycoon Samuel; and Kenneth Greenblatt, a new arrival on Broadway from the garment industry. Berlind would later become, and is still today, an important independent and ubiquitous producer of his own.

All the parties had the same goal: getting the musical funded quickly and putting it on a sound financial footing. The powerful agent Sam Cohn represented Stuart and Klaris as well as Tune. By virtue of his force of personality and razor-sharp mind, Sam effectively took the lead on one side of the negotiating table while I sat opposite him representing Nederlander, Lefrak, and, indirectly, the other producers.

Keeping in mind the *New York Times* article about *Woman of the Year*, my clients were firmly set against approving any royalty deals already based on percentages of net gross. They insisted on constructing a royalty pool, which, up to then, had been used only for straight plays and never for a musical. My instructions from my clients were simple and straightforward: unless a royalty pool was implemented, there would be no financing and no deal. Sam Cohn's marching orders from his clients were also quite simple: get the money, and quickly.

The model for royalty pools for straight plays followed what I described earlier: 40 percent to the creative team, 40 percent to the investors, and 20 percent to the theater. But when this allocation was applied to the numbers for *Nine* the results were unsatisfactory for my clients. 40 percent was too little for them to recover their investment within a reasonable period (six months or less). As a result, we hammered out a compromise with 35 percent for the creative team, 20 percent to the theater, and 45 percent to the investors.

Peter Stone, acting as spokesperson for the Dramatists Guild (of which both Yeston and Kopit were members), warned throughout the negotiations that this diminution of the authors' share of the pool was a further intrusion of the camel's nose in the proverbial tent, hastening the ultimate demise of royalties based on gross.

Sam, knowing that my clients meant to stand by their ultimatum and recognizing the economic necessity for the pool, pushed ahead and approved the deal.

But as we hastened to construct a pool acceptable to everyone at the table, we had forgotten to address one participant who lived six thousand miles away—Federico Fellini. His agreement, signed months earlier, provided for a royalty of 1 percent of the gross but, naturally, no provision for a royalty pool. This upended everything. To get the creative team to agree to a pool, everyone—including Fellini—had to accept being paid from the pool. Moreover, I had made my recoupment projections for the producers on the same basis. Try explaining a royalty pool to Fellini.

Keep in mind, there had been one straight play, *Children of a Lesser God*, that had used a pool. A royalty pool for *musicals* was unprecedented. The idea that something this new and relatively complicated could be explained and agreed to by Fellini and his advisors within a few days seemed quixotic, at best. The negotiations were Felliniesque. Phone calls and telexes (no faxes or emails in those days) were placed frantically over a period of three or four days. To no avail.

Ultimately, both the producers and the creative team caved in and reluctantly agreed to exclude Fellini from the royalty pool—not a perfect result, but a compromise for both sides when balanced against the threat of abandoning the show. This was the lesson all of us learned from those negotiations—in the future, never sign an underlying rights deal, or any creative deal, without provisions for a royalty pool, or at least the option to use one. That is still today an absolute.

Nine opened on May 9, 1982, to mostly favorable reviews. Although Frank Rich's notice was mixed, the overall impression of his review was a qualified rave and enough to ensure a healthy run for the show:

> There are two unquestionable reasons to cheer "Nine," the extravagantly uneven musical that opened at the 46th Street Theater last night. Their names are Tommy Tune and Maury Yeston. In this, his most ambitious show, Mr. Tune provides the strongest evidence yet that he is one of our theater's most inventive directors—a man who could create rainbows in a desert. Mr. Yeston, a newcomer to Broadway, has an imagination that, at its best, is almost Mr. Tune's match.

So the race was on: *Nine* vs. *Dreamgirls*. Each vied for and received their share of the early awards that spring. But the key to real success would be the Tony for Best Musical.

Those involved with *Nine* campaigned and buttonholed Tony voters with an underdog's aggression. "*Dreamgirls* is good, but not great. It doesn't stand up to Michael's other work"; "This is Tommy Tune's chance to shine and be recognized," etc. Bernie Jacobs's lobbying efforts on behalf of *Dreamgirls*, on the other hand, backfired—many voters resented his hardball tactics—and ultimately hurt the show. As time went by, Michael increasingly became convinced that "they" would be out to get him again, and deprive him and his show of the prized award.

It's hard to describe the frenzy that often grips this tiny community during Tony season. Everything else seems secondary to those who treat the outcome of a Tony vote as nearly as important as a presidential election. It's all seemingly absurd to an outsider. But don't tell that to the producers of the musicals in contention.

That year, the excitement and tension on Tony night were palpable and, in some ways, unbearable for those closely connected to the two front-runners. Looking back on that night, I can remember feeling that nothing could stop the momentum *Nine* had built in the last couple of weeks. The new kids on the block had graduated and were challenging the "old guard." (Michael was only thirty-six years old!) My wife, Nan, and I sat off the aisle, within eyeshot of Bernie Jacobs, Michael, and Bob Avian. Behind us were Tune and his producers. I was in the somewhat uncomfortable position of having been connected to both shows, but, given my close relationship with Michael, I was rooting for *Dreamgirls* and feared the worst.

And, indeed, the golden ring went to *Nine*—Best Musical. *Nine* also took home the honors for Best Score (Yeston), Best Featured Actress (Liliane Montevecchi), Best Direction of a Musical (Tommy Tune), and Best Costume Design (William Ivey Long).

Dreamgirls was by no means ignored, nabbing six awards to *Nine*'s five: Best Book (Tom Eyen), Best Choreography (Michael Bennett and Michael Peters), Best Leading Actress (Jennifer Holliday), Best Actor (Ben Harney), Best Featured Actor (Cleavant Derricks), and Best Lighting Design (Tharon Musser).

In truth, both shows shared the glory that night. For *Dreamgirls*, response to the Tonys' TV broadcast of Jennifer Holliday's thundering climax to act 1 ("And I'm Telling You I'm Not Going") almost made up for not winning Best Musical. And for *Nine*, the producers celebrated what no one could have predicted three months earlier.

Dreamgirls ran for 1521 performances on Broadway, as compared to 729 for *Nine*.

Two interesting lessons were learned that year that continue to guide producers even today:

- *Nine* seemed to demonstrate that there was an edge to shows that opened in the second half of the season (January to May) as opposed to the fall. The theory goes that shows opening later get more momentum for the Tonys and the voters are more apt to vote for what they've recently seen.
- *Dreamgirls* seemed to prove that if you presented a musical number on the Tony's TV broadcast that resonated with the viewing audience, the show would realize a substantial uptick in sales and gain national recognition. This, in some cases, might well mitigate the disappointment of losing the coveted Best Musical prize.

10

Enter Amortization

New Twists in the Royalty Pool

I feel I ought to apologize for making our discussion of royalty pools even more complex. However, over the past decade, owing to the inexorable rise of production and operating costs, a few new elements have been introduced into these formulae.

In 1981, the production costs for musicals ranged from $2 million to $3 million. By the early 2000s, those numbers escalated to a range of $6 million to $10 million. Today, it is not uncommon to see budgets of $15 million or more. *Spider-Man: Turn Off the Dark*, produced in 2010, reportedly cost $75 million—not a pretty sight, but clearly an aberration. That book remains to be written.

Due to the inflation of weekly wages and advertising costs, and ever more sophisticated and costly special effects, we've seen a similar escalation in weekly operating costs. Musicals that had weekly costs on average of $300,000 a week in the eighties escalated to the mid-$500,000 range by 2000 and today are as much as $750,000. Not to pick on *Spider-Man: Turn Off the Dark* (why not?), but its weekly costs were said to be in excess of $1 million.

Furthermore, as we've seen earlier, due to the laws of supply and demand, the theater owners are no longer willing to participate in a royalty pool. Theaters normally get all of their expenses plus a rent factor of 5 or 6 percent of net gross plus 2 percent of gross gross as a restoration fee.

All of this has meant less money for the pool reservoir, thereby decreasing royalties to the creative team and placing a greater burden on producers to realize sufficient money to pay back their investors within a reasonable period of time.

Hence a further wrinkle was introduced to the formula for determining the royalties in a pool—amortization, which is, simply put, a weekly fixed amount of money, depending on the production costs of the show, that is paid to the investors and becomes a further deduction against the weekly net gross, prior to calculating the royalty pool's share of weekly profits.

Here's an example:

Assumptions	
Production costs	$12,000,000
Weekly operating costs (including theater costs)	$750,000
Weekly amortization	$100,000

Based on the above, if there were no amortization and in one week the show brought in a net gross of $900,000, $150,000 would be left for weekly operating profits ($900,000 net gross minus weekly operating costs of $750,000). With amortization, an additional $100,000 is deducted from the net gross and paid 100 percent to the investors. That leaves only $50,000 of weekly operating profits for the royalty pool to be divided between the royalty holders and the investors. The investors get a total of $100,000 from the amortization factor plus a portion (60 percent) of the $50,000 weekly operating profits that's shared with the royalty holders.

The amortization factor allows the production to accelerate its recovery of the capitalization—again, to the detriment of the royalty holders. A final nail in the coffin for the gospel according to Peter Stone.

The amount of weekly amortization is governed by several factors; some contracts call for an amount equal to 2 percent of the capitalization with a cap of $200,000.

Here's how that works. Let's assume production costs of $12 million. To recover that amount over fifty-two weeks, the production will need to receive as its share of the royalty pool an average of $230,000 per week. An aggressive producer might insist on having that amount fixed as the weekly amortization deduction. More often, the parties will agree to a lower amount, say, $200,000 each week, so that there is sufficient money remaining for the royalty holders' share of the pool.

Of course, in weeks when the show is a sellout, the producers receive even more than the weekly amortization since there would be a balance of weekly operating profits available to the pool over and above the fixed amortization amount to be split between the investors and the royalty holders.

In return for agreeing to this preferential treatment for the investors, the authors customarily receive:

- A higher pre-production advance against royalties—$150,000, perhaps, as compared to $60,000
- A higher weekly guaranteed minimum fixed royalty (regardless of the net gross)—$1,500 per point, perhaps, as compared to $750
- A greater percentage of the royalty pool (perhaps 50 percent) and a bonus after recoupment until they've recovered what was forfeited during the amortization period
- A reduction in the amortization when the show is above a certain capacity
- A reduction (or clawback) in the producer's share of subsidiary rights income
- A share of the net profits of the production

This all leads to lengthy and sometimes very contentious negotiations. In fact, to avoid protracted debate, particularly early in the development of the show, both sides often agree to defer good-faith amortization negotiations until budgets are finalized and the producers can make their case for a formula that will enable them to recoup within a year or so of the opening.

Some Comparisons

Just as an exercise in masochism, let's compare what a bookwriter of a musical would get under three different scenarios:

1. A net gross deal
2. A standard royalty pool
3. A royalty pool with amortization

Let's assume a weekly net gross of $800,000, a not uncommon figure for today's big musicals; weekly operating profits without amortization of $150,000; and weekly operating profits of $50,000 after deducting $100,000 amortization.

1. In a gross deal, the bookwriter would get 1.5 percent of $800,000, or $12,000.
2. In a royalty pool without amortization, the writer would get 5 percent of $150,000, or $7,500.
3. In a royalty pool with amortization, the writer would get 6 percent of $50,000, or $3,000.

The above analysis doesn't factor in the modifications I listed above that are meant, if the show is a big hit, to give back to the authors, following recoupment, the money they've forfeited during the amortization period. But it is readily apparent that over time—gross deals, then royalty pools, and now royalty pools with amortization—the creative talent has borne the brunt of the investors' increasing demands for a reasonable payback period for the investors.

While acknowledging the creative team has seen an erosion of their royalties, the producers argue that they're being asked to fund extraordinarily expensive productions and cannot do so unless they can demonstrate to their investors that there's some hope they'll get their money back within a year or so. Even then these projections are based on shows grossing $1 million or more each week, numbers that are usually limited to only six or seven shows, including three or four that have been running for ten years or more.

At the risk of hearing "foul" from my friends in the unions and theater owners, I would also point out that in the face of these reductions in royalties, theater owners' expenses and rents and salaries for cast, crew, and musicians and other union personnel have increased.

The unions' argument to producers is quite simple: none of us shares in the bounty realized by authors, producers, and investors from touring companies, international companies, TV and films, and other subsidiary rights. Authors are in a way linked to the producers as owners of the business of the play with all the financial and other benefits accruing to them from the disposition of subsidiary and ancillary rights for years to come after the show closes on Broadway. For chorus members, string players, and curtain pullers, the ability to pay the rent and put food on the table is limited solely to the show's run on Broadway. And, for that, they deserve compensation that reflects the considerable talents and expertise they contribute to the value of the owners' asset—the play.[1]

The laws of supply and demand put the theater owners at the very top of the food chain. They are beneficiaries of rents paid on the gross, 100 percent recovery of their expenses, restoration fees, and fees for credit card charges and other ticketing services. Suffice it to say, at heart they are owners of the most valuable and limited resource necessary to produce a play. Season after season, producers vie for the best theaters, or any theater, for their plays. So long as there are a finite number of theaters on Broadway and a plentiful supply of plays and investors sitting in the wings, theater owners will continue to issue rental contracts that dictate nonnegotiable terms for a Broadway house.

The permutations and complications of amortization deals are not for the faint of heart. In the last chapter, I talked about the hilarity of my late-night meetings with Blake Edwards and John Scher discussing royalty pools. Sadly, Blake's biting wit and sardonic humor are no longer with us, and John Scher has put theater producing on the back burner for now. Fortunately, amortization deals came along after their musical, *Victor/Victoria*, closed on Broadway. I can't imagine what our soirees would have devolved into had I tried to introduce these gentlemen to yet another mathematical quagmire.

---

[1] Consider the plight of the designers (sets, costumes, and lighting). While they do own their copyrights and can enjoy future income if their designs are used, they are included in the royalty pool but they do not share in subsidiary rights income.

11

Workshops

Their Use and Abuse

There was no such thing as a workshop in the theater until 1974, when director and choreographer Michael Bennett first conceived of *A Chorus Line*. Back then, the word *workshop* conjured up images of dirty, health-hazard sweatshops. After Michael's experiment with this pre-rehearsal process, workshops became de rigueur over the next ten years or so, only to fall out of favor somewhat by the nineties

For one thing, the costs began to mount, with a six-week workshop costing $500,000, or more. The alternative of presenting a tryout production at a major regional theater, such as the Old Globe or the La Jolla Playhouse, both in California, became increasingly attractive. Having the regional theater finance all or a portion of the production expenses, combined with the chance of seeing a full production with sets, costumes, and lighting in front of a paying audience, appealed to producers and directors more than attending a bare-bones workshop presentation in an over- or under-heated rehearsal room. However, there was another more basic reason for the industry's dwindling interest in workshops.

To understand how producers and directors have come to view workshops today, it's instructive to examine how they first came about.

As mentioned earlier, *A Chorus Line* began with Michael Bennett conducting personal interviews for over twelve hours in a dance rehearsal room on New York City's Lower East Side on the snowy night of January 26, 1974. Two of Michael's friends, Michon Peacock and Tony Stevens, had the original idea of convening a group of theater gypsies (dancers) to share their life stories. Michael, ever mindful of how little employment there was for Broadway dancers, was intrigued by the notion and decided to tape the sessions, sensing it could lead to something unusual. Over pizza and cheap wine, a group of dancers met and free-associated about their childhoods and early experiences as amateur and professional dancers.

Michael wasn't sure what would become of the interviews—a documentary, a film, or a play? At the beginning of the tapes, he says, "I really want to talk about us. . . . I don't know whether anything will come of this. And I think maybe there's a show, somewhere, which will be called *A Chorus Line*."[1]

Michael was advised that if he wanted to exploit the interviews commercially, he'd have to get signed releases from the dancers in order to protect against ownership or privacy claims that might interfere with his ability to develop the material later on. All of the interviewees and actors who participated in the workshops signed general releases in exchange for one dollar.

What emerged from those sessions, and several others Michael recorded later, were more than twenty hours of taped personal recollections that were sometimes tedious or commonplace, but occasionally revelatory and provocative. Taken as a whole, they were a kind of group therapy session, something common to the culture of the 1970s.

After completing the interviews, Michael sensed that something dramatically powerful was buried in those many hours of memories and anecdotes. Ultimately, those tapes became the very fabric of the musical's book and lyrics:

- Several dancers' recollections of attending ballet school as young girls were at first not particularly unique or revealing. But when they went on to describe escaping their painful home lives by "going up a steep and narrow staircase, to the voice like a metronome" and discovering that "everything was beautiful at the ballet," those ordinary events took on a dramatic significance all their own ("At the Ballet").
- When one of the dancers touted her faith in plastic surgery as a means to achieving success, her comments brought into sharp

---

[1] The title *A Chorus Line* was the original title of George Furth's play *Twigs*, which Michael directed on Broadway in 1971. Michael always loved that title. Furth told him he was free to use the title in the future.

relief the hard truth that an actor's looks, more often than not, trump her talent when she is seeking a job ("Dance: Ten; Looks: Three").

- And Nicholas Dante recounting his struggle as a young man to conceal his homosexuality from his parents while trying to figure out what it meant to be a man, suggested a common thematic thread for the show of truth and self-discovery that would resonate with audiences (Paul's monologue).

Michael knew he needed a lot of time—and money—to develop the show collaboratively with his creative team from the ground up. With Dante acting as a first-time bookwriter, Michael began to conceive a book for a musical that would celebrate, and not unduly glorify, the good and the bad and the achievements and disappointments of the life of a Broadway dancer. Later on, Michael would bring on Marvin Hamlisch to compose the music, Ed Kleban to write the lyrics, and James Kirkwood to work with Dante on the book. Taking his cue from his mentor, Jerome Robbins, Michael became conceiver, director, and choreographer (along with co-choreographer Bob Avian). He also brought on board from the outset his design team—Robin Wagner for sets, Theoni Aldredge for costumes, and Tharon Musser for lighting.

Enter Joseph Papp, founder and head of the New York Shakespeare Festival, who would become Michael's producer. Papp had heard of Michael, a Broadway wunderkind, but they'd never worked together. Actually, they came from two different worlds: Papp from the downtown not-for-profit world and Michael from the uptown Broadway-musical crowd. Neither of them identified with or understood the other's milieu. But they were also two ambitious minds who clicked on the same track and had similar theatrical sensibilities. Papp's instinct to ferret out talent, particularly those who experimented with and pushed the boundaries of the art form, caused him to support Michael. He sensed Michael might carve an unusual play out of this unformed mass of ideas, stories, and personal experiences.

As a starting point, Michael told Papp he wanted to get actors in a room not to rehearse in the conventional sense (there was really no play at this point) but to "workshop" the piece by beginning preliminary work on the staging and having the authors and design team continue their thinking about the play. Papp offered the Public Theater and $100,000 for Michael to experiment with the interview material (there were two workshops) in much the same way an architect might first create a template or model for the eventual construction of a skyscraper.

At first, Michael and the creative team needed to see if, within the interviews, they could find the dramatic and emotional core of the piece from which the book, music, and lyrics could be developed, failing which the project would be abandoned. As it turned out, as the workshops progressed, the piece began to take shape organically, and a storyline of sorts emerged that could form the basis for a viable, stage-worthy musical. What started as a series of random and disparate interviews was ultimately molded into a musical play with ten songs about seventeen dancers auditioning for a place in the chorus of a Broadway show, with the director, Zach, presiding in a chair at the back of the orchestra. The workshops proved to be a laboratory within which the creative team were able to experiment with their collective contributions, without the pressure of production deadlines or outside forces such as investors.

There was a lot of speculation and gossip about the show early on, but no one, except Papp and those closely involved in the production, sat in judgment of the material during the workshop phase. Only after Michael and his collaborators were satisfied they had something to present to the public did they tell Papp the show was ready to be produced and to embark on the traditional route of rehearsals, previews, and a fixed date for opening night.

A Chorus Line opened on May 22, 1975, at the Public's 299-seat Newman Theater to ecstatic reviews. It then moved to the Shubert Theatre on Broadway the following September and went on to win virtually every major theater award, including the Tony for Best Musical and the Pulitzer Prize for Drama. It became the longest-running musical on Broadway before being overtaken by three British imports, *Cats*, *The Phantom of the Opera*, and *Les Misérables*.

In recognition of the contributions made by the dancers who were interviewed and the actors who worked for $100 per week in the workshops, Michael established a fund into which he paid a royalty from Broadway and other first-class productions, and a piece of his share of subsidiary rights income.[2] Up to this day, the dancers continue to receive a share of Michael's unprecedented generosity from *A Chorus Line*—the most money ever paid to Actors' Equity members for participating in a workshop. No one in his wildest dreams could have predicted in 1974 that this musical would turn out to be one of the most profitable shows in the history of the American theater.

Lessons Learned and Forgotten

For Michael, the primary benefit of the workshop process was the luxury of experimenting, developing, and rehearsing an unformed collection of interviews into a fully thought-out musical play. He knew he was free to fail without losing millions of dollars, although the money Papp spent to support the workshops was not insignificant for a not-for-profit theater. And, most notably, there was no opening night looming down the road or pressure from a Broadway producer or his investors. For Papp, this was precisely the mission of the Public Theater—to nurture and support artists as they honed their craft and developed their skills in creating new and important work, free from "those uptown fellas," as Papp was fond of saying.

Armed with money from *A Chorus Line*, Michael turned to his next project as an independent producer: *Ballroom*, which I've discussed in a prior chapter on collaboration. Once again Michael wanted to workshop the musical before going into rehearsals for a Broadway production. Though he had voluntarily given the actors who participated in the workshops for *A Chorus Line* a generous financial piece of the show after the fact, the Actors' Equity Association wasn't willing to rely on the generosity of other producers or directors (or even Michael himself), who might want to avail themselves of the workshop process in the future.

At the time, I was co-producing *Ballroom* with Michael, Bob Avian, and Susan MacNair, Michael's business associate, through a newly formed production company, Quadrille Productions. A few days before

---

[2] See chapter twelve, "The Approved Production Contract," for a full discussion of subsidiary rights.

the show went into workshop, Donald Grody, the executive director of Actors' Equity, telephoned me and said he was unhappy that the actors did not have a formal, Equity-approved agreement for *Ballroom*. He was prepared to call off the workshop unless we came to an agreement governing the compensation and work rules for the workshop.

This completely blindsided all of us. We had worked up an agreement for the dancers, but it hadn't been done with Equity's approval. Among other things, Grody didn't want workshops to be used as a cheap way for producers to have an extended rehearsal period while paying the actors four times less than what they'd receive under the union agreement. He also wanted to codify the actors' entitlement to a share in the show's future income. As a technical matter, Equity had no jurisdiction over the workshops, but none of us wanted a fight with Equity, least of all Michael, a lifelong member.

Michael and I called on Bernard Jacobs, then president of the Shubert Organization, to help us mediate an agreement with Equity. Over the years, Bernie, as head of the producers' trade association, had frequently sat on the other side of the collective bargaining table from Grody, haggling over terms of the actors' union agreement. While they were both tough negotiators for their own sides, they also respected each other's sense of fair play.

Grody, Bernie, and I met in the Shubert Organization offices at around 4:00 p.m. on the Friday before the start of the workshop on Monday. By 2:00 a.m. we had hammered out an agreement that's still in use today.

The actors participating in a workshop would receive $200 per day (today, it's $400), a percentage of the gross weekly box office receipts (today payable in a royalty pool), and a share of subsidiary rights proceeds, usually shared by all of the authors and producers in a separate document. The agreement also provided for some basic work rules.

Although they would be entitled to less than the income Michael voluntarily gave for *A Chorus Line*, every actor was now assured a financial stake in the future success of a musical in consideration of his or her contributions to the development of the play during the workshop. In return, the actors waived any claims they might have against the authors for any of their contributions.

Top: Rae Allen and Ray Walston in the original Broadway production of *Damn Yankees* (1955). The audience roared with laughter when Walston, who played the devil, crossed his legs to reveal bright red socks. *Billy Rose Theatre Division, The New York Library for the Performing Arts*

Right: David Merrick, Broadway's most notorious and prolific producer of the 1950s and '60s. *Billy Rose Theatre Division, The New York Library for the Performing Arts*

Top: George Hearn (*left*) and Gene Barry with Les Cagelles in Allan Carr's original Broadway production of *La Cage aux Folles* (1983). By deploying some cunning negotiating tactics, Carr managed to outmaneuver David Merrick in securing the rights to the original French play. *Photo by Martha Swope/© Billy Rose Theatre Division, The New York Library for the Performing Arts*

Left: Allan Carr, the producer of *La Cage aux Folles*. He stunned everyone when, midway through negotiations, he fired the entire creative team and switched to another. *Photofest*

Top: Lyricist David Zippel, composer Cy Coleman, and book writer Larry Gelbart of *City of Angels* (1989). Coleman was searching for a new collaborator. He settled on Zippel, who abandoned his nascent legal career and helped propel *City of Angels* to winning a Tony Award for best musical. © *Anita & Steve Shevett*

Right: Nick Vanoff, the producer of *City of Angels* (1989). At first, I thought Vanoff was kidding when he said he needed to avoid stress because of his weak heart. He wasn't joking. *Photo by Martha Swope/© Billy Rose Theatre Division, The New York Library for the Performing Arts*

Top: Larry Morton, Dorothy Loudon, and Vincent Gardenia (*seated*) and composer Billy Goldenberg, Jonathan Tunick, and lyricists Marilyn and Alan Bergman (*standing*) at the time of the original Broadway production of the musical *Ballroom* (1978). When the authors of the musical first started working with Michael Bennett, it was a lovefest. By the time the show opened, the collaboration had collapsed in acrimony. *Courtesy of Sony Music Archives*

Left: Jerome Kass, book writer for the musical *Ballroom*. *Photo by Delia Ephron*

Philip Anglim in the title role with co-star Carole Shelley in Bernard Pomerance's play, *The Elephant Man* (1979). The melding of writing, direction, and acting comes to a breathtaking moment at the end of act one as Mrs. Kendal reaches for the Elephant Man's misshapen hand. *Billy Rose Theatre Division, The New York Library for the Performing Arts*

Author Peter Stone, Lauren Bacall, lyricist Fred Ebb, and composer John Kander (*top, left to right*) and director Robert Moore, choreographer Tony Charmoli, and actor Harry Guardino (*bottom, left to right*) at rehearsal for the original Broadway production of *Woman of the Year* (1981). When the *New York Times* article exposed the financial underpinnings of the musical, it set off a maelstrom within the industry. *Photo by Martha Swope/© Billy Rose Theatre Division, The New York Library for the Performing Arts*

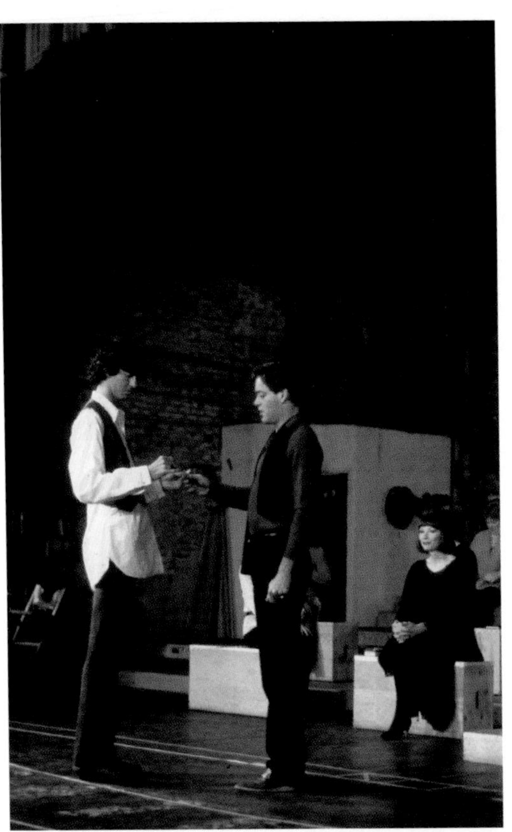

Left: Tommy Tune as director/choreographer with his leading actors, Raul Julia and Karen Akers, in the original Broadway production of *Nine* (1982). Frantic negotiations underscored *Nine*'s rush to open on Broadway in the spring of 1981, leading up to the battle of the decade between it and *Dreamgirls* for the much coveted Tony Award for Best Musical. *Photo by Martha Swope/© Billy Rose Theatre Division, The New York Library for the Performing Arts*

Bottom: Jennifer Holliday as Effie and the rest of the original Broadway cast of *Dreamgirls* (1981). Frank Rich wrote: "Mr. Bennett has long been Mr. [Jerome] Robbins's Broadway heir apparent . . . last night the torch was passed." *Photo by Martha Swope/© Billy Rose Theatre Division, The New York Library for the Performing Arts*

Michael Bennett (*center*) with Marvin Hamlisch (*right*) during a rehearsal with members of the original Broadway cast of *A Chorus Line* (1976). Bennett revolutionized the industry by introducing the workshop rehearsal process for Broadway musicals. *Photo by Martha Swope/© Billy Rose Theatre Division, The New York Library for the Performing Arts*

Michael Bennett (*left*) and Bob Avian speaking to the cast before the special performance celebrating *A Chorus Line* becoming the longest-running show in Broadway history. *Courtesy of Bob Avian*

Joseph Papp, the pioneer of the not-for-profit theater movement and the producer of *A Chorus Line*. Papp invested in Michael Bennett's talent early on as he developed *A Chorus Line*. *Photo by Friedman-Abeles/© Billy Rose Theatre Division, The New York Library for the Performing Arts*

James Earl Jones (*center left*) with the rest of the Broadway cast of August Wilson's play, *Fences* (1987). In response to some critics of his first play, Wilson purposefully structured his next one, *Fences*, in the tradition of Arthur Miller, Eugene O'Neill, and Tennessee Williams. *Billy Rose Theatre Division, The New York Library for the Performing Arts, Astor, Lenox, and Tilden Foundations*

From then on, virtually every new musical was workshopped for two, four, or even six weeks. But there were a number of significant differences between Michael's workshop and those that followed. Most significant was the need to find financing for the workshop, which could cost as much as $400,000 or more. Commercial producers paid for these costs out of their own pockets or, more often than not, sought front money from outside investors who were willing to gamble on the promise of a show in the hope that they might cash in on a bonanza like *A Chorus Line*.

Eventually, workshops became less of an opportunity for the authors and directors to experiment with and discover the work, and more of an opportunity for the producers to present the material to their investors to raise financing. Sitting on uncomfortable folding chairs in a small room watching twenty or so actors in rehearsal clothes presenting a musical with two or three musicians, no scenery, and few props was something most investors had never experienced. While it was exhilarating for some just to be a few feet away from the performers, many others found it difficult, if not impossible, to imagine the final product. And, by the way, where were the crashing chandeliers and flying helicopters?

In effect, the whole purpose of the workshop as envisioned by Michael had been turned on its head. It was no longer a private incubation process serving the artists' need to create and refine their work. Instead, it became a showcase for the producer to attract investments and stoke the interest of theater owners. Presenting a workshop to these outsiders prematurely could stifle the creative process and, in some cases, caused producers to abandon the project entirely.

One of the shows workshopped in the early 1980s was a new original musical called *Kicks*, with a book and lyrics by Tom Eyen and music by Alan Menken. Based on his workshop experience and his success with *Dreamgirls* (for which he was bookwriter and lyricist), Eyen decided to workshop *Kicks* with his own money.

The score for *Kicks* was in the tradition of Jule Styne, Cy Coleman, and Harold Rome—brassy, romantic, and danceable. Eyen's lyrics also served the story nicely and fit comfortably with the music. What needed more work, actually a lot of work, was Eyen's book, which told the back-stage story of a starstruck young girl coming to New York to seek fame and fortune by becoming a Rockette, all set against a complicated soap opera about everything from the plight of unwed mothers to the transformation of Sixth Avenue into a boulevard of characterless skyscrapers.

After six weeks of rehearsing in workshop, Eyen, who chose to direct the workshop himself, presented the work for three days to over two hundred of the most influential producers, investors, and theater owners in New York. The response was disappointing, to say the least. Everyone praised the score and liked the backstage stories of the Rockettes and the lead character. The book, on the other hand, while often quite funny and moving, was cliché-ridden, and Eyen's direction also fell short. The fact was that the show wasn't ready by a long shot to be presented as a finished work. It played like a rough first draft—too long and rambling, out of focus, and hobbled by awkward and unfinished staging and direction.

A handful of producers showed some interest, but nothing ever came of that and the show succumbed to an early death. I have an audiocassette of the workshop which I listen to occasionally. How sad that a show with such talent and promise had its progress stopped in its tracks by what I consider to have been the misuse of the workshop process.

What for Michael was a means to a creative end became for others an end in and of itself, nothing more than a tool to attract money from investors and commitments from theater owners. Producers who used workshops for this purpose truly missed the point and consequently often did permanent damage to their projects.

As mentioned at the beginning of this chapter, today there are fewer workshops and more out-of-town developmental productions in regional not-for-profit theaters. By supplementing, or enhancing, the budget of the regional theater, a producer can get a full-blown production with sets, costumes, lighting, and a fully rehearsed cast. What's more, potential investors and theater owners can view the play in an environment with which they are more familiar while also experiencing an audience's reaction. This is not to say that a musical can afford to mount these tryout productions prematurely. They still require that the authors and the producer attempt to perfect their work as best they can through a series of staged readings, for example, prior to putting the play up on any stage.

Today, workshops are still conducted, occasionally with satisfactory results. The musical *Kinky Boots* was presented in workshop before its commercial production. It was received enthusiastically by potential investors, had a successful out-of-town tryout, and went on to win the Tony for Best Musical in the 2012–13 season.

No one should gainsay the great benefits that continue to be available to authors if the workshop process is used to find the fundamental elements of the piece. For the creative team, there is simply no better option.

Michael had the luxury of Papp's patronage, both financially and spiritually. It was a partnership that started with not much more than Papp's faith in Michael and the creative process, and Michael's driving ambition to find a show. But the lessons learned from that page in Broadway history still represent a prescription for finding the idea and, as Stephen Sondheim says, "Finishing the Hat":

Mapping out the sky,
Finishing a hat . . .
Starting on a hat . . .
Finishing a hat . . .
Look, I made a hat
Where there never was a hat.

Sunday in the Park with George, act 1

A Legacy Cut Short

Michael enjoyed the trappings of making a lot of money, but he was a gypsy at heart. Jeans, sneakers, and a red baseball cap were his way of life. That wasn't going to change. He often said to me, "I'm only at my best when I need to make money." In some ways, the financial success of *A Chorus Line* became an albatross around his neck.

In 1977, I negotiated a four-picture deal at Universal Pictures for him, and he opened an office in LA to bring Broadway to Hollywood. Michael ultimately became bored with the film world, frustrated with the bureaucracy of the studio system—and he *hated* being in the relentless California sunshine. It wasn't long before he called me to say he was escaping LA and returning to New York for good. When I asked him if he had told Universal he was quitting, he said no, but he had hung a note on his office door saying, "Gone fishin'."

When he returned, he told me he had figured out on the plane trip back how to spend his money: he wanted to give back to the community that had given him so much. He bought an old factory building downtown at 890 Broadway where they still manufactured belts.

As more space became available, Michael devoted most of his time and money to establishing an artistic cauldron at 890, where composers, lyricists, directors, and designers could ply their trade in one centralized place toward the development and creation of commercial theater. If George Lucas, whom Michael greatly admired, could build a city for the commercial film industry in Marin County, California, Michael would create his own mini-version at 890 for the musical theater in New York.

One evening in January of 1978, I was flying back from LA, having just gotten Michael released from his four-picture deal with Universal. There was a snowstorm heading toward New York. I wasn't sure my plane would take off, but we did depart and land safely despite the storm. Michael called at around eight that night and said he was coming over in his newly customized van (he had long since given up his Rolls-Royce) to pick up Nan and me to celebrate his escape from LA and cruise around a snowbound city. Michael and his driver, Paul, picked us up an hour later. As we snacked on champagne and pâté, we proceeded on our own private tour of Central Park and then down Fifth Avenue. Except for a few taxicabs and the occasional skier weaving down the streets, the city was quiet and shrouded in blankets of snow.

Michael had said he had a surprise for us. I soon realized that Paul was driving us downtown, toward 890. The renovations to the fourth floor, where the first rehearsal rooms and Michael's offices would be located, were nearly complete for the beginning of the workshop for his next show, *Ballroom*.

The elevators were shut down so we climbed the four flights. As we entered the newly painted and freshly waxed floors of the rehearsal studio, Michael turned on a ghost light, leapt high in the air, ripping off the brown paper covering a wall of eight-foot-high mirrors, and began to dance, humming some tune to himself, against a backdrop of falling snow.

It was joyful and exhilarating. Michael was truly in his element, at the height of his creative prowess, and with 890 holding out the promise of becoming a unique collective artistic enterprise for the New York theater.

Michael never lived to see his dream realized. By 1987, about half of the building housed rehearsal space and offices for many artists. But by this time, Michael was quite ill, and in July of that year, he succumbed to AIDS at the age of forty-four. Without Michael, 890 would never become what he had hoped for. Today it is only a shadow of what he envisioned, with some rehearsal space and a handful of artists' studios. What's missing is Michael's energy, vision, and genius.

For posterity, however, his groundbreaking work in *Follies*, *Company*, *A Chorus Line*, and *Dreamgirls*, unsurpassed in their originality and invention, will be his everlasting artistic legacy.

12

The Approved Production Contract

For better or worse, the Dramatists Guild's Approved Production Contract for Plays and Musicals (known as the APC) continues to be the contract used most often by producers to engage a bookwriter, composer, and lyricist for a Broadway show.

As I'll discuss in more detail below, the Dramatists Guild is not a union. Consequently, it does not have the legal power to force producers to use its contract as compared, say, to the directors' or designers' unions, whose agreements are the product of collective bargaining with the Broadway League, the trade association of producers and theater owners. Nonetheless, the Guild requires its members and their agents to use the APC. If a member fails to obtain certification of his or her contract by the Guild, the member can be expelled from Guild membership.

Use of the APC is also seen as a practical tool for producers and authors' agents to expedite an understanding between the parties, even though the form contract is outdated in many ways and replete with ambiguous and byzantine provisions. However, the basic terms regarding advance payments, option periods, royalties, subsidiary rights, expenses, and billing are convenient jumping-off points for reaching an agreement without forging entirely new ground.

This chapter highlights the essential terms and conditions of the APC for Musical Plays. Many parts of the APC do not require explanation, so I've focused here only on those sections that are most critical to the producer, particularly the special provisions of article XXII, which amend and supplement the form contract.[1]

[1] There are two forms: one for dramatic plays and one for dramatico-musical plays. Many of the provisions in the dramatic play contract are very similar if not identical to those in the musical contract.

Finally, in order to fully appreciate this chapter, the reader is urged to first read or reread chapter five, "Securing the Rights," which deals with the acquisition of rights in an underlying work. Much of the terminology, words of art, and definitions addressed below are introduced in the former chapter.

But first, some history.

The Dramatists Guild, founded in 1921, is a professional organization dedicated to advancing the interests of playwrights, composers, lyricists, and bookwriters active in the American theater.[2] Since it is not a union, and therefore not exempt from the antitrust laws, it does not have the legal power to organize authors as a collective bargaining unit nor does it have the legal right to force producers to use the APC.

In 1983, Richard Barr, an independent producer and president of the then-called League of New York Theaters and Producers, sued the Dramatists Guild and three of its members, claiming they were in violation of provisions of the Sherman Antitrust Act.[3] Barr alleged, among other things, that the defendants had conspired to fix minimum prices and other terms set forth under the Minimum Basic Production Contract (MBPC), a predecessor to the APC, which had been negotiated between the Guild and the producers back in the early 1920s. The Guild counter-claimed, accusing the producers of conspiring against Broadway authors and violating the Sherman Antitrust Act.

The lawsuit became a lightning rod for both sides to air their grievances publicly, particularly in the press. Keep in mind this occurred soon after the contretemps surrounding *Woman of the Year* and the emergence of the now ubiquitous royalty pool. The producers were becoming increasingly frustrated and fed up with the Guild's insistence on minimum, nonnegotiable terms that hampered the parties' freedom to negotiate the most suitable terms on a case-by-case basis, especially for royalty pools.

---

[2] A predecessor to the Guild was the Authors League of America, founded in 1912. It represented book authors as well as dramatists. In 1921, the dramatists split off from the League and formed the Dramatists Guild to represent only authors who wrote for the theater and authors of radio drama.

[3] The Sherman Antitrust Act, passed by the US Congress in 1890, prohibits certain anticompetitive activities, such as price fixing and other monopolistic practices. A recognized union is exempt from its provisions.

The parties eventually settled, thereby avoiding a court decision on either party's allegations. As part of the settlement, the parties to the lawsuit developed a new model contract which replaced the MBPC: the Approved Production Contract.

This new agreement included many of the same terms that were in the MBPC, but it altered and improved, among other things, the minimum financial terms for the authors' option payments, advances, and royalties. It also reworked the vesting requirements and percentages for the producer to share in the subsidiary rights income of the authors. Remarkably, it did not address royalty pools, although they were already widely used at the time the APC was introduced. It was a document that gave homage to the past but ignored the business realities of the present.

Because the APC emerged as a result of a lawsuit, it was negotiated behind closed doors with a few producers, the theater owners and their lawyers on one side of the table and Peter Stone, president of the Guild, and the Guild's lawyers on the other side. Absent were the agents, managers, and lawyers specializing in the theater who spent each day grappling with many of the MBPC's ambiguities and woefully outdated provisions. Many asked, "Exactly *who* approved this new Approved Production Contract?" Not surprisingly, what resulted was an even more dense and confusing document that managed to inject more uncertainty alongside the byzantine and obscure provisions of the old MBPC. It raised minimum option payments and royalties, but it failed to provide any guidance on royalty pools.

An open town meeting of sorts was held for the industry in a Broadway theater when the APC was first unveiled in 1985. Most who attended the meeting were annoyed, if not downright angry, that so few people had been involved in or consulted about the negotiations. The APC was being presented as a fait accompli with no opportunity to object or recommend changes. The community was told that, since the new contract arose out of the settlement of a very contentious lawsuit, participation by outside parties would have been neither appropriate nor productive. In other words, the so-called Approved Production Contract hadn't been approved at all, except by a handful of lawyers not particularly conversant with day-to-day negotiations in the theater, a few producers, and one writer—Peter Stone.

There's no doubt that Stone was a knowledgeable negotiator in his own right and that the theater owners and Richard Barr were also conversant with the salient issues, but to have unleashed this convoluted document on the industry with little or no consultation did not bode well for its future use or efficacy. What's more, the settlement did nothing to abate the age-old charges coming from both camps that the other side acted improperly and illegally in its contract negotiations—charges that would once again hit the *New York Times*'s Arts and Leisure section nearly ten years later.

Since the APC did not address minimum terms for royalty pools, the Guild, frustrated at what it believed were unfair demands by the producers on its members, persuaded Senators Ted Kennedy and Orrin Hatch in 2004 to co-sponsor a bill in the Senate to exempt the Guild from the antitrust laws so that it could bargain collectively with the producers on all contracts.[4] In effect, the Guild wanted to become a legally empowered union having the same collective negotiating force as the stagehands, musicians, and actors.

Arthur Miller, Stephen Sondheim, and Wendy Wasserstein testified at the Senate hearing in favor of the bill while Gerald Schoenfeld, chairman of the Shubert Organization, and Roger Berlind, by then a well-respected and prolific independent producer, presented the producers' case. Probably due to the strong lobbying efforts both sides brought to bear on the Senate, the bill ultimately died and never reached the floor of either house of Congress. Another great example of our government at work—or not.

So, today, the APC continues to be used by the industry, warts and all, mostly out of necessity—there's nothing else. No one is happy with it, especially not the agents and theater lawyers who continue to struggle with its arcane terms and irrelevant provisions. There have been many in the community, including this writer, who have attempted to bring both sides back to the table to negotiate a clearly written, up-to-date document that can be a truly useful guide for negotiations. All such attempts have failed to gain any traction. How discouraging it is to watch artists and producers glare at each other across the table, negotiating with one another as if they were garment workers trying to gain a living wage from their rapacious employers. Suspicion and even paranoia lurk behind

[4] It's title was The Playwrights Licensing Antitrust Initiative Act.

so many negotiations, when in truth both producers and authors mostly wish to sort out their business dealings quickly and fairly so they can get on with the important work of creating good theater. Having worked and broken bread with so many authors and producers over the years, I believe a new contract could be negotiated which would serve as the basis for guarding the interests of authors while also according the producers the flexibility to produce plays on an economically viable basis.

At the very least, wouldn't it be nice to finally get a definition of a "first-class production"?

The APC Terms

The APC can be broken down into three sections:

1. Articles I through XXI constitute the basic form contract.
2. Article XXII includes additional production terms that amend and supplement the basic form contract.
3. Exhibits A, B, and C are essentially out of date and largely ignored.

Since article XXII is a rider supplementing articles I through XXI, our discussion will combine the form provisions with their amendments and additions.

Grant of Rights

As we saw with the underlying rights agreement, the APC initially grants the producer the exclusive right to present the play for one or more "first-class performances" in the United States and Canada within specified option periods, failing which the rights revert to the authors.[5]

Options and Payments

The minimum terms include non-returnable advance payments, in total for all three authors, of $18,000 for the first twelve months, $9,000 for

[5] See chapter five for a full discussion of what constitutes "first-class performances."

the next twelve months, and $900 per month for a maximum of another twelve months. This assumes a completed play (at least an eighty-page script plus a minimum of twelve songs) has already been delivered to the producer. If the play is still to be completed, the option time periods begin with its delivery to the producer. For first-time authors, minimum payments are customary, while agents typically negotiate higher payments for more established authors.

Prior to rehearsals, the producer is required to pay the authors an additional advance equal to 2 percent of the capitalization (amounts raised to produce the show) with a cap of $60,000. Given the cost of production these days, the cap is almost always reached. However, these payments are usually increased to six figures in consideration of authors bearing an amortization factor in a royalty pool prior to recoupment.

Royalties

Article IV sets out the aggregate minimum royalties for all three authors of 4.5 percent of gross weekly box office receipts (the net gross), increasing to 6 percent following recoupment of production costs. These royalties are usually divided in equal shares among the three authors, but that may vary depending on the experience of the authors.

I won't examine the other provisions of this article since, as discussed in prior chapters, most musicals don't pay royalties on the basis of net gross, but rather on the basis of weekly operating profits within a royalty pool. What's relevant here is that the 4.5 or 6 percent royalty represents the minimum number of "points" the authors receive in the royalty pool in the same way that 1 percent to 2 percent is the number of points in the pool allocated to the underlying rights owner.

General Production Provisions

- *Approvals*. The authors have the right to approve the cast, director, choreographer, all designers, and any replacements. Approval of music personnel such as the conductor, music supervisor, orchestrator, and musical arrangers is usually within the province of the composer and lyricist. The authors can vote as one (unanimously, by majority, or any other way they choose). The important thing to recognize is that neither the authors nor the producers can impose any of the foregoing personnel on the other. Mutuality between the authors, on the one hand, and the producer, on the other, is always required.

Most important, after the delivery of the completed play to the producer, there can be no changes or alterations to the book, music, or lyrics without the approval of the producer and the author whose work is affected.

- *Expenses.* Article XXII will usually expand upon the form's provision for expenses. The authors have the right to attend auditions, all rehearsals, and preview performances prior to the official opening. If an author does not reside within a fifty-mile radius of New York City, the producer is required to provide for first-class hotel accommodations (or a fixed amount), travel expenses, and a per diem of $100 to $200. Transportation can be first class or more often business class, when available.

  Authors are usually also entitled to be present at rehearsals and previews for the first national tour and the opening in London or other major foreign cities. To protect against runaway expenses, the producer will often limit to twenty-one the number of days the authors will be reimbursed for these expenses.
- *Authors' billing.* The authors almost always receive credit in a size equal to 50 percent of the size of the title of the play, on a separate line and immediately below the title. On very rare occasions, for very well-known authors, the billing can be 60 percent of the size of the title. The billing usually appears whenever the title is used except for so-called teaser ads, where only the title and the theater are credited, and on marquees, unless anyone else receives billing.[6] There may be exceptions

[6] At an advertising meeting I attended along with twenty-five people credited above the title as producers, one of them whispered to me during a discussion of signage outside the theater, "What's a marquee?" I stared at her for a few seconds and then said, "It's probably something to do with royalty pools."

for major above-the-title stars, especially on small marquees, ads on the sides of buses, and small print ads.

ABC listings (the daily directory ads in the Arts section of the *New York Times*, for example) usually exclude credits, except the authors may require billing in the Friday and Sunday editions. Over the past few years, some producers have begun to limit ABC listings to matinee days and weekends, reflecting a growing trend of reducing print advertising in favor of less costly (and more effective?) Internet and other media buys.

- *House seats*. Each author is entitled to have reserved for all regular performances of the show at least two pairs of seats (known as "House Seats") located in the center section of the orchestra at regular box office prices. These seats are held for the author until forty-eight or seventy-two hours before the day of performance. In addition, five complimentary pairs of seats are usually given to each author for the official opening night performance, along with an equal number of passes to the opening night party.

Cast Album

The producer acquires from the authors the primary right to produce an original cast album containing the score of the musical and incidental dialogue. The grant of this right is subject to the following author approvals:

1. The recording company. Most major labels are preapproved.
2. The album producer. Experienced composers often request the right to produce or co-produce the album.
3. The financial terms. The royalty terms, such as 12 percent of retail price or 24 percent of wholesale, with escalations based on sales, may be preapproved.
4. The liner notes (written synopses of the show or other commentary). The bookwriter may require that he write the notes.

In addition, the authors usually require a direct accounting of royalties and the right to inspect the books and records of the record company.

Decades ago, record companies not only competed aggressively for cast albums but also invested in the shows themselves. In 1956, Columbia Records was one of the first record labels to invest in a show (*My Fair Lady*), followed by other labels in the ensuing decades. Today record companies rarely invest in a show. Cast albums have never competed well against pop music albums, but with the general decline in sound recording sales and the other seismic shifts in the music business, cast albums have been dealt a particularly hard blow. For many shows, unless they turn out to be blockbuster hits (*Lion King*, *Hamilton*) or they have pop scores, such as those written by ABBA (*Mamma Mia!*) or the Four Seasons (*Jersey Boys*), securing a cast album deal can be extremely difficult. As a result, producers have begun to produce cast albums independently, more for the purpose of marketing their shows than making money. These self-produced albums are released through distributors who advance marketing and advertising monies to reach the small market that still exists for cast albums. For the composers and lyricists in particular, these recordings are still prized items. They memorialize their work in perpetuity, regardless of the success or failure of the show.

The economics of a standard cast album deal are quite simple. The recording company advances the recording costs, which are then recouped against the royalties payable to the production. Those costs can be anywhere from $250,000 to $450,000 or higher. Total royalties usually start at 12 percent of retail price (or 24 percent of wholesale) escalating to as much as 16 percent of retail (or 32 percent of wholesale) based on actual sales up to one million copies. Few albums ever reach that number.

Royalties are split between the authors and the producer on a 60/40 basis, respectively. If there is an underlying rights owner, the owner and the authors will share in the 60 percent proportionately based on their respective percentage royalties. Additionally, as we will see in chapter sixteen, “The Director,” directors may also share in these royalties.

The 40 percent payable to the producer will go into the pot of money available to his investors for recoupment and net profits. Given that few cast albums earn enough to recover their recording costs, a more important provision for the producers is one requiring the recording company to commit to spending a minimum amount ($250,000, for example) for advertising and promotion.

Replacement of an Author

A little understood but important clause in the APC is section 8.20 dealing with the unusual case of a producer requesting the replacement of one or more authors. This option is limited to a musical adapted from an underlying work, such as *Kinky Boots*, and is not available to a producer of an original musical.

The options available to the producer are based on when the producer decides to reject the book, music, or lyrics:

1. **Replacement before first rehearsal:** Any rejection of book, music, or lyrics by the producer is subject to the approval of the remaining authors. For example, if the book is rejected by the producer, the composer and lyricist must also reject the book in order for the producer to replace the bookwriter. In this case, the rejected author retains any option payments previously paid to him and forfeits any billing, future advance payments, royalties, or subsidiary rights income. Any material contributed by the rejected author is retained by him, with the exception of any material the retention of which would violate the rights of the producer or the owner of the underlying work. In other words, the rejected bookwriter cannot use any copyrightable elements of the underlying work that he might have incorporated into his adaptation.

   The above is easier said than done. The authors as a team usually form a strong bond among themselves. A producer will usually find it extremely difficult to obtain approval from two authors to reject a third, even in cases where everyone acknowledges that the work of the author in question isn't terribly good.

   Moreover, assuming the producer rejects the book, neither he nor the new bookwriter can use any of the original material contained in the rejected book. Regardless of how bad the rejected book is, it may have new material that the remaining authors, the new bookwriter, and the producer might want to use in the show. If the musical is successful, there's the risk that the rejected bookwriter could claim ownership of some elements of the new book. As a result, in most cases, rather than risk a lawsuit, the producer will negotiate a settlement with the rejected author giving him a modest participation in the proceeds of the musical in return for the right to use any or all of the elements in the rejected book.

2. **Replacement during rehearsal but before the first paid public performance:** In this case, provided the remaining authors agree to a replacement, the rejected author retains any advance or option payments already received but forfeits any future advance payments and automatically receives a reduction of one-half of his share of royalties and subsidiary rights income and any other monies payable under the APC. The rejected author remains one of the authors, although he is not entitled to exercise any control over, or participate in, any decisions with respect to the future exploitation of the musical. The rejected author has the right to reject or accept billing. The form of such billing is usually negotiated by the producer, the rejected author, and the new author.
3. **Replacement from the first paid public performance until the day prior to the official press opening on Broadway:** Obviously, this is very late in the day to make a replacement. It could occur during out-of-town tryouts, for example. In this case—again, only with the approval of the other authors—the producer may reject any one of the components (music, lyrics, or book) and replace the author thereof. However, the rejected author retains all of his compensation and rights in the play, except for an amount equal to up to one-sixth of the authors' combined subsidiary rights income, borne by the three original authors and the producer in the same proportion as the authors and the producer share in such compensation. For example, if the authors and producer share 50/50 in income from a film version of the musical, the one-sixth of the authors' share payable to the new author will be borne one-twelfth (50 percent) by the producer and one-twelfth (50 percent) by the authors. If, in order to hire a new author, the producer is required to pay more than one-sixth of subsidiary rights income to the new author, that excess share

is borne solely by the producer out of his share of subsidiary income.

Although this last scenario is rarely used, the APC omits mention of at least two remaining issues:

1. How are future decisions as to the exploitation of the musical affected by the addition of a fourth author? Does a new book-writer, for example, have an equal say with the original book-writer? Or must he share his vote with the old author?
2. The share of subsidiary rights income payable to the producer in many cases expires after a certain period of time. When it expires, if the producer has given the new author a share of his subsidiary rights income, how is this share to be borne by all of the authors when the producer is not entitled to receive any further income?

These and a host of other issues that are not addressed in the APC when a new author is introduced into the equation naturally lead to one grand negotiation between the producer, the new author, and all of the other authors. The authors' and producer's attorneys need to think through all of the ramifications of replacement if they wish to avoid future disputes.

Introducing a new author into the mix can be a highly disruptive and contentious proposition, leading to acrimonious debate between the creative team and the producer. Such drastic action, especially close to an opening, usually means the show is in serious trouble. However, if it is clear to the producer that his multimillion-dollar show will flounder and ultimately fail due to a deficient book or weak lyrics, he may have no choice but to insist on a replacement or threaten to close the show. In the end, this is something every producer must understand: his only real power to force decisions on the authors lies in the threat of abandoning the play or shutting it down after it opens—not an enviable position, to be sure, and a decision rarely taken unless it is patently obvious to everyone that the show is on life support and in critical need of new blood. In that case, regardless of their loyalties to the rejected author, the authors will undoubtedly recognize the need to cooperate with the producer by using section 8.20 as a blueprint for moving forward with a new author.

Additional Production Rights

Provided the producer has opened the musical as a first-class production in the United States or Canada, he may secure options to produce additional first-class productions of the play in other English-speaking territories: Great Britain, Ireland, Australia, New Zealand, and South Africa. Producers regularly add further options for foreign-speaking territories (Europe, Asia, and South America) in the hopes of having the kind of mega-hit (*The Lion King*, *The Phantom of the Opera*) suitable for worldwide exploitation.

The APC sets forth minimum option terms, advances, and royalties for the additional English-speaking territories. These are often increased since the amounts involved reflect norms set in 1985. As for royalties, producers will attempt to impose the same royalty pool as utilized for Broadway. By and large, authors will accept use of a pool in the UK and perhaps Australia, but they usually resist agreeing to the same amortization structure, since the budgets and economics of a West End production are usually substantially different from (and less costly than) a Broadway production.

The option payments for foreign-speaking territories can be quite substantial, ranging from $25,000 for Spain or the Benelux countries (Belgium, the Netherlands, and Luxembourg) up to $250,000 or more for Germany and Japan. If the producer is confident his show has strong international appeal, he will advance these monies in the expectation of entering into co-production agreements with foreign producers down the road. If he forfeits these options, he will nonetheless share in the income the authors ultimately derive when they license these foreign productions to third-party producers.

Pre-First-Class Production Rights

The APC has only one brief section (section 9.11) dealing with out-of-town, non-first-class developmental productions. Article XXII usually supplements this provision, allowing the producer to present staged readings, workshops, and regional not-for-profit productions during the developmental process. Up until the 1960s, most Broadway plays had first-class out-of-town tryouts in cities such as New Haven, Philadelphia, and Boston prior to opening on Broadway. There's no better snapshot of that ritual than the scenes that take place in New Haven in the film *All about Eve*, or in Moss Hart's book, *Act One*. However, following Michael Bennett's workshop experience with *A Chorus Line* in 1975 and the emergence in the 1950s of innovative not-for-profit theaters such as Joseph Papp's Public Theater and Zelda Fichandler's Arena Stage in Washington, DC, the traditional out-of-town tryout fell out of favor with most Broadway producers owing to high costs and other practical considerations.

In the next chapter, I'll have much more to say about workshops and the key role played by the not-for-profit theater community. For now, suffice it to say the producer must have the right to conduct readings (staged readings are governed by Actors' Equity), produce workshops (lasting anywhere from two to six weeks), and present the musical in smaller regional theaters—all for the purpose of offering himself, his investors, and, most important, the artists a chance to put the play "on its feet," make changes to the show (even replace an author?), and assess its readiness to meet the ultimate test of a major Broadway production.

Subsidiary Rights[7]

In order for the producer to become entitled to share in the subsidiary rights income derived from future dispositions of rights in a musical, he must become "vested" or qualified by running the play for a certain number of performances.

Section 11.02 sets forth five ways to vest:

1. Ten preview performances plus opening officially in New York City
2. Five preview performances plus an official opening in New York City and five regular performances

---

[7] See the definition of subsidiary rights in chapter five, "Securing the Rights."

3. Five out-of-town and five preview performances plus an official opening in New York City, provided there are no more than forty-two days between the last out-of-town performances and the first preview in New York City
4. A rarely used option—five previews plus the official press opening in New York City if the play has been presented previously by someone other than the producer, with a number of provisos, including that the play be presented with substantially the same cast and designers
5. Sixty-four out-of-town performances, regardless of a New York City opening, provided the sixty-four performances were given within eighty days of the first performance

If a producer qualifies under one of the above prerequisites (the first being the most common), he becomes entitled to share in subsidiary rights income. The sharing arrangements and the percentage split between the production and the authors are set out in detail in section 11.03. The producer has the option to choose from three alternatives in this section. The producer's shares range from a high of 50 percent in perpetuity for film and TV rights to as low as zero for amateur performances under alternative II.

Choosing which alternative is best for the producer can be tricky. If the musical has strong film potential, alternatives I and II are favorable since alternative III gives the producer only a 30 percent participation in film proceeds rather than 50 percent. If the show is particularly suitable for performances by children and other amateur groups, alternative II is usually rejected, since it does not provide for participation in amateur performances.

In most cases, producers will choose alternative I. It gives a 50 percent share in film and other media revenue and a participation in all forms of stage exploitation.

Merchandising Rights

Vesting is not necessary for the producer to exercise merchandising rights, or, as the APC refers to them, "commercial use products." The producer owns and controls these rights regardless of the length of the run, subject to paying the authors the following shares of income:

1. For sales in the theater, 10 percent of the gross retail sales (less taxes) not to exceed 50 percent of the producer's license fee
2. For sales in other locations, 50 percent of producer's net receipts (all amounts paid to the producer less all third-party costs for the creation, manufacture, and sale of products)

In the case of long-running hits, such as *The Lion King* and *Wicked*, the income from these sales can be very substantial, running into the millions of dollars. For most shows, however, unless they have the kind of merchandise attractive to younger audience members, the income is not a significant factor, particularly for the producer and his investors. As mentioned earlier with respect to cast albums, these products are viewed mainly as marketing tools for the show (and good Christmas gifts for the cast).

The rest of the APC contains a number of provisions that, while technically part of every APC agreement, are so fraught with either ambiguity or incomprehensible conditions that the parties ignore them (with the acquiescence of the Guild). There is a provision in exhibit B that affords a producer who has motion picture backing for his play preferential treatment in the event of a sale of film rights in the play. The APC calls for a "negotiator" (in the past, a lawyer appointed by the Guild) to serve as a mediator of sorts in setting a fair price for the film sale, although, today, the negotiator no longer exists. The parties sort out their negotiations for film deals themselves and authors usually agree to accord motion picture–backed producers certain first refusal rights in any film sale.

The APC also makes mention of the "Theatrical Conciliation Council," the members of which are listed in exhibit A—seven representing the authors and seven for the producers. The council was originally set up to arbitrate disputes between the parties to the APC. In my experience, it has never been utilized by either authors or producers to resolve a dispute.[8] Even if someone wanted to call upon its members today, it would

[8] Disputes between authors and producers are normally arbitrated pursuant to the rules and regulations of the American Arbitration Association.

be rough going, since the majority of members of the council are now deceased. Now there's a really good reason to revise the APC.

Summary

Every producer should be familiar with the terms and conditions of the APC. The producer's lawyer and the GM will negotiate its terms with the authors' agents and lawyers. It can be a very lengthy and arduous process, even given the general framework already set out in the APC. Along with the underlying rights agreement, the APC governs the financial structure of the production and defines not only the rights and obligations of the creators of the play, but also the investors' entitlements to income from the authors' future exploitation of the show.

13

Not-for-Profit Theaters vs. the Commercial Theater

An Uneasy Alliance Born of Necessity

The late chairman of the Shubert Organization, Gerald Schoenfeld, was fond of saying: "There's no profit like not-for-profit."

It's a great sound bite, maybe not for the layman, but surely for a theater insider. It says much about the uneasy and ambivalent relationship that has existed between the commercial and not-for-profit worlds for many decades. For one thing, it's a playful swipe at the increasingly critical role the not-for-profit theaters have played, sometimes in competition but more often in alliance with commercial producers, both for straight plays and musicals. It also goes to the heart of something all commercial producers envy about their not-for-profit brethren—they pay *no* taxes. Whenever Gerry Schoenfeld spouted this aphorism, I'd remind him that, as chairman of one of the largest not-for-profit foundations in the city, the Shubert Foundation, he would surely know better than most.

As the mutually dependent relationship has evolved over the years, an infrastructure has developed that makes it possible for Broadway producers to discover new artists and their work, mostly free of charge, and thereby open the way for profitable runs in the commercial sector. On the other hand, the not-for-profit theaters have also benefited from the relationship, both by often receiving money for their productions from commercial producers and by being entitled to share in the royalties and subsidiary rights income from the future exploitation of a Broadway or other commercial transfer.

To fully appreciate the dynamics between these two competing forces, it's necessary to examine the legal underpinnings of not-for-profit companies and the genesis of their flirtation and eventual uneasy alliance with the commercial theater.

Forming a Not-for-Profit Company and Obtaining a Tax Exemption

My purpose in this section is not to make the reader an expert in corporate or tax law. Rather, it is to describe the fundamental laws and rules that govern not-for-profits so that the reader may gain an appreciation of the important role they play not only in the theater but also in our society at large, and to compare their eleemosynary mission with the purely commercial interests of their counterparts.

A not-for-profit company (or NFP) is a product of both corporate and tax laws. Every state permits the formation of an NFP by founders (sometimes called members) who adopt a charter (akin to a certificate of incorporation of a private corporation) and elect a board of directors or trustees who are responsible for managing the affairs of the company, much in the same way a board of directors manages the affairs of a for-profit corporation. The critical difference, however, is that an NFP has no shareholders to whom the board must answer. Instead, it's ultimately answerable to the attorney general of the state in which the NFP is formed, who represents the public's interest in seeing that an NFP is faithful to its charter and mission.

Forming an NFP under state law is a relatively simple process. What is more difficult and time-consuming is obtaining recognition from the Internal Revenue Service (IRS) as a tax-exempt organization. Without this exemption, an NFP cannot accept charitable contributions, nor can any potential contributor benefit by taking a deduction for a donation on his or her tax return.

The IRS application for recognition as a tax-exempt entity is usually prepared and filed by a lawyer specializing in NFP law, in close consultation with the NFP's founders. If, when conducting an audit of the company's activities, an IRS agent should find that the NFP has not conducted its activities in accordance with its rules, the NFP risks losing its tax-exempt and not-for-profit status.

This is the ultimate sword of Damocles hanging over the board of every NFP—losing its tax exemption. As such, it is incumbent on the board to hire managing and artistic directors who are experienced and conversant with state and IRS requirements, since they are responsible for the day-to-day operations of the company. However, if the staff's activities should run afoul of either the state's laws or the IRS's rules or regulations, the board is ultimately held responsible. The board and the staff should communicate frequently so there are no surprises down the road when it may be too late to rectify any missteps.

So what are the possible missteps?

An NFP must be organized and operated exclusively for tax-exempt purposes. The Internal Revenue Code provides that NFPs are charitable organizations that have scientific, literary, and educational purposes. Although not specifically mentioned in the code, the regulations of the IRS have long recognized that cultural and arts organizations qualify as charitable organizations.

Promoting the arts, or, for purposes of our discussion, operating a theater for the production of plays that would not otherwise be produced by commercial producers, is a common tax-exempt purpose recognized by the IRS. Other related tax-exempt activities would include educational programs directed toward introducing young audiences to the theater arts and developing young playwrights.

Although the code says that an NFP must be operated "exclusively" for these purposes, in practice, the IRS regulations have qualified this to mean that the *predominant* activity of the NFP must be devoted to these purposes. Thus, for example, an NFP *may* sell merchandise, a purely commercial activity, provided it is only an incidental activity of the NFP and the NFP pays taxes (unrelated business income tax) on the net proceeds it earns from those non-tax-exempt activities.

There is one question that is fundamental to the age-old debate about the role NFPs play in the theater: What is a permissible NFP activity for a tax-exempt entity?

When *A Chorus Line* moved to Broadway and began to earn millions of dollars in net profits for the tax-exempt New York Shakespeare Festival, many began to question whether this was a permissible activity for an NFP theater. Indeed, during the musical's fifteen-year run, the Public Theater was audited by the IRS several times for this very reason. The Public obtained a clean bill of health each time—the IRS found it to be operating within its tax-exempt purposes, in spite of the fact that its production was an enormous success. Equally important, the IRS examined what the Public had done with its earnings. Section 501(c)(3) of the code specifically provides that the net earnings of an NFP cannot "inure to the benefit of any private shareholder or individual."

Reading this literally, one might assume that an NFP cannot compensate its employees or purchase materials from a vendor. Again, the IRS has qualified this language from the code, permitting an NFP to pay reasonable salaries to its management and staff and otherwise incur reasonable and necessary operating expenses in order to conduct its business as would any other private corporation.

As for the Public, Joseph Papp, its founder and producer, and its staff were paid yearly salaries and, in some cases, bonuses, which were found to be reasonable given relevant factors such as the organization's annual budget, the responsibilities of the staff, and the compensation given to other executives and staff members at comparable charitable organizations. Neither Papp nor anyone else associated with the theater received the equivalent of what a commercial producer would have received by way of royalties from the commercial run of a multimillion-dollar-grossing musical. After paying for all of its reasonable operating expenses and salaries, the Public retained all of the net earnings (or net profits) of the musical to be used in furtherance of its mission and purposes—to develop new American plays and playwrights, make plays and musicals accessible to widely diverse audiences, and produce works of art not immediately recognizable as commercial properties.

You might also question how the Public would be allowed to pay millions of dollars in royalties and rent to outside individuals who were not employees of the Public, such as the authors, Michael Bennett, and the theater owner. Surely, one would think, here is a clear case of an NFP having its earnings inure to the benefit of private entities. Not so.

The compensation paid by the Public to these outside individuals and vendors was equivalent to what they would have received if a commercial producer had hired them or rented the theater. The Public was not bound to pay substandard royalties, salaries, or discounted rent to third parties who had no conflict of interest with the Public. It was no different from paying standard rates for utilities, or hiring architects or contractors at their usual rates to build the Public's offices.

Equally important, the Public gave employment to thousands of actors, crew members, ushers, and others as a result of its having taken a risk with Bennett and the authors that few, if any, commercial producers would have taken.

The IRS agents found that, regardless of the millions of dollars earned by the Public: (1) the Public's business was operated in a manner consistent with its charter and for tax-exempt purposes, and (2) none of its net earnings had inured to the benefit of any private interests. Consequently, the Public was entitled to maintain its good standing as a qualified 501(c)(3) organization and continue to be exempt from paying any taxes on its earnings from *A Chorus Line*.

In the end, Schoenfeld was actually correct when he offered that there is no profit like not-for-profit. The Public's "profit" was not paid out as dividends to shareholders, nor was it used to benefit its founder or board with seven- or eight-figure bonuses or stock options. Such is also the case with the hundreds of other NFP theaters in New York and throughout the country that are dedicated to supporting worthy plays and musicals and advancing the careers of theater artists.

Collaborations between NFPs and Commercial Producers

After *A Chorus Line* opened, the Public became the envy of every other NFP theater in the country. How could they imitate the success of the Public with their own workshops and development of projects that might not necessarily appeal to commercial producers? Also, once they had produced a critically successful show in their own theater, how could they secure a share of the future income that would accrue once the play moved to a commercial venue and earned income from the exploitation of its subsidiary rights?

Again, the Public was a precedent setter by developing a standard production contract that secured from authors: (1) options to transfer plays to commercial venues following their run at the Public, and (2) a participation in royalties and subsidiary rights income from authors and third-party productions if commercial producers, and not the Public, transferred the plays. These types of contracts soon were adopted in similar form by most other major NFPs in New York, such as the Manhattan Theatre Club, Playwrights Horizons, the Second Stage Theatre, the Roundabout Theatre, and others. They were also adopted as standard operating procedure for major regional theaters such as the Goodman Theatre of Chicago, La Jolla Playhouse, and the Old Globe in San Diego, to name just a few.

The purpose of these contracts was quite simple: they secured the right of the NFP to transfer and exploit a successful play to the commercial arena after it had developed and produced the play in its own theater. If the NFP was not capable of producing a commercial transfer itself, these contracts ensured that when a commercial producer picked up the commercial transfer rights, the NFP would be tied financially to the future commercial exploitation of the play and thereby benefit from its economic success.

Here's a summary of the essential terms of these contracts:

- Following the run of the play at the NFP theater, the NFP retains options to transfer the play to commercial venues, both Off-Broadway and Broadway.
- If the NFP does not exercise its options to produce the play itself in a commercial venue, it nonetheless retains the right to receive income from a commercial producer who produces the play within a specified period of time after the close of the run at the NFP theater. The NFP is usually entitled to a royalty of 1 to 2 percent of the gross weekly box office receipts, payable in a royalty pool, provided all the other royalty participants are also paid in a pool, and 5 to 10 percent of the net profits of the commercial production.
- Depending on the number of performances of the play at the NFP theater, the NFP usually vests in a 5 to 10 percent share of the future subsidiary rights proceeds of the play. To avoid what is sometimes referred to as a "double dip," the NFP may agree to take either a share of the net profits of a subsequent commercial production or its share of subsidiary rights proceeds,

since the net profits of the commercial production usually include a share of the authors' subsidiary rights income.

- Depending on the leverage of the NFP, it may insist on retaining approval of the important artistic elements of the transferred play, such as any replacement of cast, director, or designers. It may also ask for approval of the budgets to ensure that the play is sufficiently funded.
- The NFP usually receives credit above the title of the play and after the commercial producer's billing as follows: "The [NFP] production of. . . ."

Enter Enhancement Deals and Co-Productions

Unlike Papp, most NFPs did not have the resources to finance commercial transfers of their plays themselves,[1] so, by and large, the vast majority of plays that were transferred to Broadway in the seventies and early eighties were produced by commercial producers subject to paying the NFP the participations outlined above. By the mid-eighties, two significant developments occurred: (1) producers began to seek a competitive edge by securing options to move plays even before the opening of the NFP production, and (2) the NFP theaters began to explore the option of being more of an active "partner" in the commercial move alongside the commercial producer.

Producers began to negotiate for the option to move a play commercially prior to the NFP production by paying to the NFP so-called enhancement money up front. This could be anywhere from $50,000 to as much as $200,000 for dramatic plays and $1 million or more for musicals. These monies are used by the NFP to enhance or improve the quality of the NFP production. In fact, in some cases, the NFP might not be able to mount a particular play at all without these monies. In return, the NFP assigns the commercial options it received from the authors to the commercial producer, subject to obtaining the authors' approval.

---

[1] It was through the largesse of LuEsther Mertz, one of the Public's benefactors, that Papp financed the move to Broadway.

Although receiving enhancement money undoubtedly benefits both the NFP and the authors, it does limit their options once the play opens and receives favorable reviews. The deal with the producer who supplied the enhancement money will have been signed before the play opens at the NFP and, therefore, so long as that producer exercises her/his option to move the play, the terms of the deal for the NFP, including its share of the gross, net profits, and subsidiary income, will have already been settled. Of course, the producer assumes the risk that the play will open to poor reviews thereby having little or no commercial future.

Playing with Other People's Money

In the nineties, some of the major New York NFPs began to explore the option to produce commercial transfers themselves, using third party investors' money for financing. This option is usually reserved for those few New York NFPs that have both the experience and resources to produce and manage a Broadway transfer. The Manhattan Theatre Club's productions of *The Tale of the Allergist's Wife* and *Proof* and the Public's production of *The Wild Party* are examples of NFPs managing Broadway productions themselves.

An important component of these deals is to ensure that the NFP's resources and assets remain exclusively in its control and are not put at risk by ceding any control to the investing partners. To do so could jeopardize the company's not-for-profit status. It is more than theoretically possible that the objectives of the NFP theater may at some point be at odds with those of the commercial producer who presumably has as a primary objective the maximization of the profits of the production.

As an example, several seasons ago, a major NFP theater produced a musical on Broadway, acting as the sole managing partner while bringing on several passive commercial investors. Under the investment agreement, the commercial producers and investors acknowledged that the NFP had the right to make all business decisions and that, given the company's status as a 501(c)(3) organization, those decisions might not necessarily be in the best commercial interests of the investors.

The show opened to mixed notices. It was doing poor business, incurring weekly losses and using up the limited reserves it had in the bank. The commercial producers wanted to cut their losses and close the show as soon as possible. The NFP, on the other hand, thought it important to run the show for its subscribers and to give the authors and actors an opportunity to have more audiences appreciate their work. After all, that's the mission of NFPs. The clash between the NFP's mission and the commercial investors' desire to protect their investments couldn't have been clearer. But that was precisely why the enhancement deal between the parties specifically provided that the investors had to accept ceding control to the NFP with the risk of conflicts arising between its mission and their interests. The NFP prevailed; the show ran for several more weeks, losing additional money, but all of the NFP's subscribers and more members of the public had a chance to see the show.

Joint Ventures between NFPs and Commercial Producers

Another variation on these themes involves the NFP partnering with a commercial producer. In this case, the NFP is indeed putting its assets at risk by agreeing to share control with commercial interests.

The solution is for the NFP to form a wholly owned, subsidiary, for-profit corporation to act as a co-producer with the commercial producer of the Broadway transfer. While a couple of board members from the NFP can sit on the for-profit board (usually the artistic and managing directors), the majority of board members must be independent of the NFP board. The for-profit corporation then in turn enters into a co-production agreement with the commercial producers pursuant to which the parties can share artistic and business control of the commercial production and all the proceeds.

The creation of a for-profit subsidiary is not a cut-and-dried matter. The for-profit company needs to be funded adequately so that it can bear the costs and expenses associated with the personnel and resources it shares with the NFP on a reasonable arms-length basis. The companies should maintain careful records, and their accountants need to make appropriate allocations at the end of each year.

The distinct advantage for the NFP is that any profits earned by the subsidiary company from the production of the commercial play can be sent up to the parent company by way of dividends on a tax-exempt basis. Any profits remaining in the subsidiary company would be subject to regular corporate income taxes.

In my career, I have probably cobbled together a couple of hundred of these deals between an NFP and one or more commercial producers. In the end, most of the time, everyone at the negotiating table has the same goal—the production of a play or musical of artistic merit. Reaching that objective requires each side to appreciate the other's legitimate concerns and special interests.

The commercial producer needs to understand the underpinnings and rationale of a tax-exempt organization. It is really the antithesis of a commercial company, not because it can't or doesn't want to earn profits but because its mission and purpose have more to do with the advancement of the arts than increasing a revenue stream.

And for the NFP, if it wishes to secure the benefits of private money to advance its mission, it needs to willingly embrace commercial producers in the development process while still maintaining its independence and decision-making authority. A true collaboration between these competing interests arises from the NFP's need to secure for itself a fair share of the bounty generated by future exploitation of its work, and the commercial producer's desire to judge a play in an NFP production prior to taking on the somewhat reduced risk of a commercial transfer.

A Word of Caution

The transactions I've summarized above between NFPs and commercial producers became very common over the past twenty years. They still occur today, but not quite as frequently. In seeking enhancement deals and other relationships with the commercial sector, NFP artistic and managing partners, as well as board members, need to keep in mind that their charter and tax-exempt status are based on their activities being predominantly charitable and not for the inurement of any private individuals or entities.

The kinds of relationships that have been summarized in this chapter will most likely pass muster if audited even though there is an argument that, to a lesser or greater extent, they do inure to the benefit of the private commercial interests. But so long as these deals do not come to dominate the activity of the NFP, it will probably survive an audit. To use an extreme example, making deals with commercial producers for all of its plays for one or more seasons would effectively transform the NFP into a mere laboratory for producers to get a free or deeply discounted preferential look at plays for future commercial exploitation. Surely that was not the intent of the NFP founders. It was most definitely not the kind of activity that would have been approved by the IRS when it first issued its tax-exemption certificate to the NFP. Where the line is drawn is never an easy question. Can it be 25 percent of the NFP's activity, or only 10 percent or maybe 40 percent? In the end, all of the activities of the NFP need to be examined as a whole—not only its play production but also its educational efforts, workshops, and other programs in furtherance of its charitable purpose.

Another related issue is diverting the resources and personnel of the NFP in seeking commercial alliances and thus distracting them from other pursuits. I've seen NFP executives become slightly schizophrenic when they are seeking charitable contributions to the NFP from the theatrical community and then, later in the day, discussing with those same parties investment in a commercial transfer. If I get this party to invest in the play on Broadway, they wonder, how can I go back to him/her later and ask for a $25,000 table for our gala?

My advice to NFPs and their boards has always been the same—be true to yourself; let your mission and charitable objectives be your first priority. There isn't an NFP that I've worked with that organized its company with the purpose of producing Broadway plays. On the contrary, supporting and cultivating playwrights and other artists in an environment free from financial and other external pressures, and allowing them to fail without causing irreparable damage to their careers, are at the very core of what all theatrical NFPs strive for. They are not meant to be a water carrier for commercial producers on their trek to Broadway.

Of course, the lure of breaking the bank with a commercial smash hit is something every theater hopeful dreams about, regardless of the origins of that success. And once every decade or so, it happens, whether the show springs from an NFP theater—such as the Public Theater with

A Chorus Line and *Hamilton* or the New York Theatre Workshop with *Rent*—or from the commercial sector, with shows such as *Wicked* and *The Book of Mormon.*

Becoming a manager of an NFP doesn't mean your dream of walking down the aisle opening night on Broadway or picking up a Tony Award on a Sunday night in June has vanished. In my experience, keeping steadfast and clearheaded at what you originally signed up for inexorably leads to commercial success in one form or the other, and at a time when you least expect it.

14

What's a Commercial Hit?

(Or, I *Don't* Know It When I See It!)

My plane was late, so I hired a taxi to take me directly to the Soldiers and Sailors Memorial Hall and Museum, an imposing, late nineteenth-century sandstone building located in downtown Pittsburgh. When I got there, I was directed to a large auditorium where a hundred or so people had already arrived—friends, clergymen, actors, directors, and other New York theater denizens. As I entered the cavernous room, I saw a line leading toward the stage where, in an open coffin, lay one of America's greatest playwrights, August Wilson.

When I received the invitation to attend the ceremony, I didn't realize it would be both a funeral and a memorial service. At first, the open coffin took me aback. Had August asked for this? He knew he had terminal cancer months before his death, so I assumed he had had time to tell his wife, Constanza, what he wanted for his funeral. Viewing dead bodies in open caskets is something I'm at least ambivalent about. For some, viewing the deceased's physical remains can be a cathartic ritual, but, personally, I can't imagine why anyone would want to have a total stranger, a mortician, determine one's final public appearance.

As I stepped up on the stage and made my way past the casket, I realized, if August had not willed it himself, Constanza and his daughters, Azula and Sakina, had made the right decision. His visage was the one I had known for more than thirty years. He appeared serene, peaceful, and, characteristically, a bit removed from the events unfolding around him. It was as if he were in his habitat—a local bar in Pittsburgh—chain-smoking, writing, and observing the bartender, the funeral director, or the local raconteur, all of whom would later become characters in one of his plays.

When I took my seat, I sat behind Gordon Davidson, the producer and artistic director of the Ahmanson Theatre in Los Angeles, and next to Michael Maso, managing director of the Huntington Theatre Company in Boston, both of whom had worked with August during a long career that now seemed tragically all too short. The three of us exchanged our favorite anecdotes about August. My favorite, often told by August himself, was about his being a teenager in Pittsburgh and making the long trek up what is known as the Hill to spend all his savings on an old cast-iron typewriter from the local pawnshop. It was on that machine that August began to compose his early writings. It was that experience and others that remained stark reminders of August's Horatio Alger–like beginnings.

We then settled back to listen to a dozen or more tributes and eulogies, punctuated most memorably by Wynton Marsalis playing "Danny Boy" (not a dry eye in the house), followed by a gospel number that had the entire congregation up on their feet clapping and cheering. There were many tributes but, not surprisingly, nothing was nearly as eloquent as a passage from one of August's plays, quoted by someone in attendance.

Throughout the ceremony, I couldn't help but rewind the tape, going back to my first encounter with August and the many events we shared over more than two decades.

A Rare Opportunity

In 1984, soon after the opening of August Wilson's first Broadway play, *Ma Rainey's Black Bottom*, I received a telephone call from Ben Mordecai, managing director of the Yale Repertory Theatre, and Lloyd Richards, its artistic director. They asked if we could set up a meeting with August to discuss his future plans.

Although *Ma Rainey* had not been a commercial success, it had received favorable reviews and would go on to receive a Tony nomination for Best Play and win the prestigious New York Drama Critics' Circle Award for Best Play of the 1984–85 season. Frank Rich of the *New York Times* wrote: "Mr. Wilson has lighted a dramatic fuse that snakes and hisses through several anguished eras of American life. When the fuse reaches its explosive final destination, the audience is impaled by the impact."

When these three gentlemen arrived at my office from New Haven later that week, I didn't know what they would tell me or ask of me. It didn't matter much; getting a chance to talk with August, not to mention Lloyd Richards, the renowned director of *A Raisin in the Sun* and *Ma Rainey* and, at the time, dean of the Yale School of Drama, was reason enough for me to be excited about getting together. The three of them had a unique working relationship. Lloyd had first met August at the National Playwrights Conference at the Eugene O'Neill Theater Center in Waterford, Connecticut. It was there that he read two short plays by August and suggested they be combined into one play—*Ma Rainey's Black Bottom*. The Yale Repertory Theatre produced the play with Lloyd directing and Mordecai acting as managing director. Later, Mordecai, on behalf of the Yale Rep, assigned the Broadway transfer rights to two commercial producers, Robert Cole and Fred Zollo. Although different commercial producers were involved, this process became the model for developing and producing all of August's plays over the next twenty years.

The meeting began somewhat awkwardly. August seemed particularly uncomfortable and reticent. Lloyd also seemed uneasy. A lawyer's office on the thirty-first floor of a midtown Manhattan building did not provide the most convivial atmosphere for a meet-and-greet session. Mordecai began by explaining that August's experiences with his two former literary agents had been anything but satisfactory. I don't remember their names, but his first agent never read any of his work and the second was also dismissive and neglectful. In short, August had written off hiring another agent. I'd learn later on that once August made up his mind up about something, no one could convince him otherwise. Based on Mordecai's and Lloyd's advice, however, he was willing to consider hiring a lawyer to represent his interests.

Mordecai went on to explain that August had already written his second play, *Fences*, and had ideas for many more. They asked me if I would take him on as my client. I looked at August directly and said I would be pleased to act for him. I promised I would try to earn his trust and confidence and help bring his plays to the stage. He smiled and thanked me. He still hadn't said more than a few words during the whole meeting. I understood from the look on his face that he appreciated the sentiment but, based on his past experiences, he would reserve judgment for the time being. It was also made clear to me that August didn't have the resources to pay my usual hourly fees. I said that I rarely, if ever, worked on a contingency basis, but in August's case, I would be happy to do so. That was the end of our meeting.

Thus began a professional and personal relationship between us in which I had the privilege of observing the maturation of one of the greatest dramatists in the American theater. The sheer magnitude of August's creative output (a ten-play cycle written over two decades) is dwarfed only by his profound and trenchant portraits of the black man's suppression, perseverance, defeats, and triumphs in twentieth-century American society. Never before had a playwright spoken to all Americans so eloquently about a subject matter that, until then, had not entered the mainstream of our dramatic culture.

August had been stung by some of the criticism leveled against *Ma Rainey*. Some thought its dramatic structure, cobbled together from two plays, unwieldy and too unconventional for the commercial theater. He told me that with *Fences* he set out to demonstrate that he could write a conventional story of a black family with characters, a plot, and a dénouement worthy of the grand tradition of Arthur Miller and Tennessee Williams. In a way, August put his own dramatic instincts on hold while writing *Fences* in order to earn respect from those who were still reserving judgment. In his next play, *Joe Turner's Come and Gone*, considered by many to be his masterpiece, August would unleash his own distinctive brand of dramaturgy, introducing a vernacular of mysticism, lyricism, and realism as no other playwright had done before or has done since. Somewhat ironically, however, none of August's plays would achieve the commercial success of *Fences*. But that's the story I'm about to tell.

August admired other black playwrights, such as James Baldwin, whose plays were praised critically but were never embraced by a wide audience. While August also chose to write only about one segment of our society, his narrative, while occasionally angry, was revelatory and often quite funny, never didactic or intimidating. Seeing a Wilson play could at times seem like attending a Baptist revival meeting with both black and white audiences joining together to celebrate the shared heritage of a distinctly American culture. By virtue of this, August's plays were accepted by and widely accessible to all audiences.

Without an agent, it was left to Mordecai and me to find a commercial producer for *Fences* after its premiere at the Yale Repertory Theatre.

Although *Ma Rainey* had been a critical success, it had lost all its money. The street's postmortem was that it was too great a stretch for a predominantly white Broadway audience. There was also Shubert Alley loose talk that the play was anti-Semitic in its portrayal of the recording industry's subjugation and exploitation of black singers in the 1920s. We knew that it would be an uphill battle to find a commercial producer willing to gamble on his next play.

We made the round of calls to all of the usual suspects. Most of them admired August's writing but considered the subject matter more suitable for a not-for-profit theater than for Broadway. One producer offered an embarrassingly low advance of $2,500. I rejected it out of hand and never told August, knowing he would have considered it insulting. August was one of the most proud and self-confident men I've ever known. In any event, we all recognized the play needed further development. We decided to delay Broadway and instead bring it to the prestigious, not-for-profit Goodman Theatre of Chicago.

At around the same time, one of my other clients, Carole Shorenstein Hays, contacted me, saying she had decided to expand her theater-producing activities. Carole was the daughter of billionaire real estate magnate Walter Shorenstein, who, at the time of his death in 2010, was the largest landlord in San Francisco. What the Rudin, Tisch, and Rose families are to New York real estate, the Shorensteins are to real estate in San Francisco. Walter Shorenstein's holdings at the time included a partnership with James Nederlander Sr. of New York, through which they jointly owned three of San Francisco's major theaters—the Curran, the Orpheum, and the Golden Gate. Carole still runs these theaters along with the Nederlanders. Her first foray as a lead producer of a Broadway play was a co-production revival of the musical *Oliver!* with Cameron Mackintosh. It was a largely uninspired affair that had a brief and unprofitable run.

She was eager to do something new and of high quality. She favored straight plays over musicals, being drawn to strong characters and storylines. I suggested she consider *Fences*. I didn't do this without some second thoughts. My first instinct was that Carole and August might not be a match made in heaven. This play would be a big gamble and I wanted Carole's first production to be a positive experience. But, despite the risks, she kept emphasizing her desire to find new writers whose plays would offer something more to Broadway audiences than the usual fare. *Fences* seemed to fit the bill.

I filled Carole in on the background and suggested we meet in Chicago for the opening, all the while cautioning her that what she was going to see was not necessarily a big commercial hit, but was nonetheless a play of great artistic merit with a powerful performance by James Earl Jones in the leading role.

Ten days later, Carole and I met in Chicago. I was very nervous. I had dragged her from San Francisco to Chicago on what I knew was more than a long shot. As we took our seats, I whispered to her, somewhat defensively, that the play would need more development and some cutting.

Nearly three hours later, as the audience rose cheering to its feet at the curtain call, Carole turned to me and said, "I want to do it. Get the rights." She had no second thoughts, no questions about cost or timing or anything else. She had become an August Wilson convert.

Everyone was elated, of course. And Carole didn't want to waste any time. It was already February and she wanted to have an out-of-town tryout at the Curran Theatre in San Francisco and then open on Broadway before the Tony deadline in early May. One of the most difficult things to maneuver for most independent producers is getting a theater, especially late in the season. Carole had a leg up on that—actually two legs up. She co-owned the Curran and she got the Richard Rodgers Theatre on Broadway from her business partner, James Nederlander.

When I returned to New York from Chicago, I got a call from Walter Shorenstein asking me to fly out to San Francisco to discuss his daughter's new theatrical venture. Being the astute businessman and protective father that he was, Walter wanted to get a quick primer on producing. After all, up to now, as far as he was concerned, this was a business in which he collected rent and recovered all of the theater's expenses while the producer bore all the risk of production. Now his daughter was putting herself on the line like all those other producers.

Walter took his daughter, one of his associates, and me to the top floor of the Bank of America skyscraper, which is etched into the San Francisco skyline. During our lunch, he pointed out the other buildings he either owned or managed around the city. Already impressed by what I had read about Walter's holdings, I found sitting atop the Bank of America building while he gave me a Cook's tour of his empire a powerful reminder that he was someone who took his business and money very seriously.

We soon got down to brass tacks. Walter wanted to know more about August, the history of the play, and something about my role as a lawyer in the whole affair. I tried to tread carefully, giving him all the information straight and to the point—no wavering or beating about the bush. Just the facts. When we got on the subject of financing the play, Walter wanted a lot of detail about budgets, how money was raised, and the split of revenue and net profits. Here's where I could speak his language, given that limited partnerships (the vehicles used for theater investments) were also commonly used for real estate deals. Among other things, I explained that theater deals commonly split the net profits 50/50 between the producer (in this case Carole) and the investors.

Walter said he wanted to offer the investment to his friends and 50 percent seemed too little. Why not increase it? I assumed he wanted to bring in his friends to reduce Carole's exposure. I told him there was no magic to 50/50, but, given the risky nature of the business, producers looked to a 50 percent share to make up for years of flops and developmental work when there is little or no money. Walter understood all too well about risk, but wasn't this play a relatively *safe* bet? (Uh-oh.)

I then felt I had to give Walter some sobering facts. Although I had introduced the play to Carole and thought highly of August, I wasn't about to let Walter Shorenstein, mega-mogul that he was, plunge into these waters on my advice without making him aware of all the shoals and sharks out there. I think the tide turned when I said that more than 90 percent of all plays on Broadway lost either all or most of their investments. Walter stared at me and said, "Well, I can't ask my friends to invest in this play. What's the point? If they lost their money, I'd just give it back to them." With that, Walter said his daughter would put up 100 percent of the financing.

Over the years, I got to know Walter and became quite fond of him. We had lunch at the Four Seasons in New York at least once a year. He was street-smart, a perceptive judge of character, and a wily negotiator. He would ask me about his daughter's ventures and I would try to pick his brain on just about any subject. He started with $1,000 in his pocket, as he was wont to remind everyone, and ended up owning most of San Francisco.

Walter died in 2010 at the age of ninety-five. At his ninetieth birthday party, also at the Four Seasons, Hillary Clinton spoke eloquently about her fondness for him, and President Clinton sent his greetings via live video. For several years, Walter was one of the largest contributors to and fundraisers for the Democratic Party. When I asked Carole one January how she and her husband, Jeff Hays, had spent New Year's Eve, she told me they had attended a celebration at the White House where her father sat next to Hillary and she herself sat to the right of the president. I think Nan and I had gone to bed that night at around eleven fifteen.

Fences on Broadway

August, always mindful of his less-than-perfect experiences with theater professionals, was a bit wary of Carole, who came from a world of privilege and wealth he knew nothing about. They were about the strangest professional bedfellows one could imagine. With her somewhat shy and enigmatic personality and August's suspicions and natural reticence, they had some difficulty at first communicating with one another. But Carole has always had enormous regard for artists and a passion for their work. August sensed that and he eventually came to admire her forthrightness and candid assessment of what was necessary to achieve a commercial success for his play. In any event, how could he gainsay this woman who was about to write one big check to bankroll his next play on Broadway?

Meanwhile, we were on a very fast track to get *Fences* to Broadway. I recommended Carole hire Robert Kamlot, a veteran GM, to manage the show. He began budgeting, contracting with the actors, and planning the move from the Curran to the 46th Street Theatre (now the Richard Rodgers) on Broadway.

By and large, everything went smoothly until we started performances at the Curran. The play got generally favorable notices, but some of Carole's subscribers complained about the show. They found it too long and sometimes offensive, particularly in August's frequent use of the

N-word. Carole and Kamlot were worried. They began to question the script. While I was in San Francisco for the opening, Carole and Kamlot asked to meet with me privately. When I walked into Kamlot's office, he handed me the script of *Fences* with dozens of notations in yellow and pink Magic Marker. Kamlot told me these were the cuts and changes he and Carole wanted August to make in the play. I knew we were in trouble.

It takes a long time, sometimes years, for a producer to earn an author's trust enough that he or she will agree to specific changes in a script. And, even then, I'd never known any producer to hand a playwright a marked-up script with changes marked in yellow for "required" and pink for "recommended." I knew this would not sit well with August. I tried to dissuade Kamlot and Carole from giving their annotated script to him. They implied that unless he was open to those changes, they would abandon their plans to bring the play to New York.

August and Lloyd Richards met with Kamlot and Carole. August said politely that he and Lloyd were already making some cuts and changes. They listened to what Carole and Kamlot had to say and then went about doing what they thought was best for the show. For the time being everything seemed to have blown over.

I returned to New York. It was spring break so I took my family for a week's vacation in Key West. Halfway through the vacation, I received a frantic call from Carole. The show had begun previews on Broadway. At the note session after that night's performance, August and Kamlot had come to near physical blows over the changes Carole and Kamlot were still insisting on. What appeared to have been resolved in San Francisco had now resurfaced in New York with renewed sound and fury.

You may recall that I mentioned in an early chapter that entertainment lawyers often help bring their clients' works to the stage by introducing them to other clients so they may collaborate on a particular project. *Fences* was one of those projects. August and Carole were both my clients—so were the Goodman Theatre and the Yale Repertory Theatre. This became a true nightmare for me while I juggled phone calls from both sides in Key West.

Lawyers are bound to apprise their clients of any conflicts. In this case, both Yale and the Goodman used their own lawyers in New Haven and Chicago, respectively. However, Carole and August refused to retain other counsel and agreed to waive any conflict of interest. What lawyers can do in this instance is to build figuratively what's referred to as a Chinese wall within their firm, separating the lawyers representing the two clients. I assigned one set of lawyers to represent Carole and another to represent August. I would act as advisor to both of them. Everyone signed off on this arrangement, but when I tried to present both sides of the argument to Carole and August, I suspected they felt I was at fault for bringing them together in the first place. It turned out the best thing for me was to be 1,500 miles away. I realized later on that I was an easy scapegoat, since I was far from the fray and it's always easier to blame the lawyers (if not kill all of them).

While my family slept, I spent most of the night speaking by phone to everyone. After a few days, everything calmed down and peace was restored. August and Lloyd continued to make changes in the script and Carole wisely realized that not only the baby and the bathwater but everything else onstage would be thrown out if she didn't back off from pressing for more changes.

Opening Night

Previews continued. Audiences were jumping to their feet every night at the curtain, but the show was losing money each week owing to weak ticket sales. Unless the show got rave reviews, it would never survive.

Fences opened on Broadway March 26, 1987. It got across-the-board rave reviews and went on to win the Pulitzer Prize for Drama, the Tony Award for Best Play, and just about every other award that season. Carole made all her money back, and then some. What started out as a play no one thought would be commercially successful turned out to be one of the most critically and financially successful Broadway dramas of all time.

But the "too good to be true" story doesn't end here. As an extra bonus, Bob Wachs, a former Paul, Weiss entertainment associate who was then acting as Eddie Murphy's manager, called me to say that Murphy thought *Fences* was the best play he'd ever seen and wanted to buy the film rights.

When I told August about Murphy's proposal, he smiled and said wryly, "I'd like to meet this guy." So off we went, chauffeured in a stretch limo, to Murphy's newly built home in New Jersey. When we arrived, we could see the house was new indeed—not much landscaping yet—but, from afar, we saw a huge garage with more than a few new sports cars parked alongside one another.

We walked into the foyer and were led into a library, which had an enormous full-length portrait of Murphy above the fireplace, reminiscent of the portrait of Laura in the eponymous noir classic. Some time passed before Murphy arrived, manicured and decked out meticulously. He was quite nervous and extremely deferential toward August, which slightly amused August but also made him able to relax and open up about what he wanted for the film. Murphy readily agreed to everything, including August's saying that he would require a black director for the film—a surprise to me and something that would affect plans to produce the film for years to come.

When I got back to New York, I negotiated the deal with Paramount (Murphy's studio) for the rights in the play, as well as a screenwriting deal for August. With Murphy calling the shots, Paramount agreed to my proposal with little hassle, paid seven figures up front for the rights and a hefty six figures for August to write the screenplay. Thirty years later, *Fences* has still not been produced as a movie.

Carole was thrilled with the play's success, and so was Walter Shorenstein. At the opening night party, he pulled me aside, put his arm around my shoulder, and thanked me for my help with the show. He then added, "I do have one bone to pick with you, however. You should have insisted that I let my friends invest in the show. Now they'll all be mad at me for not being in on the biggest hit on Broadway."

15

Finding the Money

A Gathering of Angels

Hollywood has long portrayed Broadway producers as cigar-chomping, fast-talking con men who spend most of their time auditioning chorus girls on their couch and duping widows and orphans into making dicey investments. Mel Brooks's hilarious take on these flamboyant crooks in *The Producers* pretty much imprinted that stereotype in our minds for all time. Max Bialystock raised more money than he needed for his show, hoping for a flop so he could run off with the extra funds. Instead, he got a hit. Could there be any better example of the futility of predicting which shows will work and which won't?

If I've accomplished anything in this book so far, I hope it's been to give the reader an appreciation for what producers in the real world need to know and do in order to bring a project to fruition. They need to be imaginative (having the idea), relentless (getting the rights), discerning (hiring the writers), and either very rich or, what this chapter will address, resourceful (getting the money).

I'll discuss organizing the financing vehicle for raising money for the show, as well as the federal and state laws and regulations governing the manner in which funds may be raised from the public. Your lawyer will take responsibility for drafting the offering literature based on budgets and other pertinent information supplied by the GM and you. She also needs to be knowledgeable and experienced in the issuance of theatrical securities so she can instruct you on the dos and don'ts of raising money. It is vitally important that you become educated about these matters since you, as the lead producer, will be legally responsible if your offering violates any of the applicable securities laws.

Federal and State Securities Laws

Until the Great Depression, there was little, if any, government oversight for raising money for commercial ventures, including theatrical productions. In the theater, investors, wealthy individuals accustomed to investing in small risky ventures, were commonly referred to as "angels." The term is still used today, particularly in the context of new real estate companies trying to get a foothold in the financial markets.

The agreements with angels in the theater were little more than a couple of pages stating the producer's intended use of the funds, the amount being invested, and the angels' share of profits. Today, the offering literature for a Broadway show usually consists of, at a minimum, fifty pages, including a partnership agreement, investor questionnaire, and subscription contract. These offerings are regulated by both the federal government and every state in which an offering is made.

The Securities Act of 1933 and the Securities Exchange Act of 1934 are the two applicable federal statutes. The individual states' securities laws are usually referred to as "blue sky" laws, a term first coined in 1917 by US Supreme Court Justice Joseph McKenna in *Hall v. Geiger-Jones Co.* (242 U.S. 539): "The name that is given to the law indicates the evil at which it is aimed, that is, to use the language of a cited case, 'speculative schemes which have no more basis than so many feet of "blue sky"'; or, as stated by counsel in another case, 'to stop the sale of stock in fly-by-night concerns, visionary oil wells, distant gold mines and other like fraudulent exploitations.'"

As various states began to enact laws regulating the issuance of stock, such laws continued to be referred to as blue sky laws, the term no longer having a negative connotation but serving to distinguish them from federal laws. In New York, there is a statute that specifically addresses raising money for theatrical productions: the Theatrical Syndication Financing Act under article XXIII of the Arts and Cultural Affairs Law. Consequently, every offering of an interest in a Broadway play (all of which are considered "securities") must comply with these laws and other blue sky laws of other states in which money is raised.

Thirty years ago, preparing and complying with the various securities laws was a long and arduous process. For example, musicals requiring more than $1 million were considered public offerings and as such were required to submit their offering literature to the Securities and Exchange Commission in Washington, DC, the New York State attorney general's office, and attorneys general in other states in which the securities were to be offered. It would often take weeks or months before receiving comments back from these authorities. Working with the SEC could be particularly frustrating as low-level examiners, who had little or no experience with theatrical offerings, would often be assigned to comment on the offering. New York examiners were more knowledgeable, but their comments could result in complicated negotiations over whether certain information was material and/or over the specific wording of various disclosures. All of this resulted in substantial legal fees and long delays, sometimes forcing producers to postpone, or even abandon, their productions.

Today, the situation is quite different. As a result of a number of federal exemptions (Regulation D Rules 505 and 506 of the Securities Act of 1933) certain offerings are no longer required to submit offering literature to the SEC or the states' attorneys general for review and comment. A simple form, Form D, is all that is required to be filed with the SEC. Regardless of the exemption, the federal and state disclosure and antifraud provisions still apply to all theatrical offerings. Consequently, the offering should provide sufficient disclosure of all the material terms and conditions of the offering to all the investors.[1]

No producer is expected to have an intimate knowledge of all these legal requirements and the supporting case law. This is the responsibility of your lawyer, who must determine whether or not your offering material is in full compliance with the law. However, her review is only as good as the information you and your GM supply to her. If she is to protect you from claims of securities violations by the authorities or disgruntled investors, it is imperative that she be confident you and your general manager have fully disclosed all relevant information and that no misleading or fraudulent statements are included in the offering material. In the end, if a court should find that there has not been full disclosure

[1] Under both Rules 505 and 506, an unlimited number of "accredited investors" may invest in the production and up to thirty-five "unaccredited investors" may invest. An accredited investor is one who meets certain minimum financial criteria.

or fraud has been committed, you, as producer, will be liable for any such omissions or commissions, both civil and criminal.

In terms of disclosure, the New York State securities law sets forth the minimum information that should be disclosed to theatrical investors. Other states often look to these requirements when considering full disclosure, since it is widely recognized that New York has the strongest interest and experience in protecting the public from fraudulent theatrical offerings. In some cases, when peculiar circumstances arise, you may be required to disclose certain information that at first may not appear to be particularly relevant.

Here's an example:

In my representation of a prospective major investor in a Broadway show several years ago, nothing appeared to be out of the ordinary, at least as far as the financing papers were concerned. Right before my client made a final decision about whether or not to invest, I discovered, through my due diligence, that the booking contract for the theater in which the play was to be presented stipulated that the producer would be required to vacate the theater three months after the opening. I had never encountered such a situation. I brought this information to my client's attention, since it had a direct bearing on the merits of the investment. If the show flopped, it would all be moot. If it was a huge hit, the show would probably find another theater, although that wasn't a sure thing if there was a booking jam on Broadway. What I was more concerned about was a situation in between—where the show was doing so-so business but not selling out, earning a modest profit each week but facing the prospect of losing the theater in three months. If the show was forced to close, the investors would be deprived of any further return on their investment. More important, even if another theater was available, the producer would need to spend $750,000 or more to pay for the costs of closing, moving, and reopening in another theater. Although no one could predict the outcome, under the circumstances, everyone agreed it was unlikely those additional monies would be forthcoming from the original or new investors.

My recommendation was that the offering material be amended to include this disclosure. To ignore it, I believed, would have been the basis for a securities claim of fraud and failure to disclose a material fact if, in fact, the scenario outlined above actually occurred. After some back and forth, everyone agreed to the wording of the amendment. I explained the risks to my client, who eventually decided to invest in the show. Sadly, the show got middling reviews, did little business, and closed within the three-month period.

Front Money

To quote Max Bialystock's words of wisdom, "Never put your own money in a show." That may be sound advice, but for some nascent producers, doing so may be unavoidable. Yet many new producers don't have the money to cover even the initial start-up costs. The seed money, or "front money," required for a musical can be as much as $250,000 to cover a legal retainer, initial fees to a GM, advance payments for underlying rights and to the authors, and the costs of readings. Under the New York securities law, producers are permitted to raise front money to cover these early costs and are exempt from any filing requirements, provided the offers are made to no more than four offerees.

As the offeror, the producer is limited to no more than four "offers"—not four investments. For example, if you make an offer (that is, ask for a sum of money in return for a specific return from the show) but the offer is refused, that would account for one of the four offers—and it doesn't matter if that offer is in writing or made orally. It's pretty clear that the maximum of four offerees could be exceeded very quickly. A producer needs to discern, before making an offer, the level of interest the potential investor may have in the show. There is no prohibition on the producer providing information about the nature of the show and a general description of its financial and economic components. To raise front money, some producers will have a private presentation to a dozen or so friends and family with two or three singers performing selections from the score. The producer needs to guard against making any specific offering to those in attendance, but it can be an effective method of introducing the show to those who are serious about getting involved at an early stage.

Of course, investing front money in a show at its earliest formative stage is an extremely risky proposition. However, a typical front money agreement will reward this high degree of risk with an enhanced participation in the production's net profits.

Here are the basic components of a front money agreement:

1. The investment is on a "most favored nation" basis. This means that the terms of the deal for the investor will be improved automatically if any other party investing the same amount of money or less is offered more favorable terms.
2. The funds invested may be used only for the purposes set forth in the New York securities law. They include fees and advances for obtaining underlying rights, engaging creative personnel, renting a theater, retaining lawyers and accountants, preparing offering documents, covering the costs of workshops, and other purposes reasonably related to the business of the production company. The law prohibits the use of front money to pay any fees to the producer or to reimburse him for costs of travel, lodging, or meals, unless permission is expressly granted by the investor.
3. In return for the investment, the investor is given a share of adjusted net profits of the show, based on the proportion that the front money bears to the total capitalization of the production. As an example, if the amount of the front money is $200,000 and the capitalization of the show is $10 million, then the investor would receive a 2 percent share of adjusted net profits payable to all of the investors. In recognition of the highly risky nature of the investment, the producer usually doubles this share, known as a "kicker," which in this case would be increased to 4 percent.
4. Once the offering literature is prepared, the investor will be offered the right, but not the obligation, to make an additional investment in the Broadway production. Again, the producer normally would offer the investor a kicker on this second investment, usually on the basis of one for two, meaning that if the investment yields 2 percent of the adjusted net profits, the bonus would be half of that percentage, or 1 percent, bringing the total to 3 percent. These net profits would be in addition to the share of net profits paid to the investor for the front money he contributed.
5. Depending on the amount of the investment, the producer might also offer a small portion of his weekly royalty, but these

arrangements are usually reserved for major investors of $500,000 or more in a Broadway musical.

6. The investor acknowledges that there has been no submission to or review by any governmental regulatory authority.
7. The agreement also states that the producer may abandon the production at any time, in which case the investor waives any claim for reimbursement of the portion of his investment spent by the producer prior to abandonment.

The Broadway Investment Company

Once a producer has a completed play, has hired most of the core creative team, and has mapped out a time schedule for production, he will instruct his lawyer to prepare the formal offering literature for distribution to potential investors. The timing for raising money needs to be carefully considered. If it's too early and the producer doesn't have enough of the creative or other essential elements in place, investors may want to wait until more is known, such as the casting, or when the theater is secured. In general, investors don't want to have their money tied up for more than nine months before performances begin. If, on the other hand, you wait too long, you may miss deadlines for commencement of rehearsals and other substantial financial obligations. And, one can't rely on mere oral promises to invest. It's important to have all of your investors' cash deposited in the production's bank account as soon as possible after an investor has made a commitment.[2]

As for the type of investment vehicle a producer utilizes, Broadway plays and musicals are almost always financed through either a limited

---

[2] In the 2012–13 season, Ben Sprecher, the lead producer of a new $12 million musical based on the Daphne du Maurier novel *Rebecca*, was deceived by middleman Mark C. Hotton. Hotton claimed he had a wealthy investor, Paul Abrams, who wanted to invest $2 million in the show. In a federal court proceeding against Hotton, Preet Bharara, the federal prosecutor, showed that Abrams and others represented by Hotton were nothing more than "deep-pocketed phantoms"—figments of Hotton's imagination. Having discovered the ruse shortly before commencement of rehearsals, Sprecher was never able to replace the investment and was forced to abandon the show.

partnership or its recent cousin, a limited liability company. Both of these investment vehicles offer limited liability to all the investors, with their exposure capped at the amount invested in the production, even if the show realizes losses beyond the original capitalization. In other words, if a Broadway musical is capitalized at $10 million, the investors' liabilities in the aggregate can never exceed $10 million.

The general partner of the limited partnership or the managing member of the limited liability company controls all of the management affairs of the company and is the only partner authorized to make creative or business decisions. As compared to the limited investors, the general partner or managing partner is liable for any losses realized by the production beyond the original capitalization. The advantage of using a limited liability company is that a producer may use a thinly capitalized corporation (that is, one with very few assets) to serve as the managing member and thereby shield himself from any personal liability. On the other hand, if a corporation is used as a general partner of a limited partnership, it cannot be an asset-less shell company, and it is required to meet and maintain certain minimum net worth requirements.

For ease of discussion, from now on, I'll refer to the investment vehicle as a limited partnership (an LP).

As a result of a number of federal exemptions, in most cases, it is no longer necessary to prepare an offering circular. Instead, the nature of the production and the risks associated with the investment are all contained in the LP agreement, including a summary of the plot of the play, the contemplated uses for the funds, the costs and expenses of the production, a biographical description of the producer and the creative team (along with the compensation paid to them), and a detailed description of the division of net profits among the producer, the investors, and any third parties.

Production and operating budgets, as well as financial projections showing the potential weekly revenue and costs ranging from 100 percent capacity down to breakeven,[3] are prepared by the GM and usually included as exhibits to the LP agreement. In evaluating the prospects

[3] Breakeven is the point at which weekly net gross receipts equal the weekly operating costs, including all royalties and payments to other percentage participants.

for a play, it is a good rule of thumb to look at the projections for when a show is running at an average of 70 percent of capacity. As shows seldom run at 100 percent capacity, no such analysis of a show should be solely relied on. If the show cannot recoup (or recover its costs) within a year to eighteen months at 70 percent capacity, then there is a strong likelihood it will never recoup. It is also important to look at the post-recoupment projection. Some shows are so loaded down with third-party shares of net profits and givebacks due to amortization deals that the net profits available to the investors are almost illusory.

In previous chapters, I discussed royalty structures, royalty pools, and amortization in some detail. The reader should examine those chapters along with this one to get a full picture of the financial components of a production. At the risk of repeating some of that information, it may be useful to look at a model of a typical Broadway musical capitalized at $15 million, with a royalty pool and amortization formula.

The $15 million capitalization is used to fund the "production costs" of the show. These costs consist of all development and pre-production expenses incurred prior to the official opening of the play, including acquiring rights in any underlying literary or musical material, as well as hiring a bookwriter, composer, lyricist, and all other creative personnel, such as the director, choreographer, and the set, costume, lighting, and sound designers. Production costs also include rehearsal expenses, salaries for all the actors and technical personnel, pre-opening advertising and marketing, and management, legal, and accounting fees and expenses. Until such time as all of the production costs are recovered or recouped, there are no net profits available for the producer or any investor in the show.

An important distinction to keep in mind is the difference between "capitalization" and "production costs." The former is the amount of money raised from investors to produce the show based on the production budgets prepared by the GM. The latter refers to the actual costs to produce the show, which may be lower or higher than the capitalization. If they're lower, at the producer's option, the excess funds may be returned to the investors toward recoupment soon after the opening, or used as a reserve for post-opening expenses, such as advertising or marketing, or to cover losses later on in the run. If the production costs are higher than the capitalization, then the producer must either put up those additional funds himself or find additional investors.

The production costs are recouped or recovered by deducting the weekly operating costs of the show from the weekly gross revenue. Weekly gross revenue is defined as all of the gross income received by the producer through ticket sales, merchandising sales, and other miscellaneous income.

Weekly operating profits are calculated by deducting the weekly operating costs from the weekly gross revenue. Weekly operating costs consist of salaries to the actors, musicians, stagehands, GM, stage managers, and company manager; weekly fees to lawyers and accountants; weekly advertising and marketing costs; and, most significant, theater costs, which include a weekly fixed fee of approximately $15,000 a week, all of the theater's operating costs, plus a rent factor of anywhere from 5 to 6 percent of the weekly gross revenue. Weekly operating costs also include all royalties paid to the writers of the play, the designers, music personnel (orchestrator, arrangers), and producers.

As discussed in an earlier chapter, if a royalty pool with amortization is used for calculating royalties, a further 1 to 2 percent of the capitalization will be deducted from the weekly operating costs before the weekly operating profits available to the royalty pool (to be shared between the creative team and the investors) are calculated. The share of the royalty pool payable to the producer goes to the investors quarterly toward repayment of the original capitalization.

Here is an example of a typical Broadway musical:

Production costs	$15,000,000
Weekly gross revenue at 100% capacity	$1,200,000
Weekly operating costs	$800,000
Weekly amortization (1%) paid to investors	$150,000
Weekly operating profits (royalty pool)	$250,000
Investors' share of pool is 65% of $250,000 (or $162,500) plus amortization of $150,000 for a total of	$312,500
Creative share of pool is 35% of $250,000, or	$87,500

In the above example, the weekly operating profits of $250,000 are calculated by deducting the weekly operating costs of $800,000 and the amortization of $150,000 from the weekly gross revenue of $1.2 million.

Weekly gross revenue of $1.2 million would indicate, in most cases, a complete or near sellout for that week. In practice, that rarely occurs. However, for the super-hits (*Hamilton*, *The Book of Mormon*) and the big, long-running musicals (*Wicked*, *The Lion King*), those numbers are not uncommon. Indeed, with the sale of premium tickets (tickets priced as high as $450 each), the weekly gross revenue for major hits can be $1.5 million or even higher during holiday weeks. In the above example, with weekly operating profits of $312,500, the production costs of $15 million would be recovered within forty-eight weeks, or nine and a half months, of the opening—an extremely favorable result for a big musical.

Now look at what happens if the play is playing at an average of only 70 percent capacity with a weekly gross revenue of $840,000. The weekly operating costs would be lower than $800,000, since theater rent and some other percentage variables diminish as the weekly gross revenue declines. In this case, these costs might be in the range of $725,000. As a result, the weekly operating profits would be $115,000 (weekly gross revenue of $840,000 minus weekly operating costs of $725,000). Now there are insufficient weekly operating profits to pay the full amortization of $150,000, in which case the investors would receive all of the pool monies of $115,000 and the creative team would receive only their guaranteed weekly minimum payments. At the rate of $115,000 a week, the show would have to run at least two and a half years to fully recoup its capitalization. The reality is a show selling at an average of 70 percent capacity is unlikely to last as long as two or three years. If a musical is going to have a shot at recoupment, it must demonstrate early on in its run that it has the staying power to run at or near 100 percent capacity with a heavy dose of premium seating sales.

If a show cannot demonstrate on paper that it can recoup within eighteen months or so at an average of 70 percent capacity, it should become incumbent on the producer and the GM to go back to the budgeting drawing board by reducing either the production costs, the weekly operating costs, or both. That might require some tough discussion with the creative team, especially the designers and perhaps the authors. To do otherwise—and go out with an offering showing the need to run for two and a half years or more to recoup—will prove a very difficult sell to savvy investors and their advisors. Some offerings will show recoupment only at 100 percent or 90 percent capacity. Although, strictly speaking, this may be sufficient disclosure (I would argue with that), experienced investors, and certainly their advisors, will make their own calculations at lower capacities when assessing the economic risk of the offering.

The above examples are for musical plays. The figures for dramatic plays are quite different. The production costs are in the neighborhood of $3 million and weekly operating costs can be somewhere in the area of $350,000 unless there is a major star such as Daniel Craig or Helen Mirren involved, in which case the gross weekly revenue may be greater than $1 million and the weekly operating costs may be as high as $600,000, due mainly to the very high salary received by the star or stars. A major movie star can easily receive $100,000 or more each week for appearing on Broadway. In those cases, the commitment of the star is usually only for a twelve- or fourteen-week run; so the producer must earn sufficient weekly operating profits in a short period in order to pay back the $3 million of production costs.

Also, the weekly operating profits for a drama featuring a huge, above-the-title star may be so great that it becomes preferable to pay the creative team royalties based on gross weekly box office receipts rather than a share of the weekly profits. That is often the case for straight plays, with huge stars, that run at 100 percent capacity. These calculations demonstrate that royalty pools are most useful to producers when a show is running at 80 percent capacity or less, in which case the share of weekly operating profits payable to the creative team would be less than royalties paid on weekly gross revenues. That is also true for shows that begin by paying gross royalties, but then switch (with the permission of the royalty participants) to a royalty pool when the show softens and is no longer running at or near capacity.

Net Profits

Assuming the musical or play is a hit and continues to run profitably, how are net profits divided among the creative team, the producer, and the investors? First, you need to understand the distinction between net profits and adjusted net profits.

Net profits consist of all of the weekly operating profits earned subsequent to the recoupment of production costs. Adjusted net profits are the weekly operating profits available for distribution to the producer and the investors after payment of net profits to third parties, such as stars, authors, underlying rights owners, not-for-profit theaters, and Actors' Equity Association (due to a workshop).

If a show has net profit obligations to a star, high-profile authors, a regional or other not-for-profit theater, or Equity (due to a workshop), the share of net profits payable to those entities could total as much as 10 to 15 percent. After 15 percent is deducted from 100 percent of net profits, the remaining 85 percent is considered adjusted net profits. This then represents the pool of net profits split between the producer and his investors.

As a rule, 50 percent of the adjusted net profits are paid to the producer and 50 percent are payable to the investors. The money paid to the investors is divided pro rata and pari passu (at the same time) among them in accordance with the respective amounts contributed by each. Therefore, an investor who put up 10 percent of the production costs, or $1.5 million, would receive 10 percent of the 50 percent share of adjusted net profits paid to all of the investors, or $12,500 for that week. In effect, both the producer and the investors bear, off the top, on a 50/50 basis, all of the shares of net profits payable to the third-party participants. When assessing the profitability of a show, it is important to examine the totality of the net profits given away to these parties in order to determine how much is left for the investors to realize a return on their investment. A comparison of the amount of money in any one week prior and subsequent to recoupment can be very dramatic.

In our example above, prior to recoupment, the investors' share of weekly operating profits at a gross of $1.2 million was $312,500. Following recoupment, 15 percent of the $312,500, or $46,875, is given away to third parties, leaving $265,625 of adjusted net profits to be divided equally ($132,813 each) between the investors and the producer.

This appears to be a very favorable deal for the producer. However, in practice, it would be highly unusual for him to retain all of the 50 percent of adjusted net profits. As mentioned previously, most likely he would have agreed to pay his front money investors and other heavy-hitter investors a kicker, or an additional participation in their regular shares of the adjusted net profits. If the producer had originated the idea and developed the show himself, he might also receive what are often referred to as "torchbearer" points of 5 percent of the adjusted net profits, leaving 45 percent of adjusted net profits to be divided between himself and the investors. As much as half or more of the remaining 45 percent could be given to major investors. For example, if an investor put up 10 percent of the capitalization, he would be entitled to receive under the financing agreement 10 percent of the investors' 50 percent share, or 5 percent. To provide that investor with an extra incentive to invest, the producer might offer a kicker of one for two—that is, 1 percent of the adjusted net profits payable from the producer's share for every 2 percent the investment receives from the investors' side. Here's how the division between a producer and his investors may look:

Gross weekly box office: $1,200,000
100% of net profits: $312,000
Less: 15% of net profits payable to third parties: $46,875
Remaining 85% (adjusted net profits): $265,625
Divided 50% to investors and 50% to producer:
50% of $265,625, or $132,813, payable to the investors, divided among them pro rata based on each investor's investment amount;
and
50% of $265,625, or $132,813, payable to the producer, divided 40% to the producer ($53,125) and 60% to major investors ($79,688).

Put another way, following recoupment, the producer's share of 100 percent of net profits is $53,125 divided by $312,500, or 17 percent of 100 percent of net profits.

Owing to the high cost of raising money in today's theater, a producer who has to rely on others for most of his financing would be very fortunate to wind up with this much in adjusted net profits. The road to securing 100 percent of your financing is never easy, unless you have Helen Mirren or Bryan Cranston starring in your play, a windfall enjoyed by only the fortunate 1 percent of producers.

Ancillary, Additional, and Subsidiary Rights

As we saw in chapter twelve, "The Approved Production Contract," the production company can earn additional revenue for rights other than the Broadway run, provided the show achieves at least a moderate level of success. The producer's share of proceeds from cast album and merchandising rights flows to the LP and is shared with the investors. Those deals have been discussed in detail in the APC chapter.

Soon after a successful show opens in New York, the producer and his GM will begin to look at opportunities to mount additional first-class companies throughout the United States and Canada. Depending on the magnitude of the hit, there may be sit-down companies for open-ended runs in major cities such as Los Angeles, Chicago, and Boston.[4] This first national tour will then be followed by a somewhat smaller company, perhaps with a simpler physical production, which will play smaller cities for two- to four-week engagements. Finally, a non-equity, or non-union, company may be formed or licensed to a third party to play split weeks (fewer than eight performances) or even one-nighters in small towns and communities. The length of these runs and their profitability will depend on the strength of each show based on, among other factors, its title, cast, award recognition, and the length of its run on Broadway.

The investors in the Broadway production (sometimes referred to as the "mother company") benefit from additional companies in two ways. First, they will have an option to invest in additional first-class companies in North America, based on the amount invested on Broadway. If an investor put up 15 percent of the financing on Broadway, that investor would also have the option to invest 15 percent of the capitalization for an additional company. Second, even if an investor does not invest

---

[4] A "sit-down company" refers to a new first-class company that plays major metropolitan cities—such as Los Angeles, Boston, and Chicago—for open-ended (not limited) runs. This is as compared to first-class national tours that go to dozens of cities and are booked for limited periods of time anywhere from one to two weeks to six to eight weeks, depending on the strength of the show.

additional funds in the new company, the Broadway LP will receive a share of the proceeds earned by the producer from each additional first-class company. A typical example would be a payment to the mother company of 1 percent of the gross weekly box office receipts (payable in a pool most likely) plus 5 percent of the net profits of the additional company.

The producer will have options to produce additional companies in the other English-speaking territories—the United Kingdom, Australia and New Zealand, and South Africa. Normally, the American producer would enter into joint ventures with local producers in these territories. In some, but not all, cases, the Broadway investors would have options to invest in these territories on the same basis as they would in North America.

Although this option is not in the APC form contract, the producer may also negotiate for the right to produce additional companies in foreign-language-speaking territories, such as Europe, Asia, and South America. If the producer doesn't want to produce the show himself, he will often grant a license to major foreign producers, approved by the authors, who are experienced in these territories. Normally, the Broadway investors do not have the right to invest in these foreign companies, and none of the proceeds from those companies are paid to the mother company.

Finally, as discussed in the APC chapter, the producer and his investors will share in the proceeds the authors derive from the sale and exploitation of subsidiary rights, such as movie, TV, and non-first-class stage rights (stock and amateur rights) and foreign stage rights not produced by the Broadway producer but licensed by the authors. These participations usually run for a limited number of years, but, for a successful Broadway musical, the income can be very substantial.

In Summary

I recently had lunch with a producer of a new musical who said to me, a bit sheepishly, "You know, I'm not very good at raising money."

She and her partner needed to raise $10 million. Regardless of the strength of the play, unless you have the resources and the stomach to put up some money of your own, getting financing from others is the single most difficult task for any Broadway producer. You have to become accustomed to avoidance and rejection. While I'm on that subject: when raising money, keeping your distance from family and friends may be the better part of valor. For one thing, no one should invest in a Broadway show unless he or she can afford to lose every penny and not be affected economically in any meaningful way. If losing money in a Broadway play will change an investor's lifestyle, then the person shouldn't invest. That statement should be made to any potential investor, regardless of your familiarity with his or her financial resources. Rich people aren't accustomed to losing money; that's why they're rich.

More than anything else, as a producer, you must have a genuine and transparent passion for your show. Investing in a Broadway show is not very different from betting on that horse with long odds. Your enthusiasm and belief in a show that has both artistic merit and commercial appeal will go a long way toward persuading someone to put his money where your mouth is. For all the budgets, financial projections, and facts and figures contained in your financing papers, in the end, no one can predict a Broadway success. If that weren't the case, Joe Papp wouldn't have been the sole support for Michael Bennett on *A Chorus Line*, Carole Shorenstein Hays would have been in a bidding war to get the rights to *Fences*, and the producers of *The Book of Mormon* would most likely never have offered anyone else a chance to invest in the show.

There are at least two things to keep in mind when setting out to raise money for a Broadway show: learn from the experiences of others and try to control only those things you can control.

Learning from the mistakes of others will guide you better than trying to analyze success. It's not a bad idea to do some research on shows that have failed at the box office. It's usually pretty clear when you've seen a real bomb, critically and commercially. How often have you said, "Why was that show produced in the first place? Why would anyone invest in that?"

But failure, for many other plays, is a relative thing. Some shows never recoup, but their artistic merit and positive critical reception belie their economic failure. These are the shows that may deserve some postmortem analysis. Were their audiences too limited for Broadway? Was it relevant that the shows had no real stars and didn't have recognizable titles? Was there insufficient money in their budgets for effective advertising and marketing campaigns? Were the theaters either too small or, more likely, too large? Did the shows need more work in development before opening on Broadway? Would they have benefited from workshops or out-of-town productions? Being a Monday morning quarterback can be an easy thing, but examining shows that haven't recouped can be instructive and offer good lessons later on when you're on the line yourself.

I had that conversation with the prolific producer Jeffrey Richards about the musical *The Bridges of Madison County*, which opened in the winter of 2014 and closed after three months at a total loss. The show didn't have huge stars, but it had Kelli O'Hara, a Broadway veteran, who, along with her co-star, Steven Pasquale, delivered captivating performances for which they deservedly received glowing notices. The score was tremendous, winning both a Tony and a Drama Desk Award. What's more, the musical was based on one of the best-selling novels of the twentieth century, having sold over 50 million copies. Why didn't it sell?

I pressed Jeffrey for an answer. He said that while on the surface the novel would appear to be the strongest come-on, it probably was also a deterrent in some ways. The novel had been wildly popular with those who love romantic fiction. For women who were more discerning readers, it was essentially a guilty pleasure—something you read at home but didn't discuss with your friends.

Jeffrey said that the bulk of the novel's fans resided in the Midwest and the outer reaches of the Northeast—not a very good demographic for Broadway shows, unless you're selling a family title or a star from a highly rated TV show or series. Inveterate theatergoers thumbed their noses at the thought of attending a show based on a paperback summer novel (even though they had most likely read the book). The irony, of course, is that *The Bridges of Madison County* was probably one of the most intelligent and sophisticated musicals of the 2013–14 season.

The second bit of advice is to understand and master those things over which you have control, such as budgets, creative choices, production schedule, and advertising and marketing decisions, while not becoming distracted or obsessed by the unknown or uncontrollable—critics' reactions, competing shows in the same season, investors' gripes, the location of your theater, the weather, or Michael Riedel's tantalizing gossip column in the *New York Post* (in spite of the fact no producer on Broadway dares not read his columns each week). Fortune may favor you in some of these cases, but not often.

Above all, neither you nor the creative team should spend time worrying over what will appeal to the audience; rather, you should focus on creating a work of art the authors want to write and you want to produce. Trying to second-guess your audience is almost always a prescription for failure. It's more than a distraction—it is anathema to the creative process and can only lead to a confused and muddled vision for the show.

No one has said it better, in so few words, than our greatest living musical composer and lyricist, Stephen Sondheim, in the song "Move On" from *Sunday in the Park with George*:

> "Anything you do,
> let it come from you.
> Then it will be new."

16

The Director and Choreographer

When a producer is ready to secure a Broadway theater for his show, he and his GM will make the rounds to the three major theater owners—the Shubert Organization, the Nederlander Organization, and Jujamcyn Theaters. During the reign of Bernard Jacobs and Gerald Schoenfeld, president and chairman, respectively, of the Shubert Organization, you would make an appointment with Bernie Jacobs in his wood-paneled office sitting atop Shubert Alley. There you would be met by a heavyset, barrel-chested man with a stern grimace and severe presence. Once you got to know Bernie, if he decided you were someone he liked, you'd find that there was a gentler and kinder side of him hiding under that gruff exterior.

The fact of the matter was, if you wanted to ply your craft in the theater, you'd better have curried favor with Bernie, or at least not upset him. My twenty-year relationship with him was mercurial (as it was for many others), ranging from, "There's no one better out there. If I had my choice, you would always be the Shuberts' lawyer" to "You know, John, if I wanted to, I could crush you."

Meeting with Bernie gave you your shot at securing a Shubert house on West Forty-Fourth or Forty-Fifth Street, considered by many to be prime locations. The ever-jovial Gerry Schoenfeld might pop in at some point to say hello, but it was left to Bernie to book the houses. You would want to prepare your presentation carefully, particularly if Bernie didn't have any past experience with you. In fact, if you were new to him, you'd have to rely on your GM or lawyer to get an audience in the first place. Anyway, regardless of Bernie's familiarity with you or your colleagues, early in the conversation he would ask a question that, for him, held the key to securing a Shubert theater: "Who is your director?"

If you didn't have someone Bernie admired, both personally and professionally, or, worse, if you hadn't hired a director yet, the meeting would be over quickly. If you had a Jerome Robbins, Bob Fosse, Gower Champion, Ron Field, Tommy Tune, Michael Bennett, or Hal Prince, you'd be more than halfway to getting his attention. Such was Bernie's reliance on the reputation and track record of a director as far as betting on the success of a show.

Nothing is ever so black and white, but I tend to agree with Bernie's prejudice, especially when placing a bet on a musical. As I've mentioned before, your director should participate early on in the conceptualization of the show, not necessarily providing written material but instead contributing to the visual concept and overall style for the piece. Securing an experienced director is essential to forging a crucible in which the collaborative artistic process can take place.

As a whole, the responsibilities and burdens placed on a director for a musical are much greater than those for a straight play. The director serves as the chief organizational point person—scheduling and organizing auditions and casting, rehearsing thirty to fifty actors, and preparing for tech rehearsals, previews, and the opening. All of this requires someone who has done it all before and, preferably, more than once. Without a strong leader at the helm, you would have most likely been dismissed by Bernie Jacobs and would have had a tough time raising money for the show.

Strong business and creative management are basic criteria in any assessment of the level of risk involved in investing in what is a start-up venture. If the producer is a newcomer, it becomes critically important that he surround himself with the most able GM and a director who will guide and organize the creative and practical aspects of the show from the outset.

There is much to be said for giving young and untried talent—actors, writers, directors, or any other artist—their shot at the golden ring. However, that talent has to be nurtured and given time to mature. Broadway isn't a testing ground. Promising talent needs to be protected from being thrust prematurely into an unforgiving and ruthless arena that takes no prisoners. Putting a $15 million venture into the hands of a director who has never before been through the steamroller of creating a Broadway musical is reckless and foolhardy, both for the production and for the director's future career. Once the green button making the show a "go" is pressed, the rest is like skiing downhill on an unstable-snow-packed mountain with ever-increasing speed and pressure as you race toward the finish line—opening night. Unless everything that you *do* control has been attended to carefully and in a timely manner, the avalanche that inevitably follows will overwhelm and bury you.

The Agreement

The Stage Directors and Choreographers Society (SDC) is the union that represents theatrical directors and choreographers for Broadway, Off-Broadway, not-for-profit, and regional and dinner theaters. The most important provisions of the SDC's Broadway contract are as follows:

- Scheduling and exclusive services
- Fees and advances
- Royalties
- Participation in subsidiary rights proceeds
- Ownership of copyright
- Options to direct additional companies

Scheduling and Exclusive Services

Upon entering into an SDC contract, the producer is obliged to file the agreement with the union and pay the first one-third installment of the director's fee and advance. Some producers hold off signing an SDC contract so as to avoid making these payments early on, particularly if the intention is to have a protracted period of development, including workshops and/or regional productions. The problem is that until an agreement is fully signed and filed, the director cannot be legally bound to be available to the producer on an exclusive basis and can always take on another potentially conflicting job.

In practice, most producers assume this risk. If the director wants the show and is enthusiastic about working with the creative team, he will usually sort out his schedule and make himself available down the road. Once a schedule is finalized, the director provides non-exclusive services prior to rehearsals, which become exclusive beginning with rehearsals and continuing through the official opening on Broadway.

Fees and Advances

Directors receive up-front (prior to the commencement of performances) both a fee and an advance. Today, for Broadway, the minimum total is $65,445 split $26,180 as a fee and $39,265 as an advance. For choreographers, the minimum total is $54,405 split $21,680 as a fee and $32,725 as an advance. For those who provide both direction and choreography, the minimum total is $119,850, split $47,860 as a fee and $71,990 as an advance. These minimums are routinely increased every few years as a result of collective bargaining between the union and the producers.

In practice, agents for well-known directors with a successful track record will negotiate for greater amounts ($150,000 to $200,000) and will try to get as much as possible in fees, which are not recoupable against royalties, and less in advances.

Royalties

Minimum royalties are three-fourths of 1 percent of gross box office receipts for directors, one-half of 1 percent for choreographers, and 1.25 percent for hyphenates (director/choreographers). The union permits the use of royalty pools in lieu of paying on the net gross, but it dictates minimums of 2.5 percent of net operating profits for directors, 1 percent for choreographers, and 3.5 percent for hyphenates. Again, for those directors who are more established and have precedents with greater compensation, royalties are usually much higher—2 or 3 percent for directors, 1 to 1.5 percent for choreographers, and as much as 5 percent for hyphenates. With these higher royalties, the shares in a royalty pool will naturally be much greater.[1]

The fees payable to directors prior to the Broadway opening will depend on the length of the time commitment and the extent of work required, and are usually payable in installments over the development period. For readings, workshops, and not-for-profit productions, directors normally receive fees (for workshops) or fees and royalties (for developmental productions), subject to minimums set forth in the union contract.

---

[1] See chapter nine, "Royalty Pools."

Participation in Subsidiary Rights Proceeds

For musicals, many established directors receive a share of the authors' proceeds derived from the disposition of subsidiary rights. If the director has been instrumental from the outset in the writing of the show and provided valuable insight in developing the concept and vision for the piece, then he may be entitled to share in these continuing rights, provided both the authors and the producer agree to the manner in which this share is borne among the parties. There is usually a separate agreement for this deal between the authors, the director, and the producer.

The percentage share of subsidiary rights given to the director can either be assumed 100 percent by the authors out of their share, or deducted off the top and shouldered by both the authors and the producer. For example, assume the director is to receive 3 percent of 100 percent of subsidiary rights income, and the authors and the producer receive 60 percent and 40 percent of that income, respectively. On $1,000 of subsidiary income, 3 percent, or $30, goes to the director, leaving a balance of $970 to be divided 60 percent, or $582, to the authors and 40 percent, or $388, to the producer.

The legendary hyphenates can receive as much as 5 percent in a royalty pool and 25 percent of the authors' subsidiary rights proceeds.

An important provision that's often forgotten in these arrangements is to have a vesting schedule so that the director's full share of subsidiary income is earned in installments, beginning with the development phase through opening night. In this way, if the director is fired or quits prior to opening on Broadway, the unvested portion of the original director's share of subsidiary income could be offered to the replacement director, if appropriate.

Finally, in return for receiving a share of future income, the director acknowledges that any contributions he makes to the script become the property of the authors, thus waiving any claims of authorship in the play.

Ownership of Copyright

SDC agreements require that the producer acknowledge that the director owns the copyright in his direction and the choreographer in her choreography. The copyright law explicitly states that choreography is protected by copyright. Before there were video recorders, choreographers used Laban Movement Analysis (Labanotation) for describing and documenting their choreography. Today, if possible, filing a video of the choreography with the US Copyright Office is clearly a better option.

Copyright protection for direction is another matter altogether. Stage direction is not expressly mentioned in the US copyright law, but that doesn't necessarily mean that it isn't protectable either under the statute or by common law.[2] There have been a number of lawsuits alleging copyright infringement of direction, but all those cases were settled by the litigants, without a judge or jury making a final decision on the merits of the action.

There are those who oppose copyright protection for direction, arguing that commonplace and ordinary stage directions, such as entrances and exits, like ideas, are not copyrightable and legal protection would stifle creativity. These critics contend that protecting direction would create an overly large and undiscriminating umbrella of protection, resulting in a chilling effect on new directors reviving older works. Authors have also voiced objection, saying that a director asserting ownership of stage movement can conflict with the writer's stage directions contained in a script. Because of this concern, the second-class-rights-licensing organizations, such as Tams-Witmark and Music Theatre International,[3] no longer distribute stage manager's scripts (which contain the director's detailed blocking and staging notes) to their licensees in order to satisfy directors that they are not aiding in the misappropriation of their property.

The opposing view says that a carefully constructed statute or judicial opinion should address those concerns and also provide protection for overall original and distinctive direction, particularly when tied to a specific set design or concept. If not under the copyright law, the courts could find some kind of limited protection against wholesale copying, as they do for ideas, through theories of unjust enrichment and unfair

[2] That part of the law that is derived from custom and judicial precedent (case law), as opposed to statutes.

[3] These organizations license the subsidiary stage rights in plays and musicals, after the first-class rights have been exploited, to schools, civic and other amateur groups, and for smaller commercial productions.

competition, while at the same time avoiding vagueness and protecting the rights of authors. In the end, it would simply be a matter of fairness.

Options to Direct Additional Companies

Directors normally have the option to direct additional companies, including all first-class sit-down and touring companies in North America and English-speaking companies in the UK, Australia, New Zealand, and South Africa. The director is entitled to advance notice of the formation of these companies and has a limited period of time to elect whether or not he wishes to exercise his right to direct. If he so elects, his advance, fee, and royalty payments are usually pre-negotiated.

If the director elects not to direct, the producer has the right to use his direction in the additional companies, subject to paying no fee or advance and a reduced royalty in order to allow for compensation to be paid to a substitute director who will have the right to use all or some of the original direction. The original director will usually receive one-half of his original royalty. A formula more favorable to the original director would provide that his royalty be reduced only by the amount actually paid to the new director, with a floor of one-half of his royalty. Therefore, if the original director receives a 3 percent royalty and the new director receives 1 percent, the original director's royalty would be reduced only to 2 percent, and not by one-half to 1.5 percent.

It is rare for a director to get unrestricted options to direct productions in foreign-language territories. About fifteen years ago, however, some directors were concerned that foreign productions were using the same set designs from the original productions but not paying for the direction. The directors argued that their direction and staging were inextricably tied to one another and demanded that they receive an option to direct any additional production that used the same physical production as used on Broadway.

Authors have criticized producers for agreeing to this option. They argue that it can often be difficult to determine when these two elements are truly intertwined. To tie direction to scenery, they argue, places burdensome artistic and financial restrictions on foreign producers.

If the Broadway producer elects not to pursue a foreign production, the rights revert to the authors. Authors are not bound by the obligations found only in the agreement between the director and the Broadway producer. An independent foreign producer who is granted rights in the play directly by the authors and who also acquires design rights directly from the set designer would have the unfettered right to hire another director without any restrictions, provided, of course, the new director does not infringe on any of the original director's rights. That, of course, would bring us full circle back to our prior discussion of ownership of copyright in stage directions.

17

The Designers

The artist in me cries out for design.

—Robert Frost

All of the Broadway designers, including set, costume, lighting, and sound, are members of the United Scenic Artists, Local USA 829, an autonomous union affiliated with the International Alliance of Theatrical Stage Employees (IATSE). The union was organized to protect the craft standards, working conditions, and wages for the decorative and entertainment industries. The union sets minimum fees and advances for its members ranging from a high of $38,000 for costume designers of very large-scale musicals to a low of $9,000 for lighting designers of single-set musicals.

For *established* designers, these fees and advances can be much higher, rising to as much as $60,000 or more for scenery and costumes, and $40,000 for lighting. In addition, royalties of 1 percent of the net gross or more may be paid to the very top designers from a royalty pool.

Since designers own the copyright in their designs but do not share in the play's subsidiary rights proceeds, they often seek compensation from third parties who purchase their sets from other producers. There is often confusion between ownership of the physical set or costumes (owned by the producer) and the copyright in the designs themselves (owned by the designer). When buying or leasing a used set and costumes from another producer, it is necessary to make a deal directly with the designer for use of her copyright in the designs. In a limited number of instances, there are minimum payments set out in the union's collective bargaining agreement, but in some cases those minimums do not apply.

Nothing will guide a producer better in choosing a designer than actually seeing a designer's work onstage or her portfolio of work (in the case of costumes and sets) so that you may assess for yourself whether or not her aesthetic appeals to you. Set designers have their own signature styles. Some excel in period and traditional designs; others tend to be more abstract or less literal, while still others are eclectic. Some costume designers are particularly well known for period costumes for straight plays and others specialize in large-scale musicals. It's slightly more difficult to categorize lighting and sound designers. Ultimately, the designers' compatibility with the director and the authors' vision for the piece will dictate your choices, as will availability and cost.

Finally, as I've mentioned before, bringing the design team into the development process at an early stage is also desirable in order to start the process of physically shaping the show. It's often the case that the architecture of the set design will suggest, or even dictate, to the director his blocking and movement of the actors. As we saw in the previous chapter on directors, this is why the use of the original scenic design in later productions will perforce cause the director to mimic the original staging.

What Is the First Priority—the Play or the Set?

It's a sign of the times that many musicals today, perhaps misreading the legacy of past British musicals, often place undue emphasis on visual and other special effects at the sacrifice of the play itself in an attempt to reach an audience's pleasure zones. Rather than supporting the authors' material, the physical design can sometimes overwhelm and thereby diminish it. Perhaps the producers of these shows are responding to what they perceive as the public's demand for spectacle and pyrotechnics in return for high ticket prices.

The musical *Spider-Man: Turn Off the Dark* is a good example. On its face, it seemed like a producing coup to exploit the live stage rights to this famous Marvel franchise and to secure Julie Taymor (*The Lion King*) to direct and U2 to compose the score. Leaving aside the out-of-control budgets (both production and operating) for the show, in hindsight I wonder if it wasn't a miscalculation from the outset to attempt to compete with the original $100 million-plus film and its sequels, all of which had unlimited technical and visual effects meant to seduce and mesmerize an audience. For all the flying wizardry used in the theatrical version, it all seemed tame and anticlimactic in comparison to the blockbuster films. Once the book, music, and lyrics become secondary to the physical impact of a piece, you've effectively robbed the theater of what it has to offer better than any other medium—a live emotional intimacy and immediacy checked only by the distance between the actors and the audience. Everything else should strengthen and support that alchemy, not diminish or obliterate it.

In fact, I would argue that the true test of a musical's longevity and universality is whether or not it can withstand different directorial and physical conceptions. One example is Stephen Sondheim's masterpiece, *Sweeney Todd* (book by Hugh Wheeler). The original 1979 production, directed by Hal Prince, was presented at the Gershwin Theatre (then known as the Uris), the largest of the Broadway theaters, having a seating capacity of more than 1,900. The operatic quality of the musical material, its Grand Guignol–like theme, and the huge theater seemed to dictate that everything about the production be oversized. The scale of Eugene Lee's Tony Award–winning design was enormous, ensuring that it would "fill the space" and support the ferocity and power of the music and text.

Partly out of economic concerns, but also for aesthetic reasons, subsequent revivals reexamined the play, particularly its physical demands. Both the 1989 production (directed by Susan Schulman) and the one in 2005 (directed by John Doyle) drastically reduced the size and scope of the physical layout in very different ways—Schulman's set surrounded the audience, occupying all four walls of the Circle in the Square Theatre, and Doyle used a unit set that made simple yet clever adaptations for each scene change. These designs, in their inventiveness and simplicity, served as effective backdrops for the authors' contributions. Wheeler's book and Sondheim's score, along with riveting performances, took center stage, resulting in an even deeper appreciation for this complex work. All this is to suggest that a musical shouldn't rely exclusively on any particular design or visual concept if it wants to stand the test of time and benefit from other artists' scenic concepts.

Costumes: Where Aesthetics Meet Practicality

By and large costume designs need to adhere to the script's time and place, and to the characters' socioeconomic status. The range is enormous—the nineties attire of New York City's downtown youth in the musical *Rent* has little in common with the sartorial opulence of London society in an eighteenth-century comedy by Richard Sheridan. Of course, the producer's budget can also impose practical constraints, but the most ingenious designers somehow manage (often miraculously) to overcome even those obstacles.

Costume design can also be dictated by scenic changes and the director's staging. For example, actors playing on a raked floor (built at an angle of fifteen degrees or more) or requiring a quick change (to be effected in fifteen or fewer seconds) may well need costumes that can satisfy these temporal and physical demands. Consider Theoni Aldredge's design for Effie's costume change during the number "I Am Changing" in *Dreamgirls*. Here the character's everyday street clothes magically disappear in an instant to reveal a shimmering floor-length gown as the scene switches from an audition to a live performance at a nightclub. All this as the music modulates, the lighting's palette changes, and the lyrics tell us of the character's new point of view. Music, lyrics, set, lighting, costumes, and staging all combine within seconds to move the audience along with the narrative and the character's motivation.

Sculptors of Light and Shadows

In choosing a lighting designer, your director will want someone who will devise lighting plots that complement the set design by carving up the space onstage in a way that gives specific meaning to a scene or dramatic moment. At its most effective, lighting can tell us the time and place for the action. Consider Tharon Musser's lighting for *A Chorus Line* (still, forty years later, the primer used in most graduate school courses in lighting design). When the dancers recount their personal memories in song and dance, stepping back in time, the lighting becomes richly colorful and sculptured, as best exemplified by the Mondrian-like colored squares outlined on the stage's floor during the third montage scene of "Hello Twelve, Hello Thirteen, Hello Love." This is in stark contrast to the glaring white-hot light that washes over all of the dancers when they line up downstage and play out their scenes in real time with Zach, the director, sitting at the back of the house. By switching back and forth between white and colored light, Musser helps us to understand what is "real" and what is memory or fantasy.

Sound and Fury

Sound design can be the source of gnashing of teeth during tech rehearsals and the preview period for the creative team and the producer:

- The lyricist can't understand the words.
- The composer can't hear the brass and hates the synthesizers (but the producer won't pay for any more musicians).
- The actors can't hear themselves or the orchestra.
- The director thinks the sound is just right downstairs but inaudible upstairs.
- The producer is at his wit's end trying to calm everyone down.
- The sound designer can't understand what all the fuss is about.

Consider how relatively simple life was prior to the sixties when there were no mikes or any other amplification. In a musical, the pure, unenhanced acoustic sound of Ethel Merman's towering voice would reach the back rows of the balcony. And when we heard the forgotten pure unadorned sound of the orchestra in Lincoln Center's 2008 revival of *South Pacific*, we were reminded of the thrill of experiencing a full twenty-eight-piece orchestra playing the show's original overture.

I can recall hearing an amplified orchestra for the first time at a performance of *Promises, Promises* in 1968. I was unaware that amplified "sound" had entered the theater. When the band began playing, I thought I was listening to a record—not a live orchestra. Many around me sitting in the mezzanine were stretching their necks to see if there were live musicians in the pit. It was an odd sensation. And it became even more unsettling when the actors started to speak and sing through speakers dotted around the house. It was if they were off in some faraway place.

Today, audiences have become inured to amplification, which became ubiquitous after the introduction of rock and roll and contemporary music. But a pure acoustic sound is still uniquely and extraordinarily beautiful. Visiting the Metropolitan Opera House or Carnegie Hall to listen to unamplified sound from singers and players will demonstrate what we have sacrificed in the theater. At a concert performance given by Patti LuPone several years ago, LuPone sat on the apron of the stage and sang, a cappella and without a mike, a mesmerizing rendition of "Moonshine Lullaby" from *Annie Get Your Gun*. The audience was hearing LuPone's pure, unamplified voice for the first time that evening. All the artificiality of sound equipment had vanished and the connection between performer and audience was intimate and immediate. I'm sure for many in the audience that moment was as surprising as was the moment for me when I first heard, decades earlier, an amplified overture in *Promises, Promises*.

The best sound designers ultimately find the right balance—literally by having the sound fill the house seamlessly and metaphorically by satisfying all of the competing and often conflicting demands of the artists. Designers also have to work under severe time constraints since they must perfect everything during short tech and preview periods. Every play and every theater present their own peculiar problems for the designer. Ironically, in the end, the highest compliment one can pay to a sound designer of a straight play is to say his work is imperceptible—that is, helping the audience sense, as much as possible, that they are "hearing" the play in a pure and unadorned way. And, for a musical, if he can satisfy the audience's desire to understand and appreciate the book, music, and lyrics in equal measure, he has achieved a major accomplishment.

A Final Reflection on the Mutual Dependency between Scenic Design and the Play

There is a long-standing principle held by many architects that "form follows function."[1] Does it apply to theatrical scenic design? If a script calls for a living room for six characters, one might assume the set design would be just that—four walls, carpeting, doors, windows, and appropriate props and furniture. However, many of our great set designers do not heed that prescription. Consider Boris Aronson's checkerboard set for *Company*, where the performers played out their roles in an abstract

[1] The phrase is attributed to the late nineteenth- and early twentieth-century American architect Louis Sullivan.

setting, unrecognizable as anything literal except, perhaps, in its suggestion of the apartment complex or other urban setting specified in George Furth's book. Or consider the recent revival of *A View From the Bridge*, with an extraordinary abstract design by Jan Versweyveld in which Arthur Miller's classic realistic play is performed with nothing more than a few props within a bare bones cage-like setting.

When those designs break through the script with an independent voice, they can inspire the director and authors to explore more options to express the dramatic components of the play. Those opportunities arise only when the collaboration process takes hold early on in the development of the production, making it possible for the artistic team to stretch their creative muscles as they articulate commonly held visions. And in those cases when the design inspires, or even dictates, the director's staging of particular scenes or musical numbers, function follows form—which is a true testament to a designer's talent and wisdom.

18

The Producer's Deal

> A producer is a saboteur who tries to infiltrate the passivity of viewers and to create impressions that are lasting.
>
> —Bill Moyers

The most urgent question every producer client of mine asks me at some point is, "When do I get paid?"

After all, as a producer you've anted up for a lawyer, GM, staff, authors, cast, crew, and an army of others you may never meet. But it's not always clear if you'll ever get to the other side of the ledger where you can enter some income for yourself. I've already discussed in previous chapters the producer's share of net profit income and his relationship with his investors.[1] Here, I'll focus on the monies directly coming to the producer.

Going back to the thirties and forties, other than being reimbursed for their out-of-pocket expenses, producers looked to their share of adjusted net profits as their sole income for producing a play.[2] There were no fees or weekly royalty payments. The producer's primary motivation was to see that the play recovered its production costs—otherwise, he was left out in the cold along with his investors.

In theory, a show's net profits were divided between the sweat equity (hard work) of the producer and the investment equity (money) of the investors. If you think about this simple proposition, it made a lot of economic sense. The only expenses associated with the show were direct, out-of-pocket costs to create and build the show and manage it after the opening. The objective was to spend as little as possible so that the investors would get their money back and, thereafter, they and the producer could reap the reward of profits quickly.

---

[1] See chapter fifteen, "Finding the Money," and chapter nine, "Royalty Pools."

[2] See chapter fifteen for a definition of adjusted net profits.

Over time, as shows took years to develop and needed to run six to ten months (or even longer) to recoup their costs, producers looked to weekly royalties and eventually fees to compensate themselves during these long stretches of time before realizing any net profits.

That brings us to today, when the producer commonly gives himself the following deal:

- Fee of $50,000 to $100,000, payable out of a musical's production budget. The number is considerably smaller for dramatic plays. This is a relatively recent development (the last fifteen years or so) and is not universally taken by all producers.
- Royalty of 3 percent of the net gross, payable along with the creative talent in a royalty pool. At least 1 percent out of this royalty is often shared with so-called big-hitter investors who have a substantial financial stake in the show. On occasion, I've even seen a weekly fee for the producer, say $1,500 or more, in addition to a share of the royalty pool.
- Weekly office charge of $1,500 to $2,500 for the day-to-day expenses of running an office. (Investors should be wary of producers who take weekly office charges and *also* charge miscellaneous costs to the production.)
- A share of the adjusted net profits.[3]

At some point, a fair balance between excessive and reasonable compensation for the producer should come into play. It's easy for multi-millionaire producers to waive anything but a weekly royalty and a share of net profits as their compensation. The success or failure of a Broadway show isn't going to change their lifestyles. For many others, however, it's simply too long a wait not to receive some income. As we've seen, today it can take five years or more for a show to evolve from an idea to a production and then, after the show opens, a year or more to recover the investment and begin earning net profits. In the distant past, the whole process could take less than a year and producers produced five or six shows a year.

---

[3] See chapter fifteen, "Finding the Money," for a description of this share.

In the long run, producers should be mindful of the deleterious effect their excesses may have on attracting new investments, especially from first-time investors who often are very savvy in other businesses. They will read the show's offering literature and see that, while they wait months or years for a payday, the producer is raking in fees, royalties, salaries, and office charges (shades of *Woman of the Year*?). Both producer and investor are taking a measurable risk when a show is produced as they pool their services and money for a chance to share in the equity of the enterprise. Given the protracted time necessary to reach profits, it's not unreasonable for a producer to include a royalty for his years of hard work and to recover his expenses. Beyond that, a producer needs to pause, look at himself in the mirror, and think of the future consequences.

Billing

This is not complicated. As the lead producer, your name will be listed first, before all others. It's usually in a type equal to all other producers and always above the title of the play. If there is a mob scene of producers and investors getting credit, then the general partner or managing partner may separate himself from the others by taking the first line for himself and any other general partners or managing partners.

The type of producer credit seen in *Playbill* is usually not included in other print advertising. Most producers recognize that valuable ad space should be dedicated to billing that is either required by contract or necessary to drive ticket sales. For the public, the producers' names are mostly irrelevant. So much for fame.

19

Auditions and Casting

> An actor is totally vulnerable. His total personality is exposed to critical judgment—his intellect, his bearing, his diction, his whole appearance. In short, his ego.
>
> —Alec Guinness

Very few elements of a production are immutable: If act 1, scene 3 isn't working, ask the bookwriter to rewrite it or get the director to restage it; if a song is proving problematic, try a new orchestration or ditch it altogether; and if you can't see the actors in act 2, scene 3, turn up the wattage.

But if the casting of your show isn't right, you may be in for more serious trouble. After seeing a show, how often have you said, "He was seriously miscast," or "She can dance, but she sure can't act." Those comments are due either to a casting mistake on the part of the creative team, or to the unforeseen shortcomings of the actor. Sometimes it's a little of both.

Replacing a cast member can be costly and cause morale problems among the cast. It's never something a producer does lightly. All the more reason why selecting the right casting agent and devoting sufficient time and money to the auditioning process are as critical as any other decision you will make while producing your show.

There are only a handful of experienced casting agents for Broadway shows. Each has his or her own strengths and weaknesses and personal style of interacting with directors and the creative team. The agent will have preferences and recommendations, but, ultimately, the best casting agents let the creative team find their own way and are cautious about interfering unduly in the process unless they believe that a serious mistake in casting may occur. Guiding and advising their clients are the best talents of an agent—being overbearing or intrusive is inappropriate.

What is of particular value is the agent's knowledge about the background and reputation of an actor, information that can't be found on a resume or discerned in an audition. Before you make any final decision about an actor, it is always wise to ask your agent about what he or she has heard about the actor's behavior and work ethic in previous shows. Regardless of an actor's talent, beware of anyone who is known to breed unhappiness and discord among a cast, or is notorious for being late or not a team player. Even one chronic complainer or prima donna can poison the backstage atmosphere of a show. Since your director selects the cast (subject to the authors' and producer's approvals), it's important to hire a casting agent with whom the director will feel comfortable and, ideally, has had some previous experience. Casting a musical with thirty to forty actors is an arduous process that can take six months or more, so the director had better like your casting agent, and vice versa.

The audition process involves conducting both invited auditions for members of Actors' Equity Association (the actors' union) and at least one open call, which is an audition open to any actor, regardless of whether or not he or she is a member of Equity. For a big musical, especially one with advance word of mouth, hundreds of actors may vie for a role. Since many of them will not be suitable for a role, preliminary conferences with the director and creative team will guide the casting agent in making some initial cuts without involving the director. Even so, there are some directors who insist on attending even the so-called cattle calls, when hundreds of non-equity hopefuls audition, thinking they may discover a fresh new talent worthy of getting her first big break. Bob Avian once told me that as a young dancer, even though he had an Equity card, he'd often go to the open calls, since he figured he'd have a better chance of being singled out competing against dozens of amateurs as opposed to veteran dancers in an invited call.

After the agent has winnowed down the possibilities, the director, choreographer, authors, and producer will hold as many auditions as necessary to find the show's cast. The audition team should also include the musical director, who, along with the composer and lyricist, can assess the actors' vocal abilities. As producer, if you choose to attend auditions (and I would urge that you definitely attend the final auditions), be certain you take notes so you can share your specific comments with the others.

It will all become a blur after a while if you don't make shorthand reminders of those actors you particularly liked or disliked. I am notoriously bad at remembering names, so in addition to noting the actor's plusses and minuses, I often add visual reminders such as "dyed red hair," "crooked teeth," or "Hepburn face."

Auditions for roles that require a triple threat (a performer who can act, sing, and dance) can drag on for months. The actor will first have to pass muster with the choreographer ("Can she move?"), then the musical director ("She can sing, but does she have the vocal style compatible with this composer's score?"), and, finally, the director ("Can she convey the requirements of a particular role?"). If the actor has managed to survive all three hurdles, she's in the running for the final round of auditions.

The challenge is that the creative team has to predict which actors will be able to fulfill very specific requirements of any particular role. It may be cold comfort to those who are eliminated, but it is often the case that a performer, although an accomplished singer, dancer, and actor, simply doesn't have the right bearing or appearance for the role. Being eliminated may have little to do with the actor's overall qualifications, but rather may be due to an aspect of the character that doesn't match the actor's profile or the creative team's vision of what the role requires.

Once hired, every actor will be required to sign a contract that is either for a principal role or for chorus—a determination Equity makes after reviewing the script. For chorus, the contract is referred to as a "run-of-the-play" contract. Once hired as a member of the chorus, that actor is engaged for the entire run of the show on Broadway. Chorus members cannot be fired unless there is good cause, such as being in breach of their contracts or in violation of Equity's rules.

For principals, the length of time or term of the agreement can be as short as three months or as long as a year. During that time, the salary is fixed, as are all the other terms of the contract. The actor is bound to stay with the show during that term and the producer cannot fire the actor, unless for cause. Otherwise, if an actor has behaved properly but is dismissed because the producer or director is unhappy with her performance, the actor will be entitled to receive all of the compensation under her contract for the remainder of the term following termination. This can be a serious economic burden to the production depending on how many actors are dismissed and the compensation remaining on their contracts.

When it becomes necessary to replace a star, the stakes can be very high. Not only could the production face hundreds of thousands of dollars in damages, but the adverse notoriety for the actor and the production can be severe. A decision to replace a star is made very rarely, but, when it occurs, it is usually self-evident to everyone, including the star, that a change needs to be made.

Another non-monetary consideration—but a crucial one—is the effect firing a cast member will have on the morale of the cast as a whole. Strong emotional bonds are quickly formed among cast members, regardless of ranking or experience. They've all been in the trenches and they're the few who survived. Ideally, if the show has a star, he or she should be the leader of the company, holding it together in times of stress and supporting his or her fellow actors in times of personal hardship or injury. Hearing that an actor has been fired almost always gives rise to a crisis in morale among the cast and a fear of, "What if I'm next?" Ultimately, the cast will regroup and regain their confidence, but it is important, as the producer, to be particularly sensitive to the cast's reaction to any cast change and to give them assurances that, while regretful, a change had to be made in order to realize a long and prosperous run.

A star can be replaced at different times during the run of the play, even after a year or so. In the Broadway production of *The Producers*, Henry Goodman replaced Nathan Lane after his contract expired a year after the opening. Prior to inviting the press to review Goodman's performance, the producers decided to fire him. The show received some adverse publicity as a result, and it was obviously a blow to Goodman, a highly respected and accomplished British actor. In an interview with the *Times* of London, Goodman said: "My first reaction was to laugh out loud. Later, the thing that really hurt was the thought of my family and all those people who had faith in me."

In a peculiar way, this event was a bad omen for the play. Casting the two leads of the musical continued to be problematic for additional companies in the United States, London, and abroad. Somehow, the specific chemistry that was struck between Nathan Lane and Matthew Broderick in the original Broadway production proved to be exceedingly difficult to duplicate, and, ultimately, none of the subsequent productions could match the enormous success of the original.

Sometimes, a replacement can occur as early as a workshop. To revisit the star-crossed production of *Ballroom*: Dolores Gray, a stage and screen musical star of the forties and fifties, was hired by Michael Bennett to play the leading role of Bea. After a month of workshop rehearsals, it became clear to everyone, including Ms. Gray, that she could not handle the many demands of the role. Dorothy Loudon was hired as Gray's replacement and went on to play the role on Broadway. Since the replacement was made very early on in the development of the show, both the show and the star avoided any serious damage or undue embarrassment.

In both examples, the production (that is, the producers and the creative team) made a miscalculation—the actor appeared to satisfy all the prerequisites for the role during auditions, but somehow the end result didn't pan out. On some occasions the actor might have been unrealistic about her ability to fit the bill. Rarely, if ever, are there any invidious or nefarious intentions. In most cases, the best advice for both sides is to rise above incriminations, arrive at a fair settlement, and put the matter behind them.

Then there are those shows that simply don't try to replace a star after his contract expires either because he is viewed by the public as being inextricably tied to the title of the play, or he is of such star power that no other actor dares step into his shoes. It would have been foolhardy to have tried to replace Hugh Jackman in the bio-musical based on Peter Allen's life, *The Boy from Oz*. Such was his drawing power that the producers suspended performances when Jackman took time off for vacation rather than try to cover for him with his understudy. More recent examples of irreplaceable stars are Al Pacino in *The Merchant of Venice*, Bette Midler in *I'll Eat You Last*, and Tom Hanks in *Lucky Guy*.

The last few examples demonstrate the recent trend in producing plays that rely predominantly, if not exclusively, on the box office appeal of a star or stars who are billed above the title of the show. For plays, such stars will commit only to a term of twelve performing weeks or so, and, for musicals, nine months to a year. These are necessarily standing room only (SRO), short-lived affairs that usually recover their investments and earn perhaps a 10 or 20 percent return. Plays, particularly musicals, that do not rely on box office stars run for years, if not decades (*The Lion King*, *Les Miz*, *Wicked*, *Cats*, the revival of *Chicago* . . .)

Coda

There is probably no more humbling and even intimidating experience than having to audition in a bare room in front of six or seven people sitting behind a long table judging your every move and each sound you make. Keep in mind that except for a select group of stars who will not audition (the thought being they're too well known and famous), auditions are required for virtually every actor who seeks a role in a play, even though he or she might have performed in dozens of Broadway shows and even won one or more awards. (Can you imagine a world-class architect or the CEO of a Fortune 500 company submitting to an interview for a job?)

Given the grueling audition process, actors are almost required to have tough hides and nerves of steel. There is probably no more vulnerable or stressful experience than auditioning (although some actors will tell you they love it). And actors do it day in and day out. Throughout the process, the actor is always aware that the odds are in favor of rejection as she bares her talents to those six or seven people who will pass judgment in the most subjective possible way. It's the responsibility of the director and casting agent to make sure that the atmosphere in the room is as relaxed and supportive as possible, and that the creative team is responsive to the performance. Above all, the director must be compassionate and sympathetic, especially to an actor who may be having a bad day. There's never an excuse for being dismissive, insulting, or anything but respectful.

While preparing for the revival of *A Chorus Line* in 2005, I decided to produce a documentary about the auditioning process with the intention of chronicling, for the first time, the pain and suffering, as well as the triumph, experienced by professional actors in search of their next job. Given that the central theme of the show is reflected in the lyrics "I need this job" and "I hope I get it," it seemed an opportunity to celebrate the acting profession. With the cooperation of Actors' Equity, I was able to secure permission to film all of our auditions, from open call to final calls. The DVD, *Every Little Step*, provides a rare backstage look at what is the second-oldest profession.

20

The Star

Don't let's ask for the moon. We have the stars.

—Bette Davis in *Now, Voyager*

Bette Davis's admonition to Paul Henreid in 1942 holds true today. Producers, theater owners, investors, and, alas, audiences, are all fixated on the stars. And producers these days have been accommodating them more and more.

For as long as anyone in the theater can remember, Broadway has been known as "the fabulous invalid," a phrase taken from the title of a 1938 play by Moss Hart and George S. Kaufman. Yes, Broadway is fabulous, but perpetually said to be dying from dwindling audiences, high costs, and big losses. In spite of this lament, the American theater has survived for over a century and made handsome fortunes for producers and their investors, theater owners, and artists. But the mighty struggle is ever present. With production costs for major musicals skyrocketing toward $20 million and straight plays costing more than $3 million, the surefire means by which producers can recoup these investments have become fewer and fewer.

The fear that the straight play on Broadway will become an extinct species has always been a concern to playwrights and serious theatergoers.[1] There have been numerous attempts to address these concerns over the past five decades. John Wharton's Playwrights Producing Company in the forties, T. Edward Hambleton's Phoenix Theatre in the sixties and seventies, and Tony Randall's National Actors Theatre in the nineties were not-for-profit, subscriber-based theater companies that

[1] I'm sure some will chastise me for using this phrase. But I'm hard put to come up with anything better to distinguish the theatergoer who seeks out new plays with serious themes and strong dramatic writing, as compared to the casual ticket buyer who mostly seeks visual spectacle, big stars, and recognizable titles. Not that there's anything wrong with that.

produced classics and new straight plays on Broadway. Each succeeded to varying degrees, the Phoenix being the most successful. However, none of these companies exists today, nor are there any other companies attempting to copy these ambitions.

By and large, the not-for-profit theaters have been, and continue to be, the incubators for new work and the development of new playwrights, or at least they should be. But as we've seen in the chapter on not-for-profits, even some of those companies can lose sight of their central mission to achieve these objectives.

Look to the Stars

Always seeking a safety net for their investors, Broadway producers today increasingly rely on major film and TV stars to ensure short-term financial success. They regularly appear in Shakespearean productions, other classics, and revivals of plays from the forties and fifties by Arthur Miller, Eugene O'Neill, and Tennessee Williams. There's little risk that Al Pacino in *The Merchant of Venice* won't sell out, regardless of the critical reception, although the size of the cast and the enormous compensation paid to stars may offer little reward to the investors beyond getting their money back.

One could go one step further by saying that if you have a star such as Denzel Washington (revivals of *Fences* and *A Raisin in the Sun*), it doesn't much matter what play he's in. He could read the proverbial phone book and sell out.

Many media stars view Broadway as a way to legitimize their acting credentials. They'd like to have a Tony on their mantelpiece next to their Oscar and Emmy. But their stopover on West Forty-Fifth Street is never very long. Their West Coast agents are usually apoplectic about their clients spending six months or more rehearsing and performing in a play for $1 or $2 million when, for the same time, they could be earning $10 or $20 million for appearing in a film.

Faced with a star committing to only twelve weeks of performances, projections for recoupment become quite simple: How much must a producer earn in weekly operating profits to pay off $3.5 million in twelve weeks? That's simple arithmetic: $3.5 million divided by twelve—or

San Francisco real estate magnate, Walter Shorenstein, whose daughter, Carole, produced August Wilson's play *Fences*. When learning of the odds against a Broadway show succeeding, he elected not to offer an investment in *Fences* to family and friends. He said, "I'll only give them back all their money if it fails." *Robin Platzer/Getty Images*

Carole Shorenstein Hays, producer of the original Broadway production of *Fences* (1987). The unlikely alchemy between Hays and Wilson somehow worked to make *Fences* one of the most profitable dramatic plays of all time. *Jemal Countess/Getty Images*

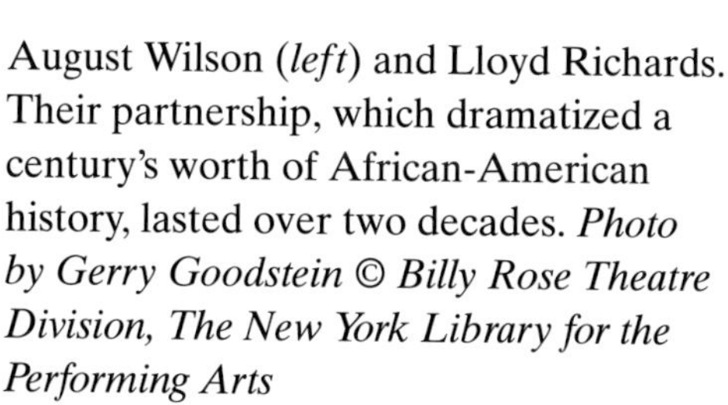

August Wilson (*left*) and Lloyd Richards. Their partnership, which dramatized a century's worth of African-American history, lasted over two decades. *Photo by Gerry Goodstein © Billy Rose Theatre Division, The New York Library for the Performing Arts*

Top: The multi-talented Mel Brooks, composer and lyricist of the musical, *The Producers*, including the song, "I Wanna Be a Producer" (2001). *Billy Rose Theatre Division, The New York Library for the Performing Arts*

Right: Michael Crawford and Sarah Brightman in the original Broadway production of *The Phantom of the Opera* (1988). Andrew Lloyd Webber ultimately persuaded Actors' Equity to permit his wife Sarah to perform the starring role in the show. *Photo by Clive Barda / ArenaPAL*

The prolific composer, Andrew Lloyd Webber. His mega-hits, *Cats* and *The Phantom of the Opera*, invaded American shores in the '80s, leaving an indelible mark on musical theater history. *Photofest*

Broadway legend Patti LuPone, as Norma Desmond, in the original London production of *Sunset Boulevard* (1993). *Photo by David Crump/© Daily Mail/Rex / Alamy Stock Photo*

Frank Langella in the 1977 Broadway revival of *Dracula*. The play was notable on the street for ushering in one of the most formidable producing teams on Broadway: Elizabeth McCann and Nelle Nugent. *Photo by Martha Swope/© Billy Rose Theatre Division, The New York Library for the Performing Arts*

The producers of the original Broadway production of *Nicholas Nickleby* (1981): Nelle Nugent and Elizabeth McCann flanked by Messrs. Schoenfeld (*center*) and Jacobs (*right*) of the Shubert Organization, and James Nederlander (*left*). McCann and Nugent managed to bring together for the first time the Hatfields and the McCoys of Broadway. *Photo by Martha Swope/© Billy Rose Theatre Division, The New York Library for the Performing Arts*

Right: Rocco Landesman, Louise Kerz Hirschfeld, Arthur Gelb, and James Binger at the Al Hirschfeld Theater in New York City. James Binger, the Brahmin head of the Jujamcyn organization, hired Rocco Landesman in 1987 to run his company, resulting in a revitalization of Broadway's third-largest theater chain. *Photo by Scott Gries/Getty Images*

Bottom: Rocco Landesman (*bottom right*) with his partners in Dodgers Productions at rehearsals for *Big River* (1985). Rocco joined the fray as the head of the underdog Jujamcyn theater chain in 1987 by attracting young producers who were seeking a change in the ways of doing business on Broadway. *Photo by Martha Swope/© Billy Rose Theatre Division, The New York Library for the Performing Arts*

Gower Champion with Wanda Richert at rehearsals for *42nd Street.* It was common knowledge that Champion was having an affair with his leading lady. *Photo by Martha Swope/© Billy Rose Theatre Division, The New York Library for the Performing Arts*

Director/choreographer Gower Champion and cast during rehearsals for the original Broadway production of *42nd Street* (1980). At the curtain call on opening night, David Merrick announced the death of Champion to a stunned audience. *Photo by Martha Swope/© Billy Rose Theatre Division, The New York Library for the Performing Arts*

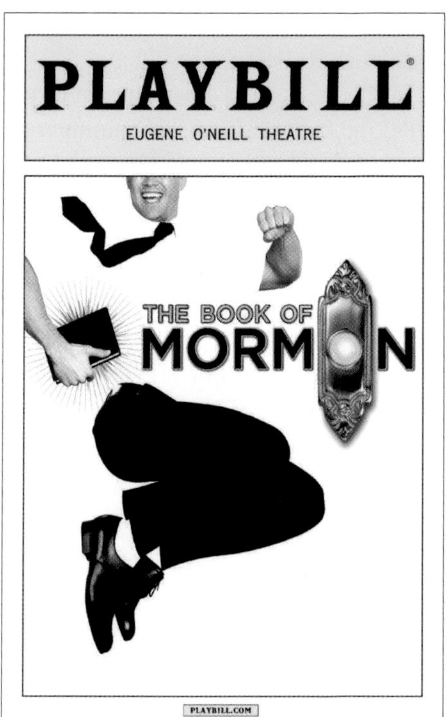

Four examples of logos that have become iconic images linked with their Broadway musicals. *Courtesy of Phil Birsch/PLAYBILL*

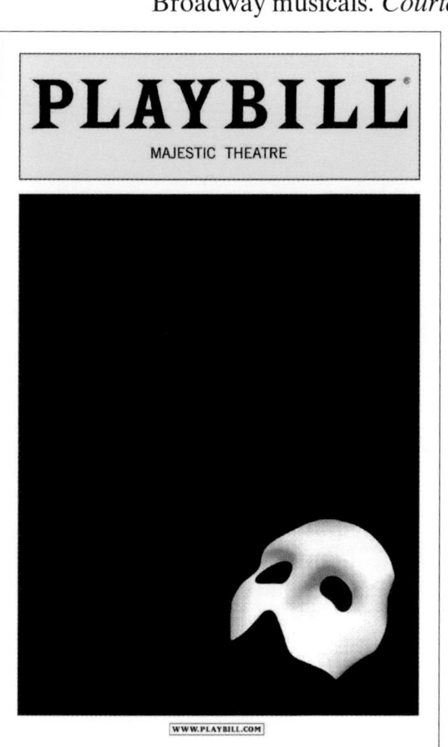

Left: Patti LuPone in the title role of *Evita* (1979). Producer Robert Stigwood and director Hal Prince turned a nervous hit into a certifiable one by devising a TV commercial that focused on LuPone's iconic victory pose and a marching chorus bearing fiery torches. *Photo by Martha Swope/© Billy Rose Theatre Division, The New York Library for the Performing Arts*

Right: Michael Bennett on Christmas Day, 1977. We had recently formed our ill-fated producing partnership, Quadrille Productions. *Photo by Nan Knighton*

Andrea McArdle, Sandy, and Reid Shelton in the original Broadway cast of *Annie* (1977). With tears in his eyes, Shelton stood atop the bar at Gallaghers Steakhouse as he read the *New York Times* rave review for the show. *Photo by Martha Swope/© Billy Rose Theatre Division, The New York Library for the Performing Arts*

approximately $290,000 per week. That's if you only want to achieve breakeven. If you'd like to get at least a 10 percent return on the investment, you'll need to make at least $321,000 in weekly operating profits each week

Those numbers, while very high, are not uncommon when plays have stars such as those just mentioned. But the number of superstars who can guarantee those grosses (so-called bankable stars), especially if the reviews are not favorable, are few and far between.

As for musicals, they too have looked to star power to provide an insurance policy for profitability. But there's a more serious economic reality for musicals. Even relatively modest revivals cost upward of $10 million, and new musicals easily cost $15 million. Stars in musicals normally commit only to a nine-month run. Unless the show is grossing $1.5 million or more each week, it is virtually impossible to recoup a musical's production costs within that short time frame. Moreover, in many cases, the original star becomes so closely associated with the play that it becomes impossible to replace him or her with someone of equal box office appeal. Stars of this magnitude simply do not replace other stars. The original star leaves and, typically, the show closes, often without recouping. Examples are Hugh Jackman in *The Boy from Oz*, Julie Andrews in *Victor/Victoria*, and Matthew Broderick in *Nice Work If You Can Get It*.

Where once Broadway was the mecca for brilliant dramas and comedies, today it is increasingly an entertainment destination not unlike Las Vegas, where tourists (domestic and foreign) flock to see headliners like Celine Dion, or spectacles like Cirque du Soleil, which are meant to dazzle the eye but never engage the intellect. I'm not suggesting that plays with celebrities credited above the title don't have a place on Broadway. On the contrary, these plays and blockbuster musicals are the engines that keep the street alive and kicking. But the plethora of these kinds of shows, as compared to the scarcity of new plays with superb veteran theater actors (not superstars), is somewhat disheartening.

The Exceptions

Every once in a blue moon, a play like *August: Osage County* comes along as the exception that proves the rule. Charles Isherwood of the

New York Times called this remarkable work by Tracy Letts "the most exciting new American play Broadway has seen in years." His review, along with dozens of other raves, assured the play a Tony, a Pulitzer Prize, and a long and profitable run. The same holds true for the British import *The Curious Incident of the Dog in the Night-Time*, adapted from Mark Haddon's novel by Simon Stephens, winner of the West End's Olivier Award and the Tony Award for Best Play. Neither of these plays employed stars. By stint of their superior writing, superb acting, and rave reviews, they attracted not only the so-called serious theatergoers but a broad-based audience of many different stripes.

As for musicals, consider *Once*, an intimate one-set musical that took the Tony for Best Musical in 2012. It had no stars and was based on an independent film that few people saw or knew about. What it did have was an appealing love story, an original score, and impeccable staging and choreography. The critics' favorable reviews put it over the top, particularly that of Ben Brantley of the *New York Times* who had given it a rather tepid review Off-Broadway ("a little too twee, too conventionally sentimental") but subsequently did a rare turnabout when he re-reviewed it on Broadway ("as vital and as surprising as the early spring"). It also benefitted and built its audiences from favorable word of mouth, not an insignificant factor in keeping a musical alive. Finally, and perhaps as important as any other factor, its operating and production costs were significantly lower than those of most other musicals.

A Star Was Born

Producers have always sought stars in musicals—Mary Martin, Ethel Merman, Robert Preston, Gwen Verdon. But a closer examination of the stars of the past versus the stars on Broadway today reveals what my good friend the producer Elizabeth McCann reminded me of the other day: "In the old days it was Broadway that *made* stars." Not today.

The Mermans and Martins were introduced to audiences and discovered on Broadway. And these stars returned time and time again to open new musicals which, in some cases, were written with them in mind by writers such as Cole Porter and Rodgers and Hammerstein. In later years, these stars attempted to parlay their fame into films, only to find that Hollywood often had its own theories of who was needed to sell a movie musical. Carol Lawrence of *West Side Story* lost the leading role of Maria to Natalie Wood in the film version. And the director Robert Wise chose Julie Andrews over Mary Martin for the role of Maria in *The Sound of Music*, an ironic twist of fate considering that ten years earlier Warner Bros. turned its back on Andrews in favor of Audrey Hepburn to play Eliza in *My Fair Lady*.

Today, it's mostly the other way around. The West Coast discovers and cultivates the stars whom producers import to Broadway for what they hope will be limited but risk-free opportunities. It's never a sure thing, but if the star is big enough, it's as close as you can get. Unknown actors still have successful debuts and breakthrough performances on Broadway, but they and their agents soon seek out a West Coast career to find financial security and wider public recognition.

There's not much point to bemoaning all of this. The positive point of view is that the live theater is slowly coming into its own as part of the worldwide media, not only as an integral part of film and TV but also the digital universe and social media. Stars such as Hugh Jackman, Helen Mirren, and Patrick Stewart have international profiles and move effortlessly and brilliantly among all media. They are box office stars who are at home both onstage and on the screen.

In the near future, Broadway plays may well find their niche in live HD broadcasts in movie theaters, in the same way operas have reached new audiences. And there may be other opportunities as Netflix, Amazon, and other streaming services expand their appetites for new programming. Mark Rylance, one of the greatest English-speaking actors today, might become a household name if his performance of *Twelfth Night* were broadcast in HD internationally or streamed on Netflix. Although the contrary view is that HD performances in movie theaters rob the theater of its unique impact as a live medium, a live broadcast can still offer a spontaneity not present in other media. A corollary benefit is to expand audiences, particularly young audiences, who otherwise cannot afford or do not live close enough to experience a Broadway show in the flesh.

Producers need to embrace these fast-moving trends if they are to compete with the sheer volume and speed with which younger audiences are bombarded by information, advertising, and marketing for their entertainment dollars. Just consider that a Broadway producer has at best $2 million for pre-opening advertising and marketing for a major musical. A motion picture studio can spend $50 million or more on its initial advertising campaign, and Apple's budget to introduce a new iPhone dwarfs the combined budgets of all plays and musicals that opened over the past ten years. The dollars for Broadway are scarce and the challenge is for producers to continue to explore new ways to reach the public through traditional means, such as print and media advertising, as well as HD, cellular, and Internet transmissions.

Compensation and Other Contractual Issues

A star's contract should be negotiated by whoever on your team has the most experience—most likely your GM with the help of your lawyer. If the star and her agent are familiar with Broadway standards, the job will be much easier than having to haggle with an inexperienced West Coast agent or lawyer. In many cases, a New York agent or a theatrical lawyer will be brought in to assist the star's representatives in negotiating the deal.

Money is, of course, of paramount concern. Unless the parties come to terms on the money, there's not much point in dealing with anything else. While gross deals are a rarified event for creative talent, getting a percentage of the gross box office receipts is the norm for big stars. For a musical, a typical deal would be a weekly minimum guaranteed salary of $50,000 until the weekly gross receipts reach breakeven ($700,000) and 10 percent of the weekly gross from $700,000 to $1 million, rising to 12.5 percent when the weekly gross is in excess of $1.2 million. These numbers and the benchmarks are all moving targets, depending on the budget of the show, the number of stars in the show (you can't afford to give this kind of deal to more than one star), the potential capacity of the theater, and the box office drawing power of the star.

In addition to the weekly salary, a star might get a percentage of the net profits of the show. Major stars have been known to receive 10 percent of the net gross from first dollar and 25 percent of the net profits. There may also be a cash bonus if the actor receives a Tony Award.

The perks for stars can be very extensive and expensive:

- Housing for an out-of-town star and her family (and for an assistant, nanny, and dog)
- Per diem allowance for food and other daily living expenses
- Private car or limousine service to and from the theater
- Choice of private dresser and hair and makeup assistants
- Private masseuse or access to regular massages
- Freshly painted and decorated dressing room with amenities
- Special security inside and outside the theater
- Special needs if the actor is asked to do promotional work and guest appearances (an essential for the producer)

Every major star I've ever represented or negotiated with comes up with his or her own unique demands. They can become excessive and unrealistic, particularly for actors accustomed to high-budget films or, worse, rock stars used to having an entourage when they're on tour. In one instance, I had to walk away from a deal with a pop star when his agent said, after weeks of negotiation, that her client needed a million dollars each week to make it worth his while. There will come a point when you or your general manager will have to say enough is enough. In most cases, so long as the production is being reasonably generous, and the star truly wants to play the role, compromises are made and a deal can be closed.

Other Issues

In addition to not giving away the entire store, be on guard for other approvals and requests that may not affect your economic bottom line directly but that nonetheless can be problematic.

If you're paying a star six figures each week, you should resist giving that star any "outs" for TV auditions, special West Coast appearances, or other similar reasons for non-appearance. This should be academic for plays, since the time commitment for the star is only a brief twelve weeks or so, but it could spell trouble for musicals, where the term can be nine to twelve months.

A star normally has the right to approve his or her co-star and the director. That's fine, of course, if these approvals are obtained early in the production schedule. But after rehearsals have begun, any such approvals should become a right-to-consultation-only in the event the director or co-star is replaced. Failing to get a star's approval of these replacements at a later date could jeopardize the entire production.

The star will insist on approval of the use of her image and likeness in advertising and marketing. Producers often ask that the star preapprove 50 percent of all photos and images prior to rehearsals to ensure they have sufficient material to mount their advertising campaign.

If the star is known for her singing ability, she will negotiate for compensation above union minimum to appear on the original cast album for the show. Actors' Equity requires all actors to receive one week's salary for each day in the recording studio. Stars will normally receive that minimum plus a royalty of 2 to 5 percent of the retail sales price (or 4 to 10 percent of wholesale) of the album.

As you might imagine, billing for a major star is never an issue—first position above the title, 100 percent of the size of the title, and appearing whenever and wherever the title appears. There is hardly ever a dispute on billing, since both star and producer want to make her name synonymous with the title of the show. In advertising prior to opening, a new musical will rely on the box office appeal of the star, particularly if the other elements are unknown commodities—all the more reason why it's so often impossible to replace a star after she leaves the show.

Billing for stars of equal stature can be problematic. Who comes first? Who's on the right and who's on the left? We read left to right, so the left is considered first position. This dilemma has been going on for decades. The producers of the 1936 Cole Porter musical *Red, Hot and Blue* came up with the ingenious solution of crossing Jimmy Durante's and Ethel Merman's names in an X pattern, in alternating black and white in the lettering and background.

Obviously, Bob Hope couldn't compete with the box office appeal of Merman and Durante, so his name was relegated to third place below the railroad crossing. But it appears that Merman got the most favorable photo placement, front and center between Durante and Hope.

A final thought: keep in mind that for your playwright, composer, lyricist, and bookwriter, the play's the thing. Stars are surely more than appurtenances, but, like all other elements in a production, they should serve the play first and foremost. And it's nice to think that the play is what comes first, and not the star who is conveniently hitched to a good title.

21

A Tale of Two Divas

Number One

Early in 1987, Andrew Lloyd Webber's production company, the Really Useful Group (RUG), announced it planned to open *The Phantom of the Opera* on Broadway at the Shubert's Majestic Theatre in January of 1988. *Phantom* had premiered at Her Majesty's Theatre in the West End of London six months earlier and was a monster hit. Later on, Andrew announced that his wife, Sarah Brightman, who originated the leading role of Christine, would recreate the role in New York.

Foreign actors cannot obtain visas from the immigration authorities to appear on Broadway without first obtaining certification from the actors' union, Actors' Equity Association. The union is required to certify that an "alien" is either a star of international stature or someone uniquely qualified to play a specific role that cannot be filled by an American actor.[1] Today, the union rules governing the exchange of American and British actors between London and New York have become more relaxed, but in 1987, American Equity tended to keep the door barely ajar for British actors, except on rare occasions.

Michael Crawford, the original London Phantom, who had international stage and film experience, was certified by Equity to recreate the role of the Phantom on Broadway. As for Sarah Brightman, Equity's Alien Committee, the committee responsible for passing on these matters, rejected her application, finding that she did not qualify either as an international star or someone with unique abilities. Although the role of Christine was demanding, the committee felt that RUG had failed to conduct a sufficient number of auditions to find an American actor capable of performing the role.

[1] An "alien" is how the Equity union contract refers to actors based in countries other than the United States.

Andrew nonetheless was adamant that Sarah be certified, failing which he threatened to abandon plans to bring the show to New York. He had written the show for Sarah and he was determined not to have anyone or anything stand in his way. Abandoning *Phantom* would deprive hundreds, if not thousands, of actors of employment in the future. And the Broadway producers, RUG, the Shubert Organization, and Cameron Mackintosh, who were still reaping millions from *Cats*, would be deprived of making a second fortune from a Lloyd Webber hit. Ironically, it wasn't lost on anyone that this contretemps was giving a nice boost to the already hefty box office advance.

No one seemed to believe that this couldn't be settled. But neither side was blinking. As a last resort, RUG decided to appeal the Alien Committee's ruling to the full Council of Equity (the governing body of the union). Brian Brolly, managing director of RUG, enlisted my counsel as well as that of Bernard Jacobs, president of the Shubert Organization, to shore up Andrew's arguments for the hearing.

We all met on the morning of the hearing in Bernie's office to finalize our arguments and strategy. I urged Brolly, as the principal producer, to take the lead in making our presentation. I thought our position was weak on the technical merits since Sarah clearly didn't meet the standards of an international star. It would also be difficult, if not insulting, to tell these actors that no American actor could perform the role. I urged Brolly to appeal to the actors' sense of fairness—this was one artist, a composer, asking other artists, actors, to have his work presented as he always intended it to be done.

The hearing began that afternoon at two. When called upon, Equity normally convenes on Tuesdays in the council room, a large space with semicircular tiered rows of seats facing a platform stage in front. As members of the council filed in to take their seats, the atmosphere was tense but also expectant. Alan Eisenberg, the executive director of Equity, well known by Bernie and me, began by giving a dispassionate and objective summary of the Alien Committee's deliberations up to that point. He was actually very helpful and influential during all of Equity's deliberations. He was well aware of the future employment opportunities for Equity's members, but he balanced those economic concerns with deference and respect for those Equity members who maintained that the principles at stake were worth the sacrifice for the greater good. A very difficult row to hoe but Eisenberg was a consummate diplomat and had years of experience jousting with producers while calming the waters at Equity.

Brolly presented Andrew's case. He was restrained, eloquent, and professorial. It's remarkable how effective a British accent and demeanor can be in persuading Americans. Brolly appealed to the creative instincts of the council. This was not a producer's plea. There were no threats of canceling the show, but that possibility was definitely the elephant in the corner of the room. Instead, as we had discussed, Brolly, speaking for Andrew, reached out as one artist speaking to another. He analogized the situation to a painter being free to use the model of his choice without interference from outside forces. He also promised that, after Sarah left the show, there would be countless American Christines and no further requests for foreign actors.

Brolly concluded by thanking the council for hearing our appeal and then opened the floor for questions.

There were a few softball questions and the reaction was surprisingly benign. I worried that perhaps they had all made up their minds to deny the application and were just going through the motions. A few hours later, Eisenberg called us at Bernie's office to say that Sarah had been certified to play the role. We immediately called Andrew, who was delighted he could inform his wife that she would indeed have her Broadway debut.

Number Two

When Andrew had the idea of adapting Billy Wilder's classic movie *Sunset Boulevard* into a musical, I'm sure he had no idea that he would be thrust into another casting maelstrom that would attract even more attention than his struggle to get Sarah Brightman on Broadway.

Gloria Swanson's film portrayal of Norma Desmond, the aging silent-screen icon, was considered a legendary performance. So when Andrew reached out to Patti LuPone to play the role, it seemed a natural choice, since she was undisputedly the Ethel Merman of the nineties and a darling of British audiences after her triumph as Eva Perón in Andrew's *Evita* years earlier. Who could ask for more?

Previews began at the Adelphi Theatre in London's West End in the summer of 1993. The tabloids were having a field day writing about the technical problems with John Napier's gigantic set. Aside from the sheer logistical challenge of moving scenery of unprecedented tonnage, the wireless communications among the technical staff backstage were constantly being interrupted by interference from passing taxis and nearby construction crews. All of this might seem funny, but it wasn't for the actors who needed to negotiate around the stage as someone hailed a cab on the corner of Piccadilly and Regent.

Opening night was July 12, 1993. The excitement and anticipation outside the theater were palpable. It was a star-studded affair, with one of the high points being Billy Wilder walking down the center aisle to a standing ovation. Everyone in the London or Broadway theater was there, including all the New York theater owners who were hoping to catch the golden ring when the show moved across the ocean. Critics were everywhere, including Frank Rich and his wife, Alex Witchel, who agreed to meet my wife and me for a late-night drink and dessert after the party.

The opening performance was flawless. Napier's set, Norma Desmond's mansion, baroque staircase and all, behaved obediently, descending effortlessly from high above the stage and then downstage as if it were nothing more than a simple scrim. The only thing onstage that could compete with the visual spectacle was LuPone's vocal power and technique, which served the score brilliantly. The show ended with a thunderous standing ovation—everyone believing they had been witness to another great British musical hit.

The party was a lavish and elegant affair held at London's Savoy Hotel. The New York theater owners were all trying to buttonhole Andrew and Patrick McKenna, Brian Brolly's newly appointed successor at RUG, to get the inside track when the show came to Broadway. Andrew would have none of it as he presided in princely manner from room to room with his new wife, Madeleine Gurdon, in tow.

Nan and I met Frank and Alex later that evening. As was his policy, Frank didn't share any of his criticism with us. For one thing, it would have been unprofessional and, for another, I'm sure he was still formulating in his mind what he thought about the show. Nan and I both sensed, however, that he wasn't much taken by the show, but we weren't prepared for what happened the next day.

The reviews were, on the whole, mixed. Frank had some praise for the show, saying that Andrew's score was "the most interesting I've yet encountered from this composer." But then he focused his attention on LuPone, and it wasn't pretty. His take on her performance can be summed up in two words from his review: "miscast and unmoving."

The British critics were much kinder to LuPone and, in many cases, praised her performance. But RUG was planning to mount the most expensive Broadway musical ever when it exported *Sunset* to Times Square and Frank's review was anything but a minor irritation.

For a while there was no word about what Andrew was going to do. LuPone's contract promised her the role in New York and, notwithstanding Frank's review, the press and everyone else expected her to repeat the role. After all, there was no doubt she wielded as much diva power (in every good sense) as Norma had in her heyday or anyone else for that matter in the English-speaking musical theater.

The axe fell early that summer when Andrew informed LuPone that she would not be performing the role in America.

A Call Not to Arms, but to Mediate

I had met Patti LuPone a few times when she was in *Evita*. I was counsel to the American production, which was produced by my longtime client Robert Stigwood. She obviously needed legal counsel to deal with her *Sunset* contract. Bob Avian, my client and old friend from *A Chorus Line*, who was also the choreographer on Sunset, referred Patti to me.

When she called, I told her that I was sure I would be disqualified from representing her since we were counsel for RUG in America, making it likely they would ask our advice on the American production of *Sunset*. Patti nonetheless pressed me to see if there was any way I could intervene.

I agreed to call McKenna to see if he would waive any conflict for the specific purpose of trying to resolve the dispute between the parties and thereby avoiding litigation. McKenna welcomed my involvement, saying Andrew wanted to get the whole thing behind him and hoped to settle amicably with Patti. Both sides agreed that if our negotiations proved unsuccessful and the parties chose to litigate, then I would be disqualified from representing either party. Patti agreed to this arrangement. She wanted to avoid a lawsuit but rightly insisted on being adequately compensated.

Patti and I met several times along with my litigation partner, Gerry Harper, to map out our strategy. It was agreed that I would go to London and meet with McKenna for so long as it took to come to an agreement.

I took the overnight flight to London. When I arrived at RUG's offices early the next morning, McKenna, the consummate gentleman and professional, welcomed me warmly and, after the usual pleasantries, we got down to the business of striking a deal. It was clear that Andrew knew he had to give Patti a generous settlement. Both sides wanted to avoid litigation, but I made it clear to McKenna that if the number wasn't a big one, Patti would go to court.

After a long day of going back and forth, McKenna conferring with Andrew in another room as I got on the phone with Patti, we struck a deal. As is the case in most situations like this one, the parties agreed to keep the terms confidential.

The next summer, Patti invited me to her home perched high on a hill in Kent, Connecticut. She led me to the side of the house and there, basking in the summer sun, was a beautiful new pool. As I looked it over, she raised her arms high above her head, à la *Evita*, and said, "Welcome to the Andrew Lloyd Webber Memorial Pool."

22

Getting a Theater

> What is a wife and what is a harlot? What is a church and what is a theatre? Are they two and not one? Can they exist separate?
>
> —William Blake

If you asked a director and a producer to describe their ideal theater, they might respond:

- Not too big but not too small
- On Forty-Fourth or Forty-Fifth Street
- Perfect sight lines
- A stage with plenty of depth and room in the wings
- A slightly raked audience so viewers can see the dancers' feet
- Comfortable seats and plenty of leg room
- Twenty-first-century restrooms
- Enough space to sell souvenirs at the back of the house
- A nice big marquee

Good luck! Finding and getting a theater that has everything you want is rarely, if ever, possible. For one thing, no one theater *has* all of these ideal attributes. Most were built one hundred or more years ago. Some are capacious but considered too barn-like for many shows. Others are more intimate but can't gross enough for the show to recoup and earn a profit. It's actually remarkable that these landmark structures are still flexible enough to accommodate $20 million musicals as well as modest, small-scale productions. To a large degree, that's a testament to the ingenuity and talent of our set designers who, faced with century-old physical plants, somehow manage to deliver miraculous scenic results.

More important, the scarcity of available theaters each season dictates that producers become beggars, and not choosers. There are a mere forty Broadway theaters in New York City deemed eligible for Tony Award consideration.[1] The Shubert Organization owns seventeen, the Nederlanders own or manage nine, and Jujamcyn owns five. The other nine are owned by not-for-profit companies and independent theater owners.

Simple math will demonstrate why there are so few theaters available each season. Leaving aside the five not-for-profit theaters reserved for their own shows, ten or more of the remaining thirty-five are regularly booked with musicals that have been running for five or more years. That leaves twenty-five theaters, most of which are filled with shows from previous seasons that run anywhere for six to eighteen months. At any one time, if your show is ready to move to Broadway, you may be shut out of getting a theater for six months or more until something closes in a theater that meets at least some of your needs. Even then, the theater owners, who tend to be risk-averse, will pick their future tenants based on a variety of factors:

- The quality of the play, its director and cast
- The experience and reputation of the producer
- The play's provenance. Is it a proven hit from London or a regional theater?

The seating capacities of these theaters vary widely from the Helen Hayes on West Forty-Fourth Street with a total of 597 seats to the largest, the Gershwin on West Fifty-First Street, with 1933 seats. All have orchestra seating and most have one balcony and several side boxes. A few theaters, such as the Belasco and the Cort, have two balconies. These theaters are usually booked only after the others are spoken for, since it's common knowledge few patrons want to sit that high up and far from the stage, unless you have a superstar, in which case you can sell seats hanging from the rafters.

Locations on West Forty-Fourth and West Forty-Fifth Streets between Broadway and Eighth Avenue, astride the famed Shubert Alley, are

---

[1] Except for Lincoln Center's Vivian Beaumont Theater (Broadway and Sixty-Fifth Street), Broadway theaters are all located between Avenue of the Americas and Ninth Avenue from West Forty-First Street up to West Fifty-Fourth Street.

considered prime real estate. However, as any theater owner will tell you, theatergoers don't go to see theaters; they go to see hit plays, wherever they may be located. They'll even seek out Lincoln Center farther uptown if that's where they can see *The King and I* or *War Horse*.

In the end, only serendipity and the gods have it in their power to make a suitable theater available on your schedule. If your show opened out of town to rave reviews, theaters suddenly become available. Stop clauses, which effectively give the landlord the right to terminate a lease, can come into play when a hot show is looking to come in.[2]

On the other hand, if there's a logjam (notwithstanding your having a potential hit), a delay can be quite costly and logistically complicated. Your cast needs to be held together, particularly a star, and your physical production might need to be put in storage. More important, advertising and marketing is put on hold, and group sales agents are unable to start booking the show.

For the shows that are struggling at the box office and barely holding on, there's nothing more disheartening than to find out the theater owner has begun to bring in other producers and directors to look at the theater for a future booking. The vultures begin to circle any theater that houses a weak show, either after a long profitable run or sometimes as soon as a week after the show has opened. It's one of the stark realities of the business. In a market with a limited supply of theaters and often a queue of shows standing in line, only the fittest survive.

And if the logjam is acute, the theater owner will offer his theater to the show he considers the strongest commercial bet and/or to the producer who has a proven track record and substantial resources to support the show during the run. Not an easy marketplace for a tyro producer to break into. All the more reason to join forces with a veteran producer and, if you don't have your own personal wealth, with well-heeled investors.

Then there's the flip side of the coin, when the theater owners compete for what they consider a surefire success. To secure the booking for the next London hit (for example, *Billy Elliot* or *Matilda*), theater owners are often willing to book one of their theaters months or even years in

[2] Stop clauses will be discussed later in this chapter.

advance, assuming the risk that the theater may lie fallow for a considerable period of time. This is sometimes necessary for shows that are technically demanding, requiring months of take-in, or when a star's availability is limited to a specific time slot.

Such was the case in 2001, when the Jujamcyn and Shubert chains were holding the St. James and Winter Garden Theatres, respectively, for *The Producers* and *Mamma Mia*.

The Producers had unusually strong word of mouth during its out-of-town tryout in Chicago. It had two stars, Nathan Lane and Matthew Broderick, and strong advance sales. The opening was the hottest ticket in town. The day after opening to unanimous ecstatic reviews, the show took in over $3 million in ticket sales, shattering every box office record on Broadway. Everyone at the opening predicted the show would run forever—and for good reason. Later, at the party, I ran into Gerald Schoenfeld of the Shubert and said to him, half jokingly, "Well, Gerry, this looks like it's the one that got away." Schoenfeld shot back, "John, just wait for the fall, when *Mamma Mia* opens." Spoken like a true competitor.

Mamma Mia was the first Broadway show to open after September 11, 2001. The town needed a feel-good musical. You could sense the critics breathing a sigh of relief that this was a show they could recommend to a community seeking an escape from the horrors of the twin towers and the city's downtown devastation. *Mamma Mia*, which opened at the Winter Garden Theatre on October 18, 2001, and moved to the Shubert's Broadhurst Theatre in 2013, ran for almost fifteen years, well outlasting *The Producers*' run at the St. James.

None of this is particularly surprising in hindsight. No one can deny that *The Producers* will go down as one of Broadway's most successful musicals. Its twelve Tony Awards alone attest to that. But as I've noted earlier, a musical like *Mamma Mia* doesn't rely on stars, nor is it a revival or a play based on another medium. What it does have is an enormous international following due to its infectious score written by the world-renowned pop group ABBA. It also benefits from a production with modest weekly operating costs as compared to most other musicals, thereby giving it the ability to sustain a long run, year after year, during stressful periods of industry-wide weak business.

Some History

Looking back over the years, it has not always been a seller's market for theater owners. Back in the 1970s, many theaters were dark. Empty theaters drained the owners' resources, what with the carrying costs of taxes, maintenance, utilities, security, and, for some, mortgage payments. James Nederlander, scion of the Nederlander family, complained to me when we first met in 1973 that he was supposed to be in the real estate business, not the producing game. "Kid," he said, "I don't want to be a producer, but I don't have a choice, unless I want to sit by and watch my theaters drive me into bankruptcy." What Jimmy and the other theater chains faced in those days was little product and very few independent producers. Nature abhors a vacuum, so he and the other theater owners often produced concerts or other limited attractions to fill the void.

Although Jimmy much preferred booking shows rather than producing them, four years later, almost by default, he became the lead producer of a musical that turned out to be one of his most profitable investments in the theater. It was January of 1977 and a new musical that had its origins at the Goodspeed Opera House in East Haddam, Connecticut, had just opened at the Kennedy Center in Washington, DC, to encouraging notices. It needed work, but Mike Nichols, who was acting in a producing supervisory role, believed in the show and was certain it would be a hit in New York. He needed a couple of hundred thousand dollars to get it there. Roger Stevens, the then head of the Kennedy Center and a good friend of Jimmy's, thought Broadway would embrace a family show, something that was rare on Broadway in those pre-Disney and *Cats* days.

Nichols and Stevens enlisted Robert Montgomery and me to represent the show and help find a white knight for New York. One of the first calls went out to Jimmy. Thinking out loud he said, "Jeez, who wants to see a show from a comic strip? I hear it didn't get great notices. But they've got Nichols. He's a smart man. Maybe I should go with him."

He did go with him. He became the lead producer and gave Nichols the money he needed to fix the show. The show moved into one of Nederlander's theaters, the Alvin (now called the Neil Simon) on Fifty-Second Street. It opened on April 21, 1977, won seven Tony Awards including Best Musical, ran for nearly six years, and spawned many touring companies throughout the United States and abroad. The show was *Annie*. Not a bad wager for a man who said he didn't want to be a producer!

Theater Owners Become Producers

So now the Shuberts had their biggest hit of all time, *A Chorus Line*, at the Shubert, and Nederlander had his biggest hit ever, *Annie*, at the Alvin. Suddenly, the fabulous invalid didn't seem all that lame. Maybe by producing themselves, the theater owners could have it both ways—reaping rents from their theaters as well as hefty profits from the shows playing there.

What followed in the late seventies and throughout the eighties was a spate of shows booked and co-produced by the Shuberts and the Nederlanders, with Bernie Jacobs, then president of the Shubert Organization, the most aggressive and acquisitive.

During that period, Bernie made it known that the Shuberts had little or no need for independent producers. He viewed producers as nettlesome middlemen standing between the theater owner and the artist. As far as he was concerned, experienced GMs, such as Marvin Krauss and Manny Azenberg, could be hired to provide all the day-to-day management needed for a production. Using corporate lingo, Bernie boasted of vertically integrating the theater business so he could control everything from creating a new project, to producing in his own theaters, to controlling the sale and distribution of all tickets.

Bernie was particularly adept at cultivating direct professional relationships with artists such as Bob Fosse, Peter Shaffer, Trevor Nunn, Michael Bennett, and Andrew Lloyd Webber. He offered James Lapine, the director and bookwriter, an in-house office at the Shubert Organization to develop new projects for which the Shuberts got first refusal to produce. By comparison, Jimmy Nederlander had more regard for the independent producer, although he too forged close relationships with artists, which helped him to secure a booking whenever it was necessary to fill an empty house. In contrast to Bernie's obsession with being in total control, Jimmy's more laissez-faire approach and self-effacing personality were often more appealing to playwrights and directors.

Where Bernie was never shy about giving a director notes after a preview performance, Jimmy usually played the role of impresario, supporting the show but allowing the artists to do their work without interference. Both personalities worked effectively in their own ways for the benefit of their respective organizations.

This was also a period when, owing to the paucity of product at home, London became a wellspring of new plays and its own brand of musicals. Every six months or so, the Berkeley Hotel in London would become the temporary watering hole for Bernie Jacobs and Gerry Schoenfeld, as well as Jimmy Nederlander. They all held court with their wives either in their suites or in the hotel's dining room, where they eyed each other as they dined with London's theatrical elite, all of whom would be looking for a home on Broadway for their latest West End hit or some new project.

During this period, it was extremely difficult for independent producers to support an office while at the same time maintaining close ties to the theater owners when it became necessary to book a theater. Even if you managed to wrestle away a hot project from the theater owners, you would rarely have first choice since the best theaters went to the owners' projects first.

There was one notable exception. In 1976, in a rather bold move, Elizabeth McCann, who was then working as an in-house producer for Jimmy Nederlander, joined Nelle Nugent, who also worked for Nederlander, to organize their own production company—McCann & Nugent Productions. Here were two women, in an industry dominated almost exclusively by upper-middle-aged men, who managed to stay in the good graces of theater owners and also independently produced a series of some of the most successful plays on Broadway. This was due in no small part to McCann's close relationships, cultivated while working for Jimmy, with many of the writers and directors in London. She was a smart, affable woman with great Irish wit who could charm the pants off the likes of Peter Shaffer, Michael Frayn, Trevor Nunn, and those who ran the prestigious London-based National Theatre and Royal Shakespeare Company. As much as the Brits knew they needed to befriend the theater owners who held the keys to Broadway, they found a good friend and sympathetic artistic ear in McCann. And Nugent, acting as a perfect counterbalance to McCann, also capitalized on her contacts in the industry, while taking a sharp blue pencil to any budget and possessing an acute understanding of the technical aspects of each production.

In 1981, McCann and Nugent helped to forge an unprecedented partnership to co-produce the Royal Shakespeare Company's production of *Nicholas Nickleby* on Broadway with both Bernie and Jimmy. It was a coup de theatre the community had never witnessed before, or since. It's also fair to say the production remains undisputedly one of the greatest theatrical achievements of all time.

A Betting Cowboy

Left out of the running for most of the hottest shows through the seventies was Broadway's third-largest theater owner—Jujamcyn Theaters. Founded by William L. McKnight, a former chairman of the 3M corporation, the Jujamcyn Amusement Corporation (as it was first known) controlled three legitimate theaters—the St. James and the Martin Beck (now the Al Hirschfeld) in New York, and the Colonial in Boston. The awkward-sounding name, Jujamcyn, was coined by McKnight for the first names of his grandchildren: Judith, James, and Cynthia.

When McKnight grew tired of the theater business in 1970, his daughter, Virginia, and son-in-law, James Binger, agreed to take it over. They sold the Colonial in Boston and, over the next decade, acquired three more New York theaters: the Eugene O'Neill, the Walter Kerr (formerly the Ritz), and the ANTA, renamed the Virginia after McKnight's daughter and later renamed the August Wilson.

Despite his deep Midwestern roots, James Binger was passionate about the theater and Broadway. On opening nights he was an unmistakable figure as he walked down the aisle to take his seat—tall, with a full mane of white hair, handsome and patrician in the mold of the then mayor of New York City, John Lindsay. It was difficult to imagine Binger messing in the day-to-day haggles of the theater business. He spent little time in New York and was rarely, if ever, seen courting British theater royalty in London. His laid-back demeanor suggested his interest in the theater was more of an avocational diversion from his primary occupation as chairman and CEO of Honeywell back in Minneapolis.

In the seventies, Jujamcyn's two Broadway theaters, the Martin Beck and the St. James, were managed by Richard Wolff, an easygoing former box office treasurer. Reflecting the low-key attitude of his boss, Wolff almost seemed resigned to the fact that producers would seek out his theaters only after all of the other theaters were booked, or after Bernie and Jimmy had turned them down. One bright moment during this time was McCann and Nugent's first production together—the successful revival of *Dracula*, starring Frank Langella, which opened at Jujamcyn's Martin Beck Theatre and ran for more than three years.

Having witnessed what can only be described as a renaissance on Broadway in the late seventies, Binger acquired the three additional theaters mentioned above and, in 1987, made an uncharacteristically audacious move by hiring Rocco Landesman, a fledgling producer who shared Binger's love for the theater and horses, to run his theaters. With a strong background in academic theater (including a PhD in drama from Yale) and a flair for betting on dark horses, Landesman took on the leadership of Jujamcyn with a determination to break out of the pack and become, if not a leading contender, a strong competitor alongside Bernie and Nederlander as they all vied for the next big hit. In his own way, Landesman also seemed an unlikely figure in the Damon Runyon atmosphere of Forty-Second Street, with his cowboy swagger (he wore cowboy boots most times, even when in black tie), infectious good humor, and refreshing transparency in business matters. He understood from the start that he needed to break new ground, and many of the young struggling producers saw in him a bright future.

Under Landesman's leadership, Jujamcyn now had an opportunity to reinvigorate Broadway by cultivating relationships with a younger crop of talent and challenging some of the tried-and-true ways of its competitors. Having produced the Tony Award–winning musical *Big River* several years earlier, Landesman embarked on the ambitious agenda of refurbishing Jujamcyn's theaters and co-producing a series of new shows, the most notable being Tony Kushner's *Angels in America* and Mel Brooks's *The Producers*. Timing is everything, and, at around this time, the market for Broadway theaters became increasingly a landlord's market, making every theater a rare commodity, including all five of Landesman's theaters.

Always a betting man, Landesman signed up to run Jujamcyn in 1987. He bargained for a first position to buy the theater chain after Binger died or if he ever decided to sell the chain. Binger died in 2004. Landesman exercised his option and became sole owner of Jujamcyn. He could now call all the shots as Broadway's number three landlord.

After he acquired Jujamcyn, Landesman's interest in and passion for the theater seemed to wane. In 2005, he sold a half interest in the theaters to Jordan Roth, the son of real estate magnate Steve Roth and producer Daryl Roth. In 2009, Landesman was appointed by Barack Obama as the new chairman of the National Endowment for the Arts, a post he held until December of 2012.

Today, Jordan Roth is the sole owner of Jujamcyn at the age of forty, more than two generations behind Philip Smith (eighty-three), the current chairman of the Shubert Organization, and Jimmy Nederlander (ninety-three). Given Roth's youthful enthusiasm and his family's deep pockets, Jujamcyn should remain a vital player on Broadway.

The Deal

The theater-booking contract will be the quickest document you will sign as a producer. Once your lawyer and GM have worked out the basic financial terms, the theater owner will prepare the first draft and you'll be told, "Sign here."

You should ask your lawyer to review the contract. However, assuming the financial deal is correctly set out, the theater owner will expect to get back the contract by return mail, if not sooner, with no changes. I'm exaggerating somewhat, but such is the case when your prayers have been answered, and you have secured a theater in any given season when a theater is hard to come by and each theater has one or two other shows waiting in the wings for a booking. Today, theater owners sit comfortably in the driver's seat with little need to woo producers or make any meaningful concessions in their booking agreements.

The financial terms of a typical theater deal are as follows:

- On occasion, a non-returnable deposit may be required up front if there is some question about the financial resources or dependability of the producer or if the producer wishes to put a "hold" on the theater for a significant period of time.

- All of the theater's out-of-pocket expenses for operating the theater are assumed by the producer (a so-called four-wall deal), including utilities, union payments for staff, maintenance, taxes, mortgage payments (if applicable), etc. These may be itemized each week, or, more commonly, there's an itemization of third-party costs and a fixed weekly amount negotiated by your GM.
- The producer pays a weekly fixed charge of anywhere from $10,000 to $20,000.
- A guaranteed minimum weekly rent is applied against a percentage of gross weekly box office receipts. In the late seventies and early eighties, when there were plenty of dark theaters, the theaters briefly participated in royalty pools, agreeing to take as rent a share (usually 40 percent) of the weekly operating profits. As soon as the market turned around in favor of the theaters, they reverted to insisting on getting a percentage of the gross as their rent. It's usually anywhere from 6 to 8 percent. The rent may be a point lower during previews and prior to recoupment as a concession to the producer before the play has a chance to realize any net profits.

A facilities fee of 2 percent of the gross is also charged by the theater for the upkeep and maintenance of these landmarked buildings.[3] For the producer, it's hard to see this as anything but an increase in rent since these funds are not earmarked for any particular use.

If a producer should modify the theater for his show, he is fully responsible for all costs to restore the theater to the condition it was in before he occupied it for his production.

Theater owners also have assumed control over credit card charges, ticketing services, and, in some cases, group sales, for which they charge fees over and above their other expenses.

---

[3] See chapter nine, "Royalty Pools," for a discussion of gross gross and net gross.

> Most of these charges are deducted from the gross receipts before the net gross receipts due to the producer are calculated.

Below is a pie chart of the fixed weekly operating expenses of a typical Broadway musical at breakeven—or when the net gross is equal to the fixed weekly operating expenses ($645,000). The theater share for rent is assumed to be 6 percent of the net gross ($38,000). When added to all other theater expenses ($154,000), the total share payable to the theater is 30 percent of the total pie (24 percent plus 6 percent).

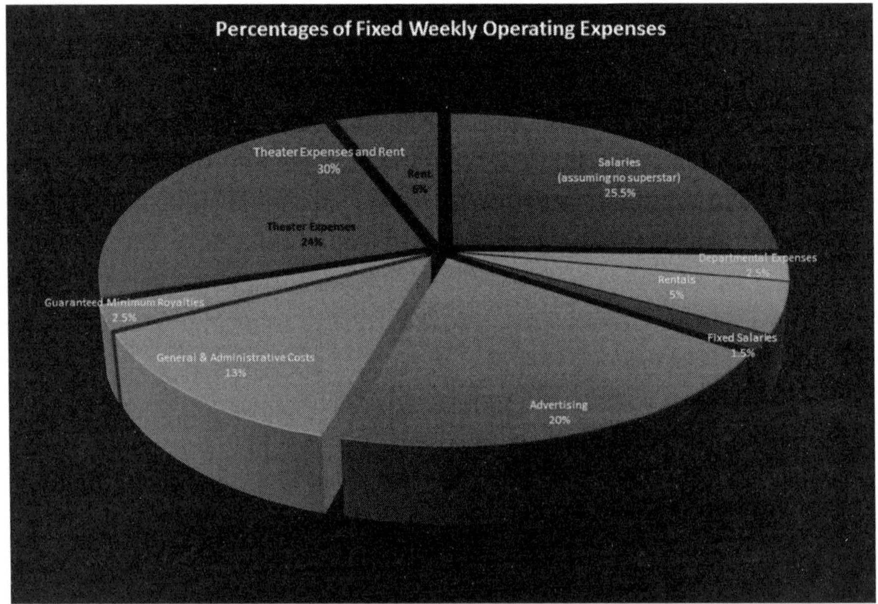

Except for a superstar's salary, theater rent (6 to 7 percent of the net gross) is the highest single item in a theater's weekly fixed expenses. And, as the above chart demonstrates, when the rent is added to all the other fees and costs of the theater, the total amount payable to the theater is the largest slice of the pie.

The Stop Clause

A booking agreement differs in several ways from most real estate leases; it is considered a license, and not a lease, and is therefore not subject to local landlord/tenant laws. Unless the play is booked as a limited engagement, there is no fixed term or period of time defined for occupancy of the theater. Theoretically, so long as the play is doing good business and the producer hasn't defaulted on any of his obligations, the show can remain in the theater indefinitely. The clause that triggers both the landlord's and the producer's rights to terminate the lease is the so-called stop clause. Second only to the money terms, the negotiation of the stop clause is the most important clause in the agreement for the protection of both the theater owner and the producer.

The concept is simple: if the net gross for any two consecutive weeks falls below a fixed amount, either party has the option of giving notice to the other party that it wishes to terminate the run of the play at the end of the following week.

Here's how it works. Let's assume the weekly breakeven, or the point at which the net gross for the week equals the weekly operating costs, is $600,000. For reasons I'll explain later, the parties might well agree to a stop clause in the amount of $550,000, in which case neither the theater owner nor the producer may terminate the agreement and thus close the play unless the net gross for two consecutive weeks falls below $550,000.[4]

For the theater owner, exercising his right to close a show when it falls below the stop clause is rather straightforward. If he has a show waiting in the wings (especially a hot show from England, let's say), he may be eager to get his theater back as soon as possible. On the other hand, if there's no one lining up for a booking, he may exercise his rights under the stop clause by giving notice to the producer but nonetheless permit the producer to continue the run. In that case, since the show was under the stop clause for two consecutive weeks, the theater owner reserves the right to close the show at any time thereafter, with one week's notice, regardless of whether the show is above or below the stop clause.

There is also another issue concerning the stop clause that seldom arises but must be kept in mind. Unless the play falls below the stop clause for two consecutive weeks, the producer cannot close the play. Why would a producer want to close the show if he's operating above

[4] Of course, if either the theater or the producer is otherwise in breach of the agreement, each has the right to terminate for cause.

the stop clause? As noted earlier, the stop clause is usually set somewhat *below* your actual weekly breakeven. The reason for this is that during hard times (the winter months or early fall, when business is usually pretty bad), the producer may want to get concessions from his vendors and the royalty participants to lower his breakeven in order to enable the show to get through these temporary tough patches. If he can reduce his weekly operating costs (usually higher than the stop clause), he may be able to reduce his breakeven, not lose any money, and still stay above the stop clause. The theater owner is usually sympathetic to this argument and therefore willing to agree to a stop clause amount that is somewhat lower than the producer's actual breakeven when there are no concessions. On the other hand, the theater owner doesn't want the stop clause amount to be too low, since the rent and facilities fees rely on high grosses. With theaters in great demand, the theater owner wants the right to terminate the agreement once the show stops yielding enough income to justify turning down new productions.

But here's a possible scenario that could give a producer a lot of sleepless nights. Let's assume the producer is unable to reduce his weekly breakeven for whatever reason—he may have miscalculated his weekly costs or he's unable to get enough concessions. In that case, he may be grossing, let's say, $575,000 each week—enough money so he's above the stop clause of $550,000, but not enough to pay his weekly operating costs of $600,000. So now the producer is hemorrhaging losses each week, but he's above the stop clause and unable to close the show. If the theater owner doesn't have another tenant waiting in the wings (these days rather unlikely), the producer could be faced with keeping the show running while weekly losses mount. This all results in a negotiating gavotte between your GM and the theater owner. As producer, you want a stop clause below your actual breakeven that you can manage to stay above, but not too high. The theater owner, on the other hand, is willing to concede a number below actual breakeven but not so low as to make it difficult to replace the show with a more profitable new tenant.

Although the consequences of falling below the stop clause may sound draconian for the producer, in practice, if the producer has been a good tenant and the show has been running for a long time, it is seldom the case that the theater owner will push a show out precipitously. Similarly, if a show is losing money but is above its stop clause, the theater owner will most likely agree to waive the stop clause if the producer wishes to close the show. This is particularly true when there is a paucity of theaters available each season. If the handwriting is on the wall, in most cases everyone will acknowledge when the time comes to close, and both the producer and theater owner will arrive at a mutually acceptable closing date without either side having to resort to exercising his options under the stop clause.

Summary

As long as theaters are in short supply, their owners will reap the highest rewards and assume the least risk in the business. Controlling distribution has always meant being in the catbird seat. It's also true of the film business, where the major theater chains siphon off their share of fees and expenses before anyone else can take their share of the pie, including the major film studios. But even movie exhibitors are constantly looking over their shoulders at competing means of distribution—DVD sales, direct-to-video, cable TV, on-demand services, and the newly arrived online streaming services such as Netflix, Amazon, and others. There are no such competing live theater alternatives.

In times of economic stress, the theaters have come to the table, as when royalty pools were introduced to level the playing field for investors. However, that was short-lived and ended as soon as the demand for theaters increased and producers began to form lines in Shubert Alley to get a chance to make their case to the wizards of Broadway—the Shuberts.

To bemoan the power of the theater owners is to ignore the basic fact of supply and demand for the finite amount of real estate available to show off your play or musical. That's one of the reasons the not-for-profit theaters have come to believe that owning Broadway theaters is a way of insuring their survival.

And that's why Jimmy Nederlander's remark to me forty years ago still rings in my ears: "I'm a real estate man. I don't want to be a producer."

23

A Theater Mystery

David Merrick, the inveterate showman of Broadway, hadn't been active for some time in the mid to late seventies when he announced the production of a new musical, *42nd Street*, which would be based on the 1933 film of the same title. The production, directed and choreographed by Gower Champion (*Bye Bye Birdie*, *Hello, Dolly!*, *Mack and Mabel*), opened at the Winter Garden Theatre on August 25, 1980, as a nostalgic spectacle with a big cast, classic tap dancing numbers, and lavish sets and costumes. It turned out to be Merrick's last Broadway hit.

There probably will never be another Broadway producer more well known to the general public or more envied and reviled by those who dared to challenge him. Much has been written about Merrick's ingenious and sometimes mischievous (some say even unethical) ways of promoting his shows and manipulating the press. Regardless of one's take on Merrick, the history books will place him among the most prolific and successful Broadway producers of all time. He also presided over the most notorious Broadway opening ever.

Stoked masterfully by Merrick, there was widespread speculation and gossip about *42nd Street* even before its premiere. There were rumors afloat about the enormity of the production, cost overruns, technical complications, and Champion's affair with the female lead, Wanda Richert, as well as questions concerning Champion's precarious health. There were frequent reports of his arriving late for rehearsals wearing layers of scarves and sweaters in spite of the hot and humid August weather.

Merrick only whetted the press's appetite by delaying the opening several times on a whim or for some other inexplicable reason, since the show appeared to be in very good shape to insiders. Finally, Merrick announced the opening.

As the formal black-tie audience filed into the Winter Garden, there was a sense of the way it used to be in years gone by. Here was Merrick, back in control, occupying his accustomed role as uber producer of Broadway. The invited audience had come to see an old-fashioned musical, one that played to the nostalgia craze embraced by the over-fifty crowd that dominated the demographics of Broadway. For a change, here was a show where money was no object and everyone could hope to identify with one of its signature songs, "We're in the Money."

Adding to the opening night high anticipation were rumors circulating among a few insiders about Champion's mysterious disappearance over the prior couple of days. As the audience settled into their seats and the curtain slowly rose to reveal what seemed to be a thousand dancing feet, everyone assumed they were about to witness Merrick's greatest triumph. The first act didn't disappoint. Every expectation seemed to be fulfilled. You can usually tell during intermission at an opening night if things are going well. If the audience is talking about the sets, the weather, or, worse, the next opening they're going to, you know you're in trouble. If they're comparing notes on their favorite moments in the first act as they rush to get back to their seats, you've got a winner.

No one doubted *42nd Street* was sweeping away the opening night audience, but spreading slowly among several people in the orchestra seats was another conversation unknown to the rest of the audience.

My wife and I lingered at our seats during intermission instead of fighting the crush of people at the rear of the house. Bernie Jacobs, looking unusually grim, was making his way up the aisle toward us. He would stop occasionally and whisper to someone he knew well and then move on. Having taken note of all of this, when Bernie got to me I wondered why he seemed so worried. After all, it was clear he had another big hit in one of his flagship theaters. What he whispered stunned me and left me speechless as I retreated to my wife and he continued to seek out fellow confidants. Bernie had asked me not to say a word to anyone. I whispered to Nan what he had said nonetheless. We sat in a state of suspended animation for the rest of the show.

When the curtain descended after the finale, there was a roar of approval from the audience with a spontaneous and legitimate standing ovation, something rarely witnessed in the theater these days.[1] The cast was taking its fifth or sixth curtain call when, from the stage right wing, out walked Mr. Merrick, appearing to be as dour and despondent as Bernie was during intermission. The audience roared its approval as Merrick took center stage with a King Lear bearing. He raised his hands to stop the cheers and bravos. After the ovation subsided, Merrick simply announced that Gower Champion had died early that afternoon.

A communal gasp was heard, followed by the kind of vocal reaction befitting the announcement of a national tragedy. Cast members cried and embraced one another. Richert bowed her head in her hands as others tried to comfort her and protect her from what had become a public spectacle of shock and grief.

The triumph of a show bathed in the giddy thrill that only a Broadway musical can create collided abruptly and brutally with the reality of the death of its ingenious creator. I don't think there will ever be a more surreal experience in the theater.

The curtain came down on cue from Merrick. Suddenly, the opening night celebration of a Broadway hit had morphed into a memorial service, as the audience left the theater following a phantom casket.

Over the following days, there was more speculation by the press and those who knew Champion and Merrick about the extraordinary confluence of events of that opening night. Champion had died earlier in the day. How did Champion get through rehearsals and previews if he was so seriously ill? How was it that no one was told or knew about it until Merrick announced it onstage? Why hadn't Merrick told the cast, or, at the very least, Wanda Richert, of Gower's death before disclosing it publicly onstage? Ironically, the tragic spectacle of watching those cast members react became indistinguishable from their performances in the show that had preceded it. Merrick surely could have come out downstage, in front of the curtain, to tell the audience the news while giving the cast their own private moment of grief.

---

[1] Standing ovations are no longer reserved for the few-and-far-between theatrical events worthy of this special approbation. Today, you know you've seen a stinker of a show if the audience *hasn't* leapt to its feet with indiscriminate abandon by the time the last actor takes his or her bow.

Leaving the civilities aside, from the point of view of a hard-nosed businessman, you had to admire Merrick's decision to risk any criticism for sensationalizing Champion's death for the benefit of gaining front-page, worldwide publicity for his multimillion-dollar investment. The day after the opening, every newspaper, tabloid, and TV news channel told of Merrick's new show and its fallen director. The reviews were mostly favorable, but that hardly mattered. Merrick had made his opening an internationally newsworthy event, the likes of which Broadway had never seen before—a fitting coda for the man whom the late drama critic Howard Kissel called the "Abominable Showman."

Final Thought

My wife and I chose to skip the opening night party. We wondered if the guests would be toasting and celebrating the show or Champion's life. I guess we thought it would be unseemly to do either. Just before we stepped into a cab on our way home, Nan pointed to a full moon in the clear sky above. We looked at each other with the same thought: Had Merrick somehow also arranged for that?

24

The British Invasion

Although it's somewhat of a sidetrack, I want to make brief mention of a sea change in Broadway history that began in the early 1980s. What many refer to as the British invasion started with Andrew Lloyd Webber's *Cats* in 1981 and was followed by *Les Misérables*, *The Phantom of the Opera*, and *Miss Saigon*. For some of us at the time, it appeared that the great tradition of homegrown Broadway musical comedy had become a lost art. There was no mistaking the crowd-pleasing and remarkable pyrotechnics employed by these shows, whether they were elevated platforms ascending inexorably to the Heaviside Layer (*Cats*), a helicopter descending from above the stage in search of Vietnamese refugees (*Miss Saigon*), or, the granddaddy of them all, the opera house chandelier crashing down from high above the audience to the stage at the end of act 1 of *Phantom*.

It was as if a new form of entertainment had been introduced to American and other theater audiences throughout the world. No one saw it coming, and it swept over Broadway like a tidal wave. Given the fact that these shows now represent three of the longest-running musical plays of all time, their scenic components cannot be the sole or even primary reason for their unprecedented success. Andrew's songs from *Cats* and *Phantom* have become part of the pantheon of the most-often-heard music anywhere in the world. Can anyone avoid hearing "Memory" or "The Music of the Night" in any cabaret, restaurant, or hotel lobby? And *Les Miz* not only continues to run in London's West End but has been revived on Broadway for the second time after the worldwide release of the theatrical motion picture version starring Hugh Jackman, Anne Hathaway, and Russell Crowe.

Whether these shows compared favorably or otherwise to the great American musicals prior to the 1980s—*Oklahoma*, *South Pacific*, *The Sound of Music*, *Gypsy*, *Follies*, *Fiddler on the Roof*, *A Chorus Line*, and *Annie*—one thing was certain: although the British shows were musicals (narrative interspersed with songs), what they couldn't be called was musical *comedies*.

These new shows were dramas with music virtually devoid of any comedy in the American tradition. It may be too simplistic a parallel, but it was not unlike the stark contrast between opera buffa and other lighthearted theater genres of the eighteenth and early nineteenth centuries and the music drama introduced by Richard Wagner and, later, Richard Strauss. Wagner wrote about Nordic myths and Valhalla; nothing lighthearted or frivolous. The British shows, particularly Cameron Mackintosh's, were dark romantic tragedies, with nary a laugh or a smile to be found, while the American tradition grew out of burlesque and vaudeville, where lovers sang and danced along with broad-based comedy.

While a lot of unemployed American writers and composers bemoaned the apparent takeover of the musical by the British, the fact is these shows resulted in thousands of American actors, musicians, and stagehands enjoying years of gainful employment and, not to be forgotten, the theater owners reaping a veritable fortune.

Some Americans writers attempted to mimic what seemed to be the British formula for mega-success, but, by and large, they were unsuccessful in developing musicals of this ilk. What did evolve were musicals that became more attuned to music of broad-based popular appeal: rock and roll. Popular music written with the AM/FM radio in mind began to complement and eventually supplant altogether the traditional music of Tin Pan Alley, as well as that of Cole Porter, Rodgers and Hammerstein, and Lerner and Loewe.

Although *Hair* and *Two Gentlemen of Verona* were early American pioneers in introducing a new "sound" to musical theater, it was Andrew Lloyd Webber who not only borrowed from the tradition of American composers but also gave theatergoers a resonance with everyday popular rock music, particularly in his early shows, *Joseph and the Amazing Technicolor Dreamcoat* and *Jesus Christ Superstar*. Andrew has often been criticized for borrowing perhaps too freely from the operatic tradition in his later shows. But it is also a hallmark of his talent and enormous popularity that he could effectively and effortlessly navigate between rock, opera, and mainstream Broadway styles of music, often within the same show.

Spectacle-driven projects are not the exclusive domain of the British—Disney's *The Lion King* and Marvel's *Spider-Man: Turn Off the Dark* are good examples. But the pendulum has swung back to a large extent during the past decade or so if for no reason other than that a production budget of $25 million or more is out of reach for all but the very few. Recent Tony Award–winning musicals such as *Once* are one-set musicals that put a premium on intimate love stories and, *A Gentleman's Guide to Love and Murder*, harkens back to good farce and slapstick comedy. What's more, *The Book of Mormon* is crafted in the best traditions of the directors of the forties and fifties—George Abbott and Joshua Logan. Those gentlemen might be surprised by some of the show's language, but they undoubtedly would be pleased to see its adherence to the grand tradition of American musical comedy. And *Hamilton* displays an ingenious melding of rap, pop, and classic musical genres into a seamless whole.

As always, what happens in the future will be guided by economics, popular taste, and, most important, artists with talent and vision.

25

Rehearsals and Previews

> An audience is never wrong. An individual member of it may be an imbecile, but a thousand imbeciles together in the dark—that is critical genius.
>
> —Billy Wilder

In an ideal world, once you've secured your financing and completed your workshop or out-of-town run, your GM will be able to finalize the schedule for studio rehearsals, the date to load in your set, the start of technical rehearsals and previews, and your official opening night.

Assuming you are among the lucky few for whom all is in order and your theater awaits you, then an inexorable process begins that's virtually impossible to stop, not unlike a locomotive going downhill—without brakes. Up until rehearsals, only a small percentage of your multimillion-dollar financing will have been spent. But from rehearsals on, the outflow of cash is nonstop—there are payments for the physical production, pre-opening advertising, weekly salaries for rehearsals and related costs, preliminary theater costs, and final fees to the creative team—all the more reason that the producer and the authors should have a high degree of confidence in the show at the conclusion of an out-of-town run or workshop. That's not to say that it must be perfect, but it's best if only some tinkering and fine-tuning of the material is necessary (as opposed to major changes) during the rehearsal and preview periods.

For a revival, the rehearsal period can be as little as five to six weeks (including technical rehearsals in the theater). For a new musical, with great technical demands, the full rehearsal period can be twelve to sixteen weeks. The original productions of *Cats* and *The Phantom of the Opera* required complicated physical changes in the theaters and onstage and thus needed many months of preparation before previews could begin.

The need for enough rehearsal time is particularly acute for any new musical that dares to come into town cold, without a fully staged workshop or out-of-town run. In some ways, when a musical has its first preview on Broadway, the word on the street and the Internet may presage the fate of the show overnight. And, although they might not admit it, the critics surely are not immune to these influences; some no doubt enter the theater on opening night with the thought, "Is it really that bad?" or "Is it really the second coming?"

In some ways, it is almost cruel to subject a cast and crew to a Broadway audience without letting the actors ease their way into their roles and the crew accustom themselves to the intricacies of the physical production. The rehearsal process, of course, gives everyone that opportunity, but much of that time is spent blocking, learning the music and choreography, keeping publicity appointments, doing costume fittings, and putting in changes as the creative team continues to work on the show.

Near the end of the rehearsal period, the director will have run-throughs and dress rehearsals from the overture to the finale. The producer(s), major investors, and theater owner are usually invited to the final run-throughs. For obvious reasons, on these occasions the tensions are high and the adrenaline is pumping for both the actors and the creative team. Savvy producers will understand the need to be supportive during this time. They should be slow to criticize what they see. There's nothing more damaging than discouraging a company with a lot of criticism so soon after they've first revealed their skills and talents to an invited audience. Chances are anything you see at this stage that needs to be addressed has already been noted by the director and the authors.

On the other hand, it is an opportunity for the producer to spot serious flaws in the material or deficiencies in the cast. Scenes that don't seem to work on any level, or performances—especially stars—that are way off the mark, may require immediate attention. Most important is to see if you, the creative team, and the director are all on the same wavelength.

This is also no time for anyone on the creative team to become a prima donna. Each author, the director, and the choreographer should remain open-minded about the changes that the team as a whole considers necessary. There has to be room for good faith and constructive collaboration among everyone. Time is of the essence, but there may still be enough time to correct the most serious concerns. In the end, the director, with the producer's money and support, will have to use his judgment wisely as to whether a cast replacement or major scene or musical rewrite will be required.

Technical Rehearsals ("Tech")

A great deal of preliminary work will have been done by the stagehands and lighting personnel after the load-in is completed and before the cast arrives. When the actors finally take the stage, tech rehearsals begin.

For anyone who has ever experienced a technical rehearsal, it becomes quickly apparent that the actors have little or no time to work on their roles. The vast majority of time is taken up setting the dozens of lighting cues, working the changing of scenes, getting the sound right, and rehearsing costume changes. It is an unavoidably tedious process that is commandeered by the director and the production stage manager. It is a race with the clock that the director must win if he is to meet the deadline of the first preview. In fact, it is not uncommon for a show to miss that deadline and be forced to cancel one or two previews. That's a real blow to the producer's bottom line (he'll have to refund tickets) and the pre-opening gossip in the press can turn negative. It may be preferable to have a rough first preview with a few fits and starts (audiences tend to be somewhat forgiving during first previews) in lieu of announcing a cancellation. However, one doesn't always have that option.

There's a truly delightful and thrilling rehearsal during the tech period referred to as *sitzprobe*—a German word meaning "a seated rehearsal." This is usually the first time the cast and orchestra rehearse together. It's often done onstage, in the theater's lobby, or in a rehearsal room. The actors are seated and perform standing in front of music stands when singing. The producers, the creative team, and others closely connected to the production are usually in attendance. To hear your cast and orchestra bring the score to full realization for the first time in a relatively small, confined space is always an unforgettable experience. It is both breathtaking in its emotional power and revelatory in demonstrating how the orchestration and arrangements intersect with the human voice. Everyone leaves the room on a high, fully aware that they may never again hear the complete score in quite the same immediate and intimate way.

If the schedule has been adhered to, there should be sufficient time at the end of the tech period to have at least one or two full dress rehearsals with the orchestra, ideally without stopping. It is only then that the entire production comes to fruition. Frantic final costume fittings, adjustments, and replacements take place. Quick changes of costume are rehearsed over and over. Orchestrations are adjusted, lighting cues are finally set, and the actors, for a few precious days, have the chance to put all the pieces together, working their way around scenery, props, glaring lights, and sometimes even ungainly costumes.

There may be a collective sigh of relief after the first dress rehearsal. For everyone involved, it seems a miracle if they got through the entire show without stopping once. That, however, is the very least the audience expects to see.

Previews

If everyone's nerves were on edge during rehearsals, there's nothing to compare to the level of anxiety backstage during the preview period. As a general rule, musicals have anywhere from four to six weeks of previews. There has been the occasional show that stretched its preview period to eight to ten weeks, hoping to stave off reviews as long as possible and benefit from high advance preview sales. That strategy is often short-sighted. It can engender ill will among the critics and press who may react negatively to being held off from reviewing the show.

The day before the first preview performance, the director and producer may decide to have what's called a "gypsy run-through." This is a free performance for an invited audience of actors ("gypsies") appearing in other shows running on Broadway, as well as the show's investors, and friends and family of the cast and crew. Ideally, it's held on a Monday night, when most shows are dark.

There is nothing quite like a gypsy run-through for a show that's ready to meet its audience. The performance is a love fest. The audiences are forgiving of any hitch in the scenery, flub of a line, or miscue. The abandon and adulation that meet each number, star turn, and scenery change are often never again experienced by the production. Such are the celebration and joy that greet a true blockbuster during a gypsy run-through. Like a tsunami, the positive word of mouth, press attention, and online chatter sweep the industry and theatergoing public. The next night, the first preview audience and those following are infected by the buzz surrounding the show, leading up, one hopes, to a triumphant opening night.

On the other hand, having a gypsy run-through is not a no-risk proposition. If the show is truly not ready for an audience, a gypsy audience will have only so much patience. They may remain polite, but a show that's in trouble, for whatever reason, cannot escape the opprobrium of any audience, no matter how well-intentioned, and the ensuing bad word of mouth, particularly on the internet, could be damaging.

While good or bad word of mouth can be influential for a show, the preview period is a time to make tough assessments of the material and, most important, to listen closely to the audience. They will usually tell you more about your show than any of your well-meaning friends who will be eager to give you notes after every performance. It's during this time that the director and the creative team need to have thick skins and clear heads to avoid being besieged with comments that are often extraneous or just plain wrongheaded. I remember comic-writing genius Larry Gelbart saying to me after a preview performance of his musical *City of Angels*, "Now it's time to stop listening to others, except the audience."

No one knows the show better than the creative team. And no one knows better the original intentions for the show. Although the process isn't scientific or foolproof, taking their cues from the audience will usually guide the creative team to making the correct adjustments during previews. Audiences are rarely wrong. They can warn you about a number of problems—including lags in momentum, confusion about the plot or the characters' motivations, poor sound, the star being upstaged (intentionally or not) by a secondary character, and the show being too long. And, being a comedy writer, Gelbart simply listened to see if his comic lines were getting laughs.

It's straightforward to note when an audience is laughing at the right times and when they react with strong and sustained applause to the musical numbers. But listening carefully when an audience is quiet is more difficult. I've often heard an author marvel that he could hear a pin drop during a certain scene. That quietude may mean the audience is enthralled, or it may mean they're barely awake or in horror at the ineptitude of what they're watching. Those reactions can easily mimic admiration. Objectivity needs to counter self-congratulation in the theater.

Here's a curious side note: I know a director who doesn't like musicals without an intermission. He maintains that audience members who truly dislike a show vote with their feet by walking out during intermission. And ask the matrons in the ladies' room what's being discussed—they'll tell you what the audience is thinking.

Even with five weeks of previews, the time rushes by almost uncontrollably. After the first preview, the cast is usually running only on leftover adrenaline in getting the show on its feet. They are exhausted and need several days to settle in. You and your stage managers should be alert to fatigue that may lead to vocal strain for your leading actors, as well as illnesses that may begin to spread among the cast.

While the director and the creative team need to consider script and scene changes, the technical team needs to make their adjustments. The production crew will usually meet with the director and choreographer in the house after each preview to hear the notes the director has taken during the performance. Afterward, the authors and the director may reconvene at a nearby bar or someone's apartment to work out additional changes in the script or score. As a result, it's usually more than a week before any significant changes can be put into the show. By the time those changes are absorbed, two weeks of previews have gone by. That leaves only two or three weeks until opening to make any more changes. But that's not really the case.

Since the early 1980s, when Frank Rich and the other major critics decided to review shows at one of the last previews rather than the official opening night, the director has needed to "freeze" the show (stop making further changes) at least a day or two before those critics arrive. That shaves off another five or six days before the official opening. Now you have, at best, ten days for any final changes before the show is frozen.

In principle, the preview period should be a time to assess audience reaction while you hone the material and work out the kinks. The reality is that there is very little time to make any wholesale changes. In truth, the preview period in New York City is a time to sharpen and refine an already completed show, fully rehearsed and vetted for flawed material or technical problems. As your preview period comes to a close, a well-prepared show will realize increased advance ticket sales as favorable word of mouth spreads, and your cast will gain in confidence as they hone their performances and become accustomed to audience reaction.

The rest is in the hands of the gods—and the critics.

26

Advertising, Marketing, and Press

If you build it, they will come.

—Kevin Costner in *Field of Dreams*

I'm not sure that either Noah or Hollywood got it right about this inevitability when it comes to the theater. Writing and producing a new musical is a Herculean task. Having accomplished that feat, you might think its success and a long run would follow naturally. But your work is only half done. As producer, your job demands that you identify and tap into your audience at an early stage and then burnish the show's reputation as a certifiable hit after you've opened. Your show will get lost in the shadows and lie fallow next to the competition unless you harness a team that can effectively advertise, market, and manage it from the first day it is announced until its last performance, hopefully many years in the future.

That team consists of three groups:

1. Your advertising agency, which will develop and create your logo and artwork (for example, the running young man of *The Book of Mormon*), as well as work side by side with your social media advisors to develop your ad strategy in print, in the media, and online
2. Your marketing group, which will identify and reach out to the demographics of your audience and also work with your online team to exploit opportunities in social media
3. Your press representative, who will manage your relations with the press from the first press release to opening night to interviews and special appearances during the run of the play

All three groups need to work as a team, never in isolation from one another, so that the show is presented to the public and the press in a coherent and compelling manner. As I've previously mentioned, a new component to the industry over the past ten years is a heavy concentration both of time and money in online ticket sales, and Internet advertising and marketing, particularly throughout the various social networks. These initiatives also need to be in sync with your overall advertising and marketing campaigns, a feat that's taken time over the years to achieve.

The Advertising Agency

It may be a while before you decide on the logo, artwork, and images to be associated with your play. Ideally, you want to find artwork that will come to identify your show in an instant—the yellow cat's eyes against a dead-black background for *Cats*, the white mask of the Phantom, the waiflike child of *Les Misérables*, or the rendition of the lion's head for *The Lion King*. These lasting images have long since taken on a secondary meaning as they relate to the title of these shows. One only has to see the image, without anything more, to identify the musical. Your logo should be registered as a trademark for protection with the U.S. Patent and Trademark Office to ward off imitators who wish to trade on the goodwill and reputation of your play. This also ties into your exploitation of merchandise, which will be enhanced by the distinctive logo and artwork for the show.

Producers frequently interview two or three agencies to represent a show. The agency's creative presentation during the sales pitch is often the most important element in winning an assignment. It's also critical that the agency's creative department read the script of the show before presenting its ideas to the producer. The producer wants to know that his agency "gets it." Many jobs have been lost by presenting a logo that is stylistically or graphically brilliant on its own merits but doesn't resonate with the play or the production team's conception of the show.

Regardless of the ingenuity or imagination of the agency, however, input from the creative team as well as the producer on how they see the show and what they consider to be its strongest selling points is essential.

After coming on board, the ad agency will devise a budget for the pre- and post-opening advertising campaigns. For a major Broadway musical, \$1.5 to \$2 million can easily be spent before the opening. If the show has a superstar above the title, the budget may be smaller simply because a few display ads in the *New York Times* may be enough to accumulate a big advance. For shows that don't have much to sell prior to opening (such as a recognizable title or star), the ad campaign will need to introduce the show, its title and subject matter, to the public. Unfortunately, these early campaigns often go largely unnoticed by a public accustomed to buying tickets only *after* the show opens and the critics have weighed in. Even then, it may be slow sledding.

A case in point is the musical *A Gentleman's Guide to Love and Murder*, which opened at the Walter Kerr Theatre in the fall of 2013. Having successfully premiered the production at the Hartford Stage in Connecticut, the creative team and the producers were confident they had a strong show with wide audience appeal. Despite getting unanimous glowing reviews after its Broadway opening (for the play as well as for its leading man, Jefferson Mays) the show struggled at the box office through the fall and a frigid winter. "Why?" the solons on the street wondered:

- Was the title too long? (It was difficult to read and see on the theater's marquee.)
- Was the TV ad unappealing? (The commercial touted the show's positive reviews but seemed to create little more than an impression of a lively old-fashioned musical—a cross between a British farce and a Gilbert and Sullivan operetta.)
- Was the word of mouth not strong enough? (Unlikely, since most people who saw the show seemed to love it.)
- Despite a performance by Mays unlike any other seen on a Broadway stage in years, was this going to be another example of a good show failing due to the lack of a major TV or movie star?

The producers persevered in the face of weak business in the hope that spring would bring them much-needed awards. Their strategy seemed to pay off when the Tony Awards Nominating Committee gave the show ten nominations, the most of any show that season. Immediately after the nominations were announced, there was a jump in the box office and the advance rose. Those numbers rose even higher when the show won the Tony and most other major awards that season for best musical. The hefty business the show realized after the Tony Awards was a far cry from the half-filled houses and weekly losses of the early days. The stark reality is that there are so many factors that lead to success—critics' accolades, strong word of mouth, great performances, and ingenious ad campaigns. But for some shows, a Tony, the industry's top honor, is often the critical component to a long run.

The Ad Budget

The line items in your production budget for advertising and publicity break down into:

- Front of house (marquee and other signage)
- Outdoor ads (billboards, posters, and window cards)
- Print (newspapers and magazines)
- TV and radio (production and media buys)
- Website, online, and social media
- Direct mail
- Group sales

How to find the right mix and allocate your limited resources must be carefully thought through. The sobering truth about theater advertising is that the funds available to the producer are a mere pittance when compared to those available to motion picture studios and many other leisure destinations (Vegas, theme parks, sports) all seeking to woo the ticket-buying public both at home and abroad. As mentioned in chapter twenty, a major motion picture company can easily spend $50 million in its initial launch of a film, while a big-budget musical needs to spread $1.5 million or so over a six-week period.

What's more, the attention span of today's consumers is fleeting. When worldwide news, opinions, and reviews appear instantly online, producers and ad agencies find themselves trying to outsmart the public to get their attention. What swept Facebook or Twitter as a hot topic today can disappear overnight. Gaining a foothold in social media is a daunting task, given the more sensational and dramatic news unfolding every minute.

The print media (newspapers and magazines) were once the mainstay of theater advertising. Full-page ads or double-truck ads (two full pages) were the norm for most musicals if they received favorable notices after they opened. The daily editions of the *New York Times* and many of the tabloids in New York City and the surrounding suburbs carried ten or twelve ads each day, and the weekend editions were filled with ads for most shows. Listing your show in the ABCs (the daily listings) of the *New York Times* was a given. Today, there is little advertising in print, and most shows aren't listed every day in the ABCs—in some cases only on Fridays and Sundays. This is the result of the rapidly rising cost of print ads and the corresponding decline of readership. The *New York Times* today charges nearly $300,000 for a full-page, color ad. A producer has to question the wisdom of purchasing these ads when few readers under the age of forty buy a hard copy of anything, no less a newspaper.

Today, the power and influence of the *New York Times* as an ad and marketing tool are a shadow of what they once were. Concerned at what appeared to be its waning power, in the fall of 2009 the *New York Times* embarked on an ill-fated attempt to demonstrate to the industry that it still held sway over the sale of tickets to a Broadway play. In an unprecedented arrangement, the paper made an agreement with Manny Azenberg, the producer of a revival of Neil Simon's *Brighton Beach Memoirs*, that in return for discounted print ads in the *Times*, he would agree not to place ads in any other paper for the period prior to the official opening. The *New York Times* was betting that their ads alone would build the advance and catapult the show into a big Broadway hit, thus demonstrating its market power.

The gamble failed. Despite generally favorable reviews, the play never built any advance and never gained much interest from theater parties and group sales. It closed a week after the opening. If anything, the experiment proved beyond a doubt what many had already concluded—that the *New York Times* print ads were largely ineffective and had lost their power and reach. The whole escapade was an embarrassment for the paper. And for Azenberg, there was the fallout of engendering bad will with the New York Times's competitors by shutting them out prior to the opening. All around, a sorry result.

The Dilemma of TV Advertising

Somewhat surprisingly, prior to the late 1970s, there was little, if any, advertising on television for Broadway plays. Two shows changed the landscape dramatically.

The Wiz, a musical adaptation of the film *The Wizard of Oz*, opened in 1975 to mixed notices. It was out of the mainstream for Broadway with its all-black cast and pop score. After the opening, the show became what is sometimes referred to as a "nervous hit"—doing pretty good business but not a sellout. It was unclear if the show would make it. The musical broke ground not only in casting but also by having a major motion picture studio, 20th Century Fox, as producers and a major investor. Although TV ads were alien to most Broadway shows, it was a natural medium for a film studio. An expensive (for Broadway) commercial highlighting one of the show's most infectious songs, "Ease on Down the Road," was produced and run repeatedly on local TV stations. The box office took off, the industry took notice, and, from then on, Broadway started incorporating TV ads into their production and operating budgets.

Another show for which TV ads had the same or even greater impact was Robert Stigwood's original production of *Evita* in 1979. Again, the show opened to mixed notices. Another nervous hit. Stigwood, with his entertainment-mogul intuition, had sensed the first impressions of the show as soft and not particularly memorable. Along with the musical's director, Hal Prince, he produced a TV commercial and placed it widely. It featured the now iconic shot of the star of the show, Patti LuPone, thrusting her arms upward in a V for victory and the cast holding aloft fiery torches, advancing toward the screen. Those ads left an indelible impression on the public and, along with a Tony for Best Musical, were responsible for the surge at the box office that followed.

Today, the public has become inured to TV ads for Broadway shows. Millions of dollars are spent each year by Broadway producers, with little appreciable result. The cost can be prohibitive for all but the well-heeled hits. Producing a compelling ad that will stand out from the crowd can easily cost $250,000, and buying time for a modest campaign is upward of $500,000. In most cases, regardless of the ad's production values, a show needs to have something truly distinctive to get the attention of the TV audience: a major star (Jim Parsons in *An Act of God*), nostalgia-driven music for the fifty-plus crowd (*Motown*; *Beautiful*), or an established reputation as the hottest and hardest-to-get ticket in town (*Hamilton*). Without one of those elements, you will be hard put to recover the cost of TV production and distribution from future ticket sales.

The Emergence of Online Advertising and Marketing

With the decline in print readership, and the prohibitive cost and questionable effectiveness of TV ads, producers have turned to online advertising and marketing to help fill the gap and tap into new and younger audiences.

There are a few independent firms that specialize in this area. In order to compete, the major ad agencies have recently created in-house departments focusing on the Internet, with varying degrees of success. No one seems to know why and how content on the Internet goes viral. Luck or timing? In any case, that shouldn't dissuade producers from attempting to harness the medium for the benefit of their shows. And whether your Internet manager is in-house or not, you need to be certain everyone works as a team so that the show's message is coordinated and consistently identifiable regardless of the venue or site.

Early on, many producers' eyes were either crossed or closed when the statistics for the number of "hits" on the show's website were discussed and analyzed ad nauseam in weekly ad meetings. Most producers could have cared less. Their concern was, and still is, how many tickets they'd sold for the thousands of dollars they'd invested in this new medium. But as the data has gotten more refined and sophisticated, and the traditional means of advertising continue to lose their effectiveness, producers have become increasingly aware of the importance of the Internet both in targeting a show's core audience and broadening audience awareness. They've become more educated and attuned to the benefits it can offer a show.

Damian Bazadona, president of the advertising agency Situation Interactive and a leader in the field, told me recently, "Our ability to track ticket sales in terms of demographics and niche marketing improves every day. Part of our challenge is to translate the data we receive into a clear message for the producer. Once he understands the benefits, both direct and indirect, he can work with us to improve the show's profile and outreach." In fact, this new awareness is now reflected in operating budgets with online initiatives accounting for as much as 25 percent of a producer's weekly ad budget.

A corollary to this trend is creating specific content for social media. Authors have been enlisted to write special promotions that particularly draw young audiences to the show's website. Once there, they will hopefully move around the site, become curious, and maybe even buy a ticket.

As for ticket sales, sophisticated online sales tools, created to compete with the brokers and discount sites, are being fine-tuned all the time and can substantially affect your bottom line. Many shows have found that it's worth paying Google whatever it takes to make certain your official website pops up first in line when anyone searches for your show.

A final word of caution: the Internet, especially social media, can bite the hand that feeds it. For better or worse, you need to be aware that you can't control the message once it's out there going viral. Today, more than ever, the message is the medium. You and your team need to be ever vigilant, tracking the Internet daily for trends and other signs of your show's reputation in cyberspace. Trying to stay one step ahead of the Internet may seem fruitless, but to ignore its widespread presence and influence is to flirt with disaster.

Marketing and Sponsorships

Working in parallel with your ad agency is your marketing group. They are responsible for tie-ins with radio stations, airlines, department stores, and other commercial partners willing to give free ad space in return for credit on programs and free tickets for their employees or loyal customers. The most sought-after partnership arrangements are with American Express, which will pick up the tab for early print ads and send out e-blasts to their members for the privilege of offering their premium card holders first-choice tickets to the most eagerly anticipated new shows, particularly those with major stars.

There was a time when Broadway dreamed of making lucrative sponsorship deals with corporations, but today those deals are few and far between. Time and time again I've seen major companies flirt with Broadway shows only to find their corporate ad and marketing divisions unwilling to draw down money from their overall budgets to spend on a play that reaches approximately 1,500 people each night, as opposed to one TV ad that will reach millions of people. They ultimately conclude that the money is better spent elsewhere where they can, in ad-speak, "get more eyeballs for the buck."

Ticket Prices: Too High or Too Low

This is as good a place as any to address ticket prices.

Every show fights to fill every seat in its theater every night. An empty seat is revenue lost forever. You can never get it back. But only a few plays each season manage to bring all the elements together for a big hit. For a hit, full-priced and premium tickets are its mainstay for as long as it's possible to fill the theater and stay well above weekly breakeven. Even when a show is earning a profit, the producer needs to remain constantly alert to any downward trends, as reflected in the daily "wraps," that suggest the play's strength and visibility may be diminishing.[1]

Sooner or later, however, your show will go soft, and issuing discount tickets will become a necessity. For example, if your houses are half-empty with little advance during the preview period or later in the run, half- or three-quarter-priced tickets can be allocated to the TKTS ticket booth located on West Forty-Seventh Street in Father Duffy Square.[2] Theatre Development Fund (TDF), the operator of the TKTS booths, also has a discount program for its membership that has helped thousands of shows over its sixty-year history. There are also scores of other discount outlets on the Internet that will aid struggling shows before they find their footing in the marketplace. Yet a new show cannot survive on discounting. There's simply not enough money to be made in a theater when most of

---

[1] A wrap is the total amount of daily ticket sales from all sources—box office, mail, online, and group sales.

[2] TKTS booths are also located at South Street Seaport and in downtown Brooklyn.

your audience is paying an average price of 50 percent or less of a full-priced ticket.

Once a show is established as a hit, the word of mouth will spread that only full-priced tickets are available, with none available at TKTS or online discount sites. For the blockbusters, it's well known that if you don't want to wait months for a center orchestra seat, you'll have to spring for premium seats, which can cost anywhere from $175 to $450 for each seat. Prior to 2005, brokers and scalpers had a monopoly on choice seats for the hit shows, buying hundreds of seats before the opening and then reselling them at a premium. When *The Producers* opened in 2005, its producers established a policy for the first time by which a select number of choice seats would be reserved for premium pricing. With the demand for tickets so great, the plan proved highly successful. Since then, every show with high demand has taken advantage of premium pricing, depriving the scalpers of their monopoly on premium seating and benefiting the show, its creators, and investors. The downside, if there is one, is the growing perception that obtaining the best seats for prime shows has now become an elitist enterprise reserved for the very wealthy and the well connected. It may be the American way, but it sometimes appears that one of the seven deadly sins—greed—has taken over the industry with abandon.

Consider this sobering calculation: if you pay $450 per seat for a family of four ($1,800), eat at a good restaurant ($250), and park your car ($50), you've spent $2,100, without having accounted for some merchandise ($50) or a coke ($10 per cup) sold at the theater. Even at regular box office prices, a family of four will spend about $1,000 and still find themselves seated in the rear or side orchestra.

Here's something else to consider: the inexorable rise of regular ticket prices along with premium tickets makes it virtually impossible to nurture younger audiences as future theatergoers. When I served as chairman of the Theatre Development Fund in the 1990s, we developed a program (born of an idea of Wendy Wasserstein) to enlist the help of theater professionals (actors, directors, playwrights) to introduce small groups of inner-city high school students to the Broadway theater. Each group of one professional and about ten students would attend six shows in a season and then go back to TDF's offices for pizza and a roundtable discussion about what they had just seen. The tickets were subsidized by TDF and the producers of shows participating in the program.

Most of these students had never been to a Broadway show or any professional play for that matter. To witness these students' surprise, wonder, and joy from what they experienced walking into a Broadway theater for the first time was a revelation for all of us at TDF, as well as for the mentors. At one show I mentored, I accompanied a high school senior from Harlem who had just been admitted to an Ivy League school. As he looked over his *Playbill* before the show began, he turned to me and asked, "What's an intermission?" When I explained it to him, he wanted to know what we would do for fifteen minutes. Here was a young man, with great intellectual talent, who had lived in New York City his entire life but had never set foot in a Broadway theater. In fact, he told me he rarely even traveled to midtown.

The Wendy Project, as it's now known, continues today. Not long before Wendy's untimely death, she said to me that we needed to take the next step with the program. It simply wasn't enough, she argued, to expose these students to the theater without giving them the chance to revisit the experience and develop their cultural awareness by seeing more shows. It struck her that it was frustrating, or even cruel, to introduce young students to something so transcendent from their everyday lives, just to have it be out of reach in the future because of such high ticket prices.

There are no easy solutions. TDF was created in 1968 to address audience development and it continues to do extraordinary work. But no one organization can do it all. It will take a concerted effort by commercial producers, theater owners on Broadway, and others around the country to devise the means by which we can attract and sustain new audiences. Many regional theaters have such programs, as do individual producers for their own plays. However, the job is one that needs to be addressed beyond the industry by the federal and local governments and the corporate sector. That will happen only with public and private leadership willing to pay attention to these concerns. Without a national imperative, the theater and all the arts will inexorably become the exclusive province of the very few while our broader culture will be increasingly dominated by a popular market mentality that seeks to please the masses.

The Press Agent

Your press agent needs to be all things to all people. He needs to coddle, schmooze, and monitor the press and the critics. More important, he needs to know their likes and dislikes. He needs to be responsive to their special requests (interviews, photo ops, guest appearances) and be aware of what prejudices (good or bad) a journalist may bring to the material or the cast. If the agent is representing a revival, he needs to figure out if the play is beloved by the critics (*Death of a Salesman*) or is a vehicle for a big TV star. In the latter case, the challenge will be not to offend those reporters or publications that don't get the first interview with the star or some other special treatment. Your agent also needs to establish a close rapport with the cast and the star's personal press agent and manager, who may have their own ideas on how best to present and protect their client.

If your play doesn't have a big star or some other high profile, you and your agent will have to figure out how best to capture the attention of the press. Here are the kinds of questions your agent will raise and then try to answer with your and the creative team's help:

- What is it about this show or the production that is newsworthy?
- Why should an editor reserve space for an article about your play?
- Is the subject matter particularly provocative or controversial?
- Are the authors old hands or are they a new breed of young talent?
- Is there something unusual about any of the design elements?
- Has the show gone through a particularly unusual out-of-town tryout that might make it the dark horse of the season?
- Or, is the show so top-heavy with big stars and a renowned director that everyone is just waiting for the mighty to fall?

A good agent with his ear to the ground will help you devise a public relations profile from your very first press release that will complement what your ad and marketing teams devise for your show. Effective press-agenting is as creative as any other part of producing a show. A press agent is invaluable, but only when he's in sync with your vision and objectives for the show.

As for opening night, it usually calls for two or three Valium or Xanax for both you and your press agent. Your agent needs to make sure the invited stars and other VIPs are happy—have Oprah Winfrey and the star's mother-in-law been put in the right seats? Will they all have their cars ready to take them to the party? Has anyone been slighted by not getting the red carpet treatment? Will the curtain go up later than a half hour after the announced time, making the audience impatient and annoyed? And during all this time, he's checking his emails to get the early reviews—elation or defeat? In any event, by the time the evening is over—pure exhaustion.

After the show opens and hopefully gets great notices, the anxieties of opening night are soon forgotten. And those first media impressions made before the show opened will naturally morph into other fresh stories that your agent will disseminate so that your show continues to receive coverage throughout the media. As a show ages, it can become increasingly difficult to get the attention of the press. A show running five, ten, or more years is old news, but a creative press agent will find clever ways of raising and revising a show's profile in conjunction with your ad and marketing teams as they renew and update your message and images.

Last sobering fact: for any new show struggling to find its way among the other thirty to forty shows that open each year, when the Tony Awards are announced at the end of the season, it will either become the show's crowning moment or its death toll. The truth is that no agent, ad rep, or marketing genius has ever been able to come up with a better slogan than "Best Musical" or "Best Play."

27

Catharsis

Opening Night

Nothing should be more liberating than an opening night. It is the apotheosis of celebration for a Broadway show—a night to congratulate the army of creators, performers, technicians, staff, and, of course, your investors, for their determination, perseverance, and faith (against all odds) in bringing an idea, conjured up years ago, to a Broadway stage. For the producer, it should also be a time to put behind all the anxieties and pent-up emotions accumulated during the many years of preparation. And for the creative team, it should be a glamorous and exhilarating experience. The truth is, however, openings are much more complicated affairs.

For the producer, high anxiety still prevails as he waits out the critics' verdicts and contemplates inheriting a flop, struggling with a middling success, or hitting the jackpot. For the authors, the same emotions take hold, but it's more personal for them. Their reputations as artists (and egos) are on the line. Veteran authors and actors know the sting of being lambasted and the unfettered joy of being praised. For the uninitiated, well, they will just have to learn what it's like either way.[1]

The celebrity of these events has faded over the years. What was once a major news story is today just another blurb in the *New York Post* and largely ignored on *Extra* or *Entertainment Weekly*, unless of course a movie star or highly rated TV personality is in attendance. Openings

---

[1] I can recall a dinner one night when a wise director was giving avuncular advice to a first-time writer whose show was about to open on Broadway. We all suspected the critics were not going to be kind. The director warned that the sting of getting bad reviews on opening night doesn't end the matter. They are followed by many other reviews that keep dribbling in for days, if not weeks afterward. It's hurtful and personal.

used to be black-tie affairs. Limos stretched for blocks as they lined up to discharge VIPs in front of the red-carpeted entrance to the theater. (It's now de rigueur to arrive in a black Escalade.) I recall, early in my career, snagging a ticket to the Broadway opening of a new play, *Dreyfus in Rehearsal*, at the Shubert Theatre. I got the seat from a friend who worked for the GM, Jack Schlissel. When we got to the theater, Schlissel stopped us at the door. He looked us over and saw we were wearing suits—not evening clothes. He switched our tickets from the orchestra to the dreaded side balcony where no one could see what we were wearing. Today, Schlissel would have been happy to see we weren't wearing jeans and a T-shirt.

In the past, the critics attended the official opening, which gave the proceedings an air of anticipation akin to waiting for the jury to decide the fate of the accused. Today, the critics attend two or three nights before the official opening, so they can ruminate and rethink their initial impressions and sharpen their knives for the kill or polish their adjectives for headline-grabbing quotes. In an instant, they can decide the fate of a show ten years in the making. I'm exaggerating somewhat. Today, as compared to twenty years or so ago, for better or worse, critics don't dictate a play's success or failure in the same way they did back then.

Many factors have come into play over the past twenty years that have diminished the power and influence of the critics: rapidly decreasing readership of newspapers and magazines; explosive proliferation of the Internet and social media, chat rooms, blogs, and other sites offer opinions from the guy next door and self-appointed critics; and, finally, the production of more musicals geared either toward younger audiences (à la Disney), or to those who care mostly about who's starring in the show or whether it's based on a popular film.

Just spend some time milling around the TKTS discount ticket booth in Father Duffy Square at Broadway and West Forty-Seventh Street before a show. The questions most often asked are: "Who's in the play?" "Did it win a Tony?" and, less often, "Did it get good reviews?" Annual surveys conducted by the Broadway League regularly report that word of mouth has increasingly become a prime consideration for selecting a show, well above critics' opinions.

This slow turnabout in the forces that shape the future of a play can also have unforeseen consequences. How else to explain the feeling of despair when a playwright has her play open to positive reviews by all the first-string critics only to play to 40 percent capacity and close within a few weeks? Years ago, favorable reviews virtually guaranteed success, and actors earned their stardom by first appearing on Broadway and then going to Hollywood. Today, an author faces the harsh reality of being told by a producer that her play, regardless of its intrinsic merits, will find an audience only by casting the right movie or TV star. And, it isn't enough just to have a recognizable name. It has to be someone who, when listed above the title, will guarantee a sell-out, not because of great reviews, but even despite bad ones.

Arriving at the Theater

By the time you've gotten to the theater for the opening, your press agent will already know a handful of reviews, but most likely not the *New York Times* (unless he has an inside mole). It's hard to recommend what to do about this. If you're tipped off about receiving generally negative notices, you will have lost the chance to indulge freely in well-deserved congratulations for everyone, free from the outside noise of the press and critics, at least for a few precious hours. There will be time enough, later that night and afterward, to bemoan a disappointing reception or revel even more in great acclaim. My advice is to tell your press agent to keep the news to himself and not meet your eyes before the evening is done, lest you pick up on his elation or despair.

As you enter the theater, don't be surprised if no one recognizes you or if the press ignores you. You're just the producer. Gone are the likes of David Merrick, David Belasco, and Flo Ziegfeld, who were recognizable figures, equal in stature and notoriety to the stars. If you have any doubt about this, watch a theatergoer stare in bewilderment as she scans the forty or so names that regularly appear above the title of a play in *Playbill*. Only one or two names listed on the first line are the general partners who have any legitimate producing authority. The others are major investors who may be consulted, but make no decisions. The man on the street is unaware of these distinctions.

While we're on the subject of title-page credits—several years ago, those responsible for administering the Tony Awards decided that anyone who received billing above the title of the play was entitled to receive a Tony Award medallion if the show won Best Play or Best Musical. Only three silver trophies are given free of charge to the winning show, but the other "producers" listed on the title page can buy a medallion for their mantle for a few hundred dollars. In a time when raising money for plays and musicals is as difficult as ever, it has become a commonplace practice to attract investors by setting minimum amounts (say, $50,000 for a play and $250,000 for a musical) in order to receive above-the-title billing and the chance to get a Tony medallion—hence, a village of producers listed in *Playbill.*

As for the rest of the credits, if you look at a *Playbill* from twenty years ago, the title page was reserved for the cast, the authors, designers, director, and, for a musical, the choreographer, orchestrators, and arrangers. With the rise of the influence and authority of GMs in the 1980s, they began to ask for title-page billing. That was followed by the press agent and advertising agencies. The floodgates then opened to virtually everyone—special-effects coordinator, hairstylist, fight director, marketing group, production supervisor, etc.

Don't misunderstand me. All of these people deserve appropriate credit for their contributions to the show. My only quarrel with the current state of affairs is that crowding sixteen or more of the show's personnel and forty or more producers on the title page necessarily diminishes the importance of those artists who have contributed, over many years, the ideas, concepts, and seminal art to the enterprise and who rightfully should enjoy a position of prominence reserved for the very few, and not for the many. In fact, with so many credits on the page, it all becomes one big blur, thereby rendering everyone's credit unreadable.

I've had this discussion many times with my colleagues, and most agree that this has spiraled out of control. It's all due to, "If they're getting credit, then I should, too." If there were a viable alternative, perhaps even those who now require title-page billing would be willing to consider it for everyone's sake. A possible solution would be to look to the film business, where billing for the so-called "below-the-line" personnel, who are mostly salaried, is distinguished from that of the players who are also paid a percentage of the film's revenues.[2] For the theater, perhaps, there could be another place in the *Playbill* to credit the salaried personnel, somewhere after the title page and right before the staff page listing at the end of the "Who's Who" section. Just a thought.

Before the Curtain

You will want to go backstage before the curtain to hug your cast and pump up your staff and crew. Anyone who has seen *The Producers* knows you never say "good luck," but rather "break a leg" or "*merde*," a superstition peculiar to the theater that's alive and well even today. You will also have had distributed opening night gifts delivered to everyone associated with the show. They can run the gamut from modest favors with the show's logo to more lavish gifts. You should splurge on your authors, director, and other members of the core creative team. Whatever the tensions and disagreements that preceded the opening, this is a time when you need to rise above the fray and show your sincere gratitude. In my view, what's even more important is to accompany your gift with a handwritten note expressing your personal thanks.

When you're finally ready to enter the theater, don't be surprised to see that not all the best seats have been reserved for your family, friends, and investors. The theater owner will have reserved dozens of seats for himself and *his* family and friends, as is his right under the booking contract. Also, as noted previously, your artistic team will have been allocated five or six pairs of house seats to which they are entitled under their agreements. Your press agent will also have set aside choice seats for any celebrities or other notable guests. Meanwhile, you had better be sure you have accommodated all of your investors by affording them seating commensurate with their level of investment. Attending opening night and the party that follows are considered inalienable rights by every investor in a Broadway show. For a producer to forget that fact is

---

[2] In a film production budget, the below-the-line artists are the cinematographer, production designer, film editor, and similar personnel. The above-the-line consists of stars, writers, directors, and producers.

to bring the wrath of God upon himself (and a sound rebuff when he asks that investor for money for his *next* show).

If your nerves will allow, you might want to mill around the front of house to greet your guests, but heaven knows you don't want to run into someone fuming over the fact that he's been relegated to the first balcony. Most producers are simply too anxious to chitchat before an opening. They prefer to be backstage with their cast and crew, almost as if they're in the labor room awaiting the birth of a baby. There'll be time enough later, at the party, to greet and mingle with everyone else. And let's not forget the deft Merrick touch of coming down the aisle to take his place in row E, seat 101, just a minute or two before the curtain rises.

28

The Opening Night Party

After the opening, the producer is expected to throw a party. You should do that. It's meant to be for your cast and crew, your investors, and everyone who has worked on the show. It's a time to celebrate your show officially entering the annals of Broadway. No mean feat.

Your GM will have budgeted about $100,000 for the party. You can spend less or a lot more, depending on the venue, the food, and the entertainment. If possible, try to get sponsorship for the party, at least for the booze.

Having attended hundreds of these affairs, I'll offer a list of don'ts. If you follow this advice, your party will be just fine:

- Don't hire an amateur to organize the party. Suzanne Tobak is the doyenne of opening night parties. You need to hire a Tobak or one of the other party managers who know the protocol and can identify the VIPs you can't afford to offend. The best sign your party is going smoothly is when Tobak is looking relaxed and happy. If there's fear in her eyes, you're probably in big trouble. At one of my parties, I spied Tobak across the room hurrying toward me, obviously with important news. Pat Schoenfeld, Gerry's wife and the ultimate arbiter of opening nights, had just given Tobak the thumbs-up and told her, "It's the best opening night party I've been to in years." Victory was ours!
- Don't forget to personally thank everyone who worked on the show, from your star to the stage doorman. They deserve your attention.
- Don't pick a venue that's too far from the theater. Your guests want to leave the theater and get to the party quickly without having to climb aboard a school bus that takes them down to Chelsea Piers.

- Don't delay serving the food (usually a buffet). The veteran opening-nighters will get to the party within minutes of the curtain and they'll expect to grab a drink and fill their plates so they can eat and run.
- Don't put "Reserved" signs on every table, leaving little or no seating for the majority of your guests. Try to limit the reserved seating to your cast and creative team. They'll get to the party later than everyone else. Nothing is worse than seeing members of your cast looking lost and bereft as they search for someplace to sit.
- Don't have the band or DJ blast the music early on when everyone wants to mingle, and the professionals want to "do the room." Later, the cast can take the dance floor and control the evening.
- Don't serve food that needs to be cut up. Serve finger food.
- Don't serve complimentary soft drinks, beer, and wine and then charge for hard booze. If you can't afford Ketel One and Chivas, okay, but you don't want your guests discussing your cheap bar.
- Don't make a speech. No one wants to hear from you.
- Don't get spifflicated yourself. Get a nice buzz on so you're congenial and relaxed. But you'll need your head on straight when the reviews come in, good or bad.
- Don't be disingenuous. If you say, "I'm not concerned about the reviews right now. What's important is that we gave them the show we wanted to do," *mean* it.

There is one thing I miss at today's opening night parties. Before the 1980s, the first-night critics attended the opening night performance. When the curtain came down, you would see them rushing up the aisle to beat everyone else out of the theater where they would catch a cab or walk back rapidly to their desks at their papers.

No one at the party knew anything about any of the reviews. Those in attendance celebrated unabashedly and in utter ignorance of the show's critical fate. All of this lent drama and tension as the evening wore on. Those who sat close to the critics in the theater would try to guess at what they were thinking, although most critics were accustomed to wearing poker faces throughout the show, except for the one or two who could be seen nodding off in the middle of act 2. They usually gave the show a rave review, at least the parts they were awake for.

I remember the opening night party for *Annie*, which was held right next to the Alvin Theatre (now the Neil Simon) at Gallaghers Steakhouse on West Fifty-Second Street. The place was jam-packed. The show had gotten a mixed reception out of town, but work had been done and New York audiences were very enthusiastic, with great word of mouth on the street. Yet there was no way of predicting how a sentimental, comic-strip musical would land with the New York critics.

At about 11:15 p.m., Reid Shelton, who played Daddy Warbucks, stood up on the bar in the front of the restaurant. Blessed with a booming bass voice, Shelton bellowed to the crowd to be quiet. He had just gotten a copy of the *New York Times* review from the show's press agent and he was going to read it out loud.

Everyone was standing and holding their breath. I knew it had to be good—Shelton wasn't so obtuse as to get up and read a pan. But, nonetheless, the tension was unbearable. I mean, how good was it, really? Just favorable? Or would it be a certifiable rave with dozens of quotes that could appear on the marquee, in print and all over town?

Shelton read the Clive Barnes review with tears in his eyes: "To dislike the new musical *Annie*, which opened last night at the Alvin Theatre, would be tantamount to disliking motherhood, peanut butter, friendly mongrel dogs and nostalgia. It also would be unnecessary, for *Annie* is an intensely likeable musical. You might even call it lovable; it seduces one, and should settle down to being a sizeable hit."

Up went a roar of approval, drinks were spilled, and everyone hugged and kissed each other. It was like New Year's Eve.

I wish that kind of celebration were possible today. Now, the critics attend performances two or three days before the opening. Except for the *New York Times*, many of the reviews are leaked ahead of publication. Press agents are prized for their ability to get advance word of the notices. By opening night, many of the reviews are already known to the producers. By 10:00 p.m., the New York Times review is online.

Word gets around the party pretty fast. Many know the verdict before they arrive. If the news is good, the party lasts until midnight and continues on to another late-night club. When it's bad, only a few stragglers are left.

There's something to be said for the way it was back then in 1977 when *Annie* opened. Our innocence often served us well. And sometimes ignorance *is* bliss.

29

The Choices We Make

> And what I really don't want to do is teach other people how to do what I should be doing myself.
>
> —Cassie in *A Chorus Line*

In the summer of 2006, I was lying flat on my back on the floor of my suite at the Clift Hotel in San Francisco. Next door, at the Curran Theatre, my new production of *A Chorus Line* was nearing the end of tech rehearsals and was about to begin previews.

My journey to the floor of this hotel started back in 2005, when I decided to produce my first Broadway show. At the time, I was chair of the Entertainment Department at Paul, Weiss. As the executor of Michael Bennett's estate, I, along with the other owners of the rights to *A Chorus Line*, was being pursued regularly to license a Broadway revival of the show.

Having practiced entertainment law for over thirty-five years, and having tutored dozens of producers, I wanted to finally try producing a Broadway show myself. But it loomed before me as a momentous decision. Could I bring myself to leave a practice I had built up for the past three decades? All for the chance to leap into the abyss of producing, with all of the attendant risks of which I was so acutely aware?

The first step was to get the consent of the other owners of the property. I convened a meeting of all the representatives in a conference room in my office. They included Biff Liff, a former associate of David Merrick and one of the best agents in the business, representing the James Kirkwood Estate along with Elisa Lefkowitz, the estate's lawyer; Ellen Mercado, Nicholas Dante's representative; Alan Stein, the Ed Kleban estate's lawyer; and Sarah Douglas, the estate's agent. I had already spoken to Marvin Hamlisch before the meeting about my intentions and had received his blessing. Bob Avian cautioned me about the risks, but ultimately supported my foray into the abyss and agreed to come out of his unofficial "retirement" to direct the revival. Although I had known all of them for decades, I had no idea how they would respond to my proposition. After all, they were entrusted with protecting their clients' interests in an American classic and needed to be sure it was put into trustworthy and experienced hands. I might have toiled in the outer fields of the theater business for years, but I had never produced before.

I opened the meeting by plunging right into the subject—it was time to revive *A Chorus Line* and I wanted to be its producer. At first, they were all taken aback. After a pause and a few questions, one by one, each of them expressed support and gave me their enthusiastic approval. I will always be grateful for the show of confidence I got that afternoon from all of those representatives. Little did they know that, underneath my seemingly calm demeanor, I had been sure they would dismiss my overture with a polite but firm denial. Theirs was the first indication of whether or not I was fooling myself that I could pull this off in the community. Without their strong endorsement, I don't think I would ever have had the gumption to move forward.

At the end of the meeting, Alan Stein, Kleban's lawyer, asked if he could have a moment with me alone in my office. Stein, now deceased, was a wise man and, at the time, an elder statesman of the entertainment bar, specializing in the music business. He could be a very aggressive adversary, but I respected his judgment and integrity. We always got along and usually agreed on most issues regarding *A Chorus Line*.

In my office, Stein reiterated his support, but then asked, "Are you ready to leave your practice? I can't understand how you can walk away from a partnership with Paul, Weiss to produce."

I explained to Stein that I wasn't going to leave Paul, Weiss, and that I had made a special arrangement with the firm to continue with my practice *and* produce the show. Instead of reacting with relief, Stein shook his head and said, "That's a mistake. You can't do both." I tried to explain. "It doesn't matter," he said, and counseled me to think long and hard about the decision. Stein had great regard for the legal profession, and, to his mind, it was inconceivable that I could keep all these balls up in the air. As he left my office, he turned and said with a mischievous grin, "Oh, and by the way, we want a $250,000 advance."

I believe the choices we make, combined with happenstance, or luck, propel us through our lives. What Stein said to me that day, more than nine years ago, has stayed with me, not so much as a haunt but more as a reminder of this period of my life when the choices I faced would dictate the rest of my professional career.

So here I was, two years later, in my suite in San Francisco, with excruciating back pain. A dozen massages, visits to several doctors and chiropractors, and a lot of painkillers had no effect. Nothing seemed to work. Maybe this was what they meant by being out of town with a musical.

I had set up a mini-office in my suite in one room, with a computer, printer, and all sorts of office supplies so I could attend to my law practice from six each morning (nine New York time) until midafternoon, when I would go to the theater for rehearsals and preview performances. After the show, Bob Avian, his partner Peter Pileski, Nan, and I would go off to the local bar to rake over that evening's performance. We weren't rewriting the show, but we would scrutinize everything else until about 1:00 a.m. or so. Then, the next morning, before everybody else got up leisurely at ten or eleven, I'd be awake by six to begin another day of reading contracts and making calls to negotiate my clients' deals. In the back of my mind I knew this was all crazy, but I was working on excess adrenaline and the truth was I was never happier than when I was at the theater.

But back to my back.

I struggled through previews and the opening, plied with codeine and whatever else I could get my hands on. San Francisco and the critics embraced the show. The *San Francisco Chronicle* has its own version of four stars: at the top of the review, near the byline, sits a little man in an armchair. Depending on whether the show is a dud, so-so, pretty good, or a smash, the little man will take on four different guises from sleeping (a flop) to leaping out of his chair (a rave). Carole Shorenstein Hays, owner of the theater, said this made it simpler for the readers to decide whether or not to see the show. There was no need to read the review, just check out the man.

The little guy was jumping for *A Chorus Line*. Our success made it possible for me to come to New York with 20 percent of my investors' money recouped. It is a testament to Bob Avian; Baayork Lee (the original Connie and choreographer of the revival); the designers, Robin Wagner (sets), Theoni Aldredge (costumes), and Natasha Katz (whose lighting stood in for Tharon Musser's original lighting plan); and the cast and crew. I also need to make special mention of Alan Wasser and Aaron Lustbader, my GMs, whose vigilance and expertise made me look good. Sorry if this sounds like an acceptance speech, but I loved working with all of these artists and appreciate that nearly perfect experiences don't come often.[1]

When I got home from San Francisco, I went to more doctors about my back including an orthopedist at Lenox Hill Hospital who ran a battery of tests only to tell me that I had the back of someone twenty years younger, with no evidence of any injury or other ailments.

The mystery was solved when my internist, having run every blood test imaginable, checked me for Lyme disease, and, sure enough, that was the culprit. I got on a heavy dose of antibiotics and was cured within ten days.

Despite a lukewarm review from the *New York Times*, the other mostly favorable notices and good word of mouth made it possible for the show to recoup in record time (nineteen weeks) and have a healthy run on Broadway and on tour. That may have also helped to ease the pain.

Lessons Learned

I felt I had gotten a new lease on life when I decided to produce. But I was also terrified. I had witnessed so much over the years standing on the sidelines—unprecedented success on rare occasions and abject failure more often than not.

I thought I was ready to try producing mainly because of the many lessons I had learned from observing hundreds of producers and artists plying their crafts. Ironically, I was concerned that perhaps knowing all

---

[1] *A Chorus Line* was nominated that season for Best Musical Revival. We lost to Stephen Sondheim's *Company*. Who better to lose to than your own client? My only regret was not being able to thank everyone associated with the show. I had to write this book to finally do it officially.

the pitfalls and dangers lurking around every corner could make for a wary traveler. I knew the attributes of a good producer included blind ambition and relentlessness in the pursuit of success against all odds.

It became quickly apparent to me that the job of producing was more than daunting. Several of my closest clients and law partners financed the show as limited partners. Otherwise, I struck out on my own with no other general partners. Looking back, I know I had to do it for myself, but I now appreciate the benefits of having producing partners that you can trust and with whom you can commiserate. Producing solo can be a very lonely affair. Both victory and defeat are better served in the company of others.

If you're going to do the job responsibly, you will find it is a full-time occupation, both before you open and afterward as you nurture the play's growth.

And Now Life Really Begins

All of this hit me like a sledgehammer in the fall of 2006 and early 2007, after the opening. My back pain might have been the result of Lyme disease, but my psyche and emotional bearings were beginning to get frazzled as I worked on the show incessantly and continued to tend to my clients. Managing a show, especially a hit, is a daily affair—checking the wraps (the amount of money coming in from ticket sales each day), watching the advance, adjusting advertising and marketing campaigns, addressing crises backstage with your cast and crew, preparing road tours, and fielding offers from foreign producers—all this and the barrage of the usual phone calls and daily crises of my clients continued unabated. I realized later that summer that I was going to have to make a choice—it was the show or my practice. I couldn't do both. Hello, Alan Stein!

I sought counseling to help me through this period. I wasn't depressed. On the contrary, I was elated while working on *A Chorus Line* and felt dragged down only by the relentless pressure and demands of my law practice. But I knew I had to turn to a third party to help me sort out my future. I struggled in the sessions with all the pros and cons, just like a good lawyer. After months of wringing my hands and tearing my hair out, I came to a very simple conclusion: I would leave Paul, Weiss and devote my full time to the show and future producing projects. It was inconceivable to me that I would turn the show over to someone else. Since I couldn't do both and I knew I faced mandatory retirement from the firm eventually, I chose producing.

Musings

Early in the book I mentioned that the stereotypical portrait of a Broadway producer as a flamboyant, reckless entrepreneur has been molded and embedded in the public's subconscious over many years. The fact is no such prototype exists. There are many types of producers who come from all different backgrounds:

- Theater owners (particularly when their theaters are empty)
- Not-for-profit theaters
- General managers (who also want to do for themselves what they've been teaching others to do)
- Hollywood independent producers (film and TV)
- Hollywood film studios (most notably Disney, but all of the other majors occasionally)
- Related entertainment companies from other media (such as Marvel, which co-produced *Spider-Man: Turn Off the Dark*)
- British and other foreign producers
- Writers (such as Andrew Lloyd Webber, Neil Simon, and Richard Rodgers)
- The rich and famous (such as Oprah Winfrey and Whoopi Goldberg)
- Former talent and press agents (and lawyers)
- Heirs, divorcées, and others who have come into substantial discretionary funds

Who's missing from the list? Just the ordinary guy, of modest means, who decides to become a producer and succeeds by dint of an education, the sweat of his brow, hard experience, an innate intelligence, and some luck. Producing in the theater has rarely been a profession available to everyone. Most come to it by way of another profession, through the back door, or by the serendipity of unearned wealth.

Even those who have earned a good living from general managing or other regular paying work rarely leave their "day jobs," knowing that earning a living wage from producing eludes most everyone. Having observed (and represented) each of the types listed above, I've tried to glean the personal qualities and temperament of a good, if not great, producer, regardless of the number of Tonys on his or her mantelpiece or the amassing of great wealth:

- *Passion.* After reading a play or musical, or attending a workshop, I ask myself, "Can I imagine getting up each morning to work on something like this? Maybe it'll make money, but how can I devote my time, money, and energy to this material?" For me, more often than not, the answer to the first question is, "No." But the never-ending search for material that strikes all the right chords, even in its infancy or rough form, is fueled by a producer's obsession to bring a show to life, regardless of those who disagree with his assessment or the odds against success.
- *Appreciation of the artist.* Most able producers crave the vicarious pleasure of nurturing and observing the artist at work. Understanding the egos and predilections of the creative team takes experience and an innate ability to balance the artists' creative freedom with a commercial agenda that recognizes the practical demands of getting the play ready for production.
- *Faith in instincts.* If you believe you have the talent and good sense to produce, then you have to make hard choices and decisions based on what is right for the show and what is consonant with your initial instinct to produce it. More often than not, when I've looked back at my mistakes, I've thought, "I should have gone with my instincts." That's not to say those instincts are always right, but that's why it's your show and not someone else's that you've invested in.
- *Financial as well as emotional investment in the show.* It's not enough just to emote to your future investors about the artistic merits of the show. If you're presenting yourself as a commercial producer, you need not only to present cogent and responsible financial projections, but also to back them up with your own

personal financial commitment (notwithstanding Max Bialystock's golden rule[2]). The level of commitment should be commensurate with your own financial wherewithal and the perception your investors have of your ability to take risk. If you are not in the position of putting up a cent, then you probably shouldn't be producing in the first place.

- *An ability to focus on what can be controlled without being distracted by what's beyond reach.* I've touched on this before, but it's worth repeating. Timing, luck, bad weather, chat rooms, and critics' reviews are unknowable variables to be reckoned with after the event, not before. You and your creative team can control every word, spoken and sung, and everything that's seen onstage. Those objectives, in and of themselves, are mammoth efforts and demand nothing but constant and relentless pursuit. Put aside the rest.

In spite of spending decades helping my clients get a play or musical onstage, I began my producing career with enormous anticipation but with an equal dose of apprehension. I knew from my experience much of what I've discussed in this book, but to actually do it myself was another thing altogether. After trying my hand at it for the past decade, I now have a deeper appreciation and respect for those who are best at it.

Many of my friends and colleagues often lament the sorry state of the theater. That's nothing new. When I first started in the business in the seventies, the predictions of the theater's demise had already been going on for decades. If this wasn't true, the New York theater would have its own version of Silicon Valley—on the west side of Manhattan between Fortieth and Fifty-Fourth Streets—with thousands of producers of every stripe.

Those of us who are fortunate, or unfortunate, enough to be besotted by the theater can't leave it alone. As producers, we need to hope that the artists will always be there, not by some miracle, but by encouraging and supporting them to examine the human condition so they can create good work, whether that be in a reading, a workshop, or a not-for-profit theater.

Or perhaps in an all-night session of dancers, downtown, talking about their lives over pizza and cheap wine.

---

[2] "Never put your own money in the show."

Epilogue

When I decided to leave my law practice and start producing in 2007, it wasn't the first time I had looked into the abyss and moved over to the dark side.

Thirty years earlier, I had left Paul, Weiss as a young sixth-year associate and joined Michael Bennett as his producing partner. Along with Bob Avian and Michael's go-everywhere and do-everything assistant, Susan MacNair, we formed a production company called Quadrille Productions.

Leaving my firm in 1977 may not have been as momentous a decision as when I left in 2007, but it was nonetheless a bold and very risky move at the time. I was newly married with a four-year-old stepdaughter, Eliza. Paul, Weiss paid its associates well, but I went from bachelorhood to being the head of a family overnight. Living in Manhattan in the seventies with rampant inflation ripping up the economy left me with little, if any, savings.

The partners at the firm encouraged me to stay. They said I was "on track" for partnership and gave me every sign that I'd be asked to join the firm as a partner in a couple of years. On the other hand, Bob Montgomery, one of my mentors at the firm, sensed that I had to try my hand at producing, and told me he understood why I couldn't turn Michael down. He told me that I would always regret not taking this chance, even if it turned out not to be the right choice.

When I told my parents what I was thinking of doing, they were horrified at the thought of my leaving my legal career behind and running off to play at producing on Broadway. They knew I loved to visit Broadway, but they didn't want me to live there.

Nan, on the other hand, knew that I wouldn't be able to pass up the chance to do what had lain in the back of my mind for all those years since I was boy. And so did Michael. They urged me to leave the firm and join him in what seemed to me at the time to be a bright and boundless future.

After all, following *A Chorus Line*, the entertainment world beckoned to Michael. He was the most sought-after director/choreographer on

Broadway. Any project could be his for the asking. As I discussed in an earlier chapter, after flirting with the film business for a year, he fled Hollywood, repelled by its corporate culture and the dominance of committee decision-making over the individual artist. When he returned home to New York, he focused all of his energies on Broadway.

By early 1978, we had set up offices for Quadrille at the newly acquired building at 890 Broadway. Since Michael now had the financial resources to do just about anything he wanted, this new company provided him the infrastructure and artistic and business independence he had longed to have for many years. The projects we began to develop included a new version of *Peter Pan* (maybe for Mikhail Baryshnikov?); an adaptation of the Jimmy Cagney–Doris Day film *Love Me or Leave Me*; a musical based on the Children's Crusade, with a score by Jimmy Webb; and a musical about a young woman who decides to leave her husband, travel to Europe, and explore her sexuality (*Scandal*). Even Irving Berlin, then in his nineties, who repeatedly refused everyone who asked permission to adapt *Easter Parade* into a musical, immediately said yes to Michael.

Somewhat to my surprise, the project Michael decided on for his next musical was *Ballroom*. I've talked about this show earlier, so suffice it to say that it struck me and others close to Michael as a peculiar choice. It was difficult to imagine him being drawn to the late-middle-aged lead characters or the plot of a widow's search for a new identity after her husband's death. Giving employment to older dancers seemed to be the one thing driving Michael to do the show, as well as his early attraction to working with Jerome Kass, Billy Goldenberg, and the Bergmans.

For me, from the first day of our partnership, I sensed that several people who had close relationships with Michael resented my presence. It was one thing to be Michael's lawyer and advisor; it was another thing altogether for us to be business partners. It threatened their sense of entitlement to have immediate and direct access to Michael. *A Chorus Line* had also made many people rich and seemed to give bleary-eyed Broadway hope for a revitalized future.

I found out later that Bernie Jacobs was apoplectic about Quadrille and the plans Michael and I were making. With Michael's penchant for identifying all those close to him as relatives, Bernie relished taking on the role of Michael's father, literally, and his godfather, figuratively. I might be a brother to Michael, but I would be no match for Bernie's obsessive power and influence over him.

Bernie's campaign to oust me started almost as soon as I arrived at 890. His wife Betty was at the time working for Michael as a reader. She supported Bernie, of course, as did Michael's accountant, Marvin Shulman, who bristled when he was told that I would be supervising and reviewing all of Michael's bank accounts. To his credit, Joe Papp never objected to my association with Michael. He knew Michael needed to spread his wings and come out from under the shadow of others, including Papp himself.

The pressure put on Michael by Bernie eventually became unbearable. Michael turned pale when I told him of being awakened one Sunday morning by an eight o'clock phone call from Bernie. I can't remember the specific reason for the call, but I do remember him saying he could "crush" me if he wanted to. I laughed it off, knowing full well this was just a misbegotten outburst of Bernie's jealousy. Nan didn't laugh. When I told Michael, he didn't laugh either. In fact, these extreme actions only fed into his paranoia at the time about Mafia figures following him and his perceived need to keep the Shuberts close to him since, as Bernie would remind Michael often, they could make or break him. As for Nan and me, we began to wonder whether the head of our dog might be found under our bedsheets one morning.

Meanwhile, back at 890, I was unhappy and disillusioned with my new career. Although, yes, I was producing *Ballroom* for Michael, it was unsatisfying and frustrating. While I was accustomed to talking to dozens of clients each day in my law practice about their projects, my day-to-day job now was one-dimensional. Michael was fully occupied and absorbed with the show, and had little time or inclination to discuss business. That was my job, and he was more than happy to trust me to do whatever I thought was right.

However, one Monday morning in late May, Michael came into my office, shut the door, and sat down. I knew what was coming. He said, "I think it's best for both of us, our sanity and our careers, that we abandon Quadrille and you go back to your practice." He looked shaken and was trembling. Gone was the joy and anticipation he had exuded months earlier when he had spoken about the newly found freedom to do whatever he chose and his chance to give back to Broadway all that it had given him. He said, "They won't let us do this. They're too powerful, and we're too young and weak to fight them."

We embraced and I left. I went home to tell Nan. We walked the streets of Manhattan reeling from the realization that in only five short months, we had gone from that exhilarating snowy evening with Michael at 890 to this moment of dejection and disillusionment.

That night, Michael called me at home at around nine. He said he needed me to come over to his apartment right away. He wanted me to listen to something. It had been an enervating day, and I had planned to go to bed early. He wouldn't take no for an answer. Nan, being her usual supportive self, encouraged me to go.

I climbed into a cab outside my apartment on East Eighty-Second Street. As we made our way down to 40 Central Park South, I asked myself what could possibly be that important for Michael to play for me at this peculiar moment.

When I arrived, Michael greeted me at the door with quite a good buzz on. His apartment reflected his personality—you couldn't tell where the windows stopped and the mirrors began. He told me to sit down and have a drink. "Listen carefully," he said, as he turned on the stereo.

Slow down you crazy child.
You're so ambitious for a juvenile.
But then if you're so smart,
tell me why are you still so afraid?
Where's the fire, what's the hurry about?
You better cool it off before you burn it out.
You got so much to do and only
so many hours in a day.
But you know that when the truth is told
that you can get what you want
or you can just get old.
You're gonna kick off before you even get halfway through.

When will you realize, Vienna waits for you?
Slow down. You're doing fine.
You can't be everything you want to be before your time.
Although it's so romantic on the borderline tonight.
Too bad, but it's the life you lead.
You're so ahead of yourself that you forgot what you need.
Though you can see when you're wrong
you know you can't always see when you're right (you're right).
You got your passion, you got your pride,
but don't you know that only fools are satisfied?
Dream on, but don't imagine they'll all come true.
When will you realize, Vienna waits for you?
Slow down you crazy child.
Take the phone off the hook and disappear for a while.
It's all right, you can afford to lose a day or two.
When will you realize, Vienna waits for you?

The song was "Vienna" from Billy Joel's new album, *The Stranger*. I had never heard it before. It left me open-mouthed and speechless. Michael said, laughing loudly, "Don't you see? It's us. He wrote this for us! Now there's nothing to worry about. It's all going to be all right. Just keep remembering, Vienna waits for us."

He was half drunk, partly joking, but mostly serious. I hadn't realized until that moment that the breakup of Quadrille was as painful for Michael as it was for me, perhaps even more so.

He went on to say, "They're all going to die. And we'll be left. Then we can do anything we want. Just be patient. They won't let us do what we want to do now."

After we broke up Quadrille, I went back to Paul, Weiss. Nine months later, Nan and I celebrated the addition of our daughter, Nola, to our small family. Sadly, my father got to hold his granddaughter only once before succumbing to liver cancer a month later. He never got to see me become a partner at Paul, Weiss. My mother was aware of the deep disappointment I went through when my producing career came to an abrupt end, but I knew she secretly rejoiced that I had returned to the law.

Michael and I continued to be close friends, brothers. I remained his lawyer and advised him for the remainder of his career. As for Bernie, after I left Michael we became closer than ever. I was no longer this existential threat to his relationship with Michael. I think he was genuinely fond of me. Perhaps he felt some guilt for what he had done. I forgave Bernie, but I realized much later that Michael never did.

In 1985, I got another call from Michael, summoning me to his office at 890. Again, I didn't know the reason for the meeting.

When I arrived, he sat me down and handed me a drink. This time we weren't going to be listening to music. This was serious. I knew what he was going to tell me a moment before he said, "I have AIDS."

A fire curtain crashed before my eyes. This was worse than cancer, a heart attack, or stroke. In 1985, having AIDS was a certain death sentence, pure and simple. Before I could react, he said, "They think I have a year to eighteen months."

Much has been written about the aftermath. Michael kept his illness hidden from everyone at first, except for Bob Avian, Robin Wagner, and me. Later on he told Bernie Jacobs and a few others. But then Michael and Bernie decided to concoct a harebrained story about Michael having a heart condition, to explain his abrupt departure from the musical *Chess* right before rehearsals began.

Michael died on July 3, 1987, in Tucson, Arizona. He had gone to a hospital that promised some experimental treatment six months earlier. On the plane trip out, Michael could hardly breathe, and it soon became clear he would never be returning to New York. He bought a sprawling ranch house in the foothills looking up into the beautiful mountainscapes that surround that city.

Michael didn't want to see many people while he lay dying. For reasons he never made entirely clear to me, he cut off ties to several people before his death, including Bernie and Betty Jacobs. He did, however, instruct me in his will to give one of his prized possessions to the Jacobses: the Tiffany silver top hat from *A Chorus Line* signed by members of the original cast.

In those nightmarish early years of the crisis, there seemed to be no mercy for any of the victims, including Michael, struck down at the age of forty-four, and the thousands of others who, almost without warning, were consigned to death by the virus. I was a close-up witness to the tragedy that robbed Michael of his dreams and deprived the rest of us of his genius. Thirty years later, it seems at long last we've recovered from the horrors of the worst days of the epidemic, although there is still no cure and much more to be done in research and education.

Those few years I knew Michael, from 1974 through 1987, shaped me, personally and professionally, more than anything else in my life. My working in the theater today is as much my desire to produce as it is a testament to Michael's ambition for both of us when we were young and naïve. Michael told me, "Vienna waits," so when I began to produce in 2005, that's what I named my company. I can't imagine what my life would be like today if Michael had lived even five more years—when therapeutic cocktail drugs were finally able to stem the virus and offer victims hope for an extended life. Broadway's talent pool was ravaged by AIDS, which wiped out hundreds of actors, writers, directors, designers, producers, and countless others in every craft within the industry. What would we have inherited from them if they had survived?

I'm older now, and maybe wiser. By writing this book, I hope that I've been able to impart to future producers what I learned from Michael and the hundreds of artists with whom I've worked over the past many years. Billy Joel says, "Dream on, but don't imagine they'll all come true." Every dream does not come true for producers, but why not try?

Acknowledgments

My hat's off to:

those who plowed through my early drafts and offered support and helpful criticism, especially my brother Jeff, Bob Avian, Ellen Conrad, Bob Harling, David Johnson, Aaron Lustbader, Chip McGrath, Peter Pileski, Alex Schemmer, Rini and Mark Shanahan, Suzanne Tobak, Alan Wasser, Helene and Francis Weld, and David Zippel;

Jonathan House, who helped me see what was always right in front of me;

Paul, Weiss partners Bob Atkins, Gerry Harper, and Jeffrey Samuels for keeping me on the straight and narrow;

Jennifer Richards for helping me spread the word;

all those at Applause, including Anne Horowitz, Marybeth Keating, Wes Seeley, and especially John Cerullo, who said YES before reading a single word;

the staff at the New York Public Library for the Performing Arts, most notably Patrick Hoffman and Jeremy Megraw, who helped me delve into the library's trove of archival photographs, and Thomas Lisanti;

three books from which I learned so much—Stephen King's masterly book *On Writing: A Memoir of the Craft*, Phillip Lopate's helpful guide to nonfiction writing *To Show and To Tell: The Craft of Literary Nonfiction*, and Mary Norris's smart and witty book *Between You and Me: Confessions of a Comma Queen*; and

the hundreds of actors, directors, writers, designers, agents, theater owners, and colleagues of every stripe and form in the entertainment community who taught me so much by demonstrating their love and devotion to their craft over the course of my career.

A special mention to the ever-patient and brilliant Annabella Cascone for her ability to turn my hacking at Word 13 into readable and grammatical prose.

A heartfelt hug to my daughters, Eliza and Nola, who urged me to write this book from the very beginning.

And finally to my wife Nan, whose talents as a *true* writer honed and shaped my early drafts, and whose love and compassion for more than four decades have kept me sane and very happy.

Index